The New
100 Years War

The New 100 Years War

by
Georgie Anne Geyer

1972
DOUBLEDAY & COMPANY, INC.
GARDEN CITY, NEW YORK

For Glen and Robert Lee

CONTENTS

FOREWORD

As I write this, the Vietnam war is drawing to a close, solved, not through victory, but by exhaustion and by a "formula" that will extricate the United States without too stricken a conscience and too brooding a remembrance of sacrifice. But the theater of war, that grisly play that finds no dearth of actors, is not closing.

Instead, it has only shifted—shifted half a world away, from Vietnam to the Middle East, where it has been smoldering in its present form for twenty years, and where it has been blazing historically for five thousand years. And here the problem of Arab against Jew is one with even deeper and more dementedly twisted roots than those of North Vietnamese against South Vietnamese, Russian against Chinese or Punjabi against Bengali. Here, in a deep religious sense and in a profound historic sense, is where the world's will to create really began and where, conceivably, it could end.

U Thant has warned that the Middle East conflict could become the new "100-year war." President Nixon has said the Arab-Israeli conflict has created the single most dangerous situation for world peace. Israeli officials will tell you privately that "If the Arabs were ever about to win, we would use the atom bomb." And before he died, President Nasser's speeches were sanguinarily veined with threats of wading to victory through a "sea of blood and a horizon blazing with fire."

Clearly, there is a madness in the mood and in the

passions that emanate so abundantly from one small piece
of land. This rhetoric is typical of the flamboyant feelings
that the Middle East seems to generate and to elicit, even
from otherwise reasonable men. There is something about
the area that evinces either the purest holiness or the most
distilled madness. It is a world we must understand, but
equally a world we cannot understand if we listen only
to the rhetoric which is so beguilingly seductive, and misleading. It is, finally, a world understood not in public
pronouncements and shameless propaganda but in terms
of glances and shudders and things not said—in terms of
shadows and whispers.

It would seem obvious, for instance, to assume that the
Arabs are doing what they seem to be doing: fighting
against Israel. Yet it became clear to me, after being in
the Middle East for a good while, that this is not true;
they are fighting something quite different, and most of
it is themselves.

It would seem obvious to most Westerners, still horrified
and guilty over Germanic barbarities in World War II
and the pogroms and lesser indignities that emerged regu-
larly against the Jews throughout East European history,
that the Jews have a total and unquestionable right to
return to the "land of Israel" and to create their homeland
there.

Yet after really studying, point by point and step by
step and exclamation point by exclamation point, the
niceties of the question of right to the land, the impartial
person can only come up with disturbing questions. Does
the fact that Jews lived in Palestine for twelve hundred
years before their Diaspora in the first century A.D. and
want this land so passionately give *them* the right to this
valuable, treasured piece of earth which always was the
hub of the Middle East? Or does the fact that many Arabs
lived there, even during that period, and that the modern

Arabs have lived there for thirteen hundred years up to the
present give *them* the right to Palestine?

It would seem equally obvious to most foreign observers
that the Palestinian commandos are a brand of fanatic
madmen excelling in many of the worst historic characteristics of the Arabs; that they are the "poor refugees" of
the world whose histrionic rage has arisen out of their
degradation. But on careful analysis they turn out to be
quite the opposite. For the most part, they are neither poor,
nor uneducated, nor without hope or future; and in fact,
their particular style of Third World revolution is one that
is more and more tautly linked up with the other young
revolutionary movements in the world, even including—
incredibly—the young New Left Jews in the United States.

But then, the Middle East has always been a mystic
and beguiling place. There is something about the pristine
clearness of the air, the dry beauty of the deserts, the
haunting, miasmic air of the Mediterranean, that made of
men equally prophets, poets and madmen.

It would seem obvious, too, from the one-dimensional
picture that is so prevalent about them, that all Arabs
are pretty much alike: in effect, fanatical, unpredictable,
proud, brutal. On the contrary, what goes under the human
title of "Arab" is an incredibly, richly mixed mosaic. The
true Arabs exist really only on the Arabian peninsula,
where they are independent warriors and superb merchants.
As to the others, the Egyptians are gentle, fatalistic, self-
reflective, humorous people who have no true Arab blood
at all but are a Mediterranean people; the Syrians are
highly intellectualized, Frenchified Mediterraneans, as are
the Lebanese; the Sudanese are an Anglicized Arab-Negro
mixture; and from Libya westward you find the Berber
tribes, who embraced Islam late and are not Arabs either.

Indeed, the "Arabs" are one of the most heterogeneous
groups, ethnically and racially, in the world, carrying within

themselves strains of the Semitic, Hamitic, Armenoid, Nordic, Negroid and Mediterranean races. It was not until
the seventh century that the Moslems under the Prophet
Mohammed, secure and fanaticized in the glow of their
new religion, established their "Arab empire" from the
Atlantic Ocean to China. It was not until after World
War I, as nationalism grew in the Middle East as a response
to British, French and Turkish colonialism, that "Arab"
was used again. The term achieved what is probably its
most correct modern use after the Egyptian revolution of
the late President Gamal Abdel Nasser, in 1952—Nasser
simply said that an Arab was a person whose native tongue
was Arabic. And that's about as realistic a definition as
one can arrive at.

On the Israeli side, the "obvious" is not so obvious
either. The reason for the existence of Israel—and thus
the reason for the entire Middle East conflagration—was
to create and nurture a Jewish homeland, a Jewish state
and a Jewish cultural renaissance. Yet what is it today to
be a Jew when most young Jews never set foot in a
synagogue, when Orthodox Jews are looked down upon
as something to excise from the body politic as soon as
possible, and when non-Jews now are able to gain Israeli
citizenship?

And what is it on the "other side," when the Moslem
commandos do not practice their religion, either? Is it
possible to have a holy war with nothing holy in it?

And why should we in the United States concern ourselves with such a troublesome place, filled with such unpredictable, temperamental people, anyway?

Why? First, there is the responsibility of the West to
Israel, a country created by the accord of the world community. But the creation of Israel is not only an attempt
to right the horrible wrongs of World War II, and, finally,
to create for the Jews a homeland of their own. Ours is
a responsibility, too, to the American Jewish community,

whose genius has contributed so much to this country, in the arts, sciences, commerce and politics.

But what is usually forgotten is that we have an equal, though more generalized and less precise, responsibility to the Arab and Moslem world. Americans need not harbor the guilt which the European colonialist nations had in their dealings with the Middle East. But we have a responsibility to the Arabs as fellow human beings and as fellow human beings whose civilization has also given us so much.

If we are to look at it only in very practical terms, the Middle East is extraordinarily important to us economically. The Middle East and North Africa are the source of some $1.7 billion in net dollar inflow each year for the United States, from trade and investments. The Arab world contains some three-fourths of the known oil reserves of the non-Communist world and supplies 42 per cent of the oil consumed in the non-Communist world plus about three-fourths of Western Europe's requirements. Nearly one-half of our income from direct investment in foreign petroleum—a total of $1.8 billion—comes from the Middle East, or about one-fifth of what the United States receives from all its direct foreign investments. Yet until President Nixon began to turn American policy around in the summer of 1970, it was clear that the Middle East was being lost to us. Since the 1967 war, diplomatic relations with nearly every Arab country have been broken.

At the same time, Russia was masterfully fulfilling its aching historic expansionist drive to the south which started with Peter the Great, who exhorted his followers to "approach as near as possible Constantinople and India, for whoever governs them will be true sovereign of the world." The Soviet descendants of the expansive Peter do not, of course, want to be "sovereign" in any obvious sense; they want spheres of influence, governments that are similar to and linked to theirs, bases and privileges and hegemony.

And this they have been getting, as government after government in the Middle East falls to new socialist military men, who look East and not West. By the 1970s, it was not too much to say that the Soviet Union had nearly fulfilled Peter's injunction, for the Red Sea, the Indian Ocean and, many believe, soon the Persian Gulf were increasingly becoming *their* waterways.

For all of these basic reasons and for many more subtle and not so obvious ones, and despite the apparent peace initiatives of 1970, the Middle East presents to us today the most tantalizingly awful perspectives. In short, it is the one area where tempers are so short, memories are so long and rationality is so rationed that it presents the real danger of a Russian-American confrontation. It is the Balkans before World War I, where intense local rivalries coupled with a lack of responsibility for the peace of the world and the lining up of characters on one or another side among the great powers presented the most frightening possibilities.

It all seems quite mad, of course, if one asks the obvious questions. What is it that motivates—drives—the Arabs in their obsessive holy war? Why do they apparently choose to destroy themselves and even their national development instead of accepting the reality and presence of a tiny beleaguered state in their midst? Who are these men who are so obsessed with "unity" but cannot sit in one another's presence for more than an hour without murderously squabbling? Why must they characterize the only thing they agree upon about Israel as the "intrusion," the "final insult of Westernization," the "ultimate slap of colonization"; and all feel it like a knife being driven into them?

And what is it that drove the Jews back to this tiny piece of land, after they had scattered throughout the world? What is it in the man or in the spirit of Judaism that created their noble and tragic history, with its attempts at assimilation, alternating with rigid Judaistic exclusivity, with apparently successful amalgamation into another nation ending only with pogrom and genocidal fury? Why did it have to be, in the beginning of the twentieth century, that the Jews—feeling it hopeless to seek a home elsewhere in the world and feeling they could preserve themselves as a people only by the establishment of a "Jewish homeland"—were driven to return to a homeland that was also someone else's homeland?

But this book is not only about the Middle East. It is also about me—about a woman foreign correspondent, who is always a strange creature in the world, attempting as seriously and searchingly as I know how, to discover even some small truths in a tormented part of the world.

I was very fortunate. The first time that I was in the Middle East—during 1969 and 1970—was probably the most important and symbolic time since the State of Israel was founded. All the fruits—robust and rotten—of the last twenty years had come to harvest. It was a magic, tortured, revealing time in which, suddenly, everything became very clear. You could see the results of the 1967 war—the "six-day" war now in its third year. You could see the demoralization that had finally afflicted both peoples. You could see, more clearly than ever before, the enormous threat posed to American interests by the increasingly aggressive Russian presence. You could see the meteoric rise—and fall—of the Palestinian commandos, representing a vibrant new Palestinian nationalism. You could see the form that the "new Arab revolutionary governments" were taking, as country after country fell to Nasserist young officers. And you could see, for the first time, an Israel that was no longer the Cinderella of the Western world but a mature and therefore troubled state.

The second time I was in the Middle East—during the spring and summer of 1971—the drama had advanced, and in many ways changed. Other figures representing other elements had marched to front stage to play out

their days, and suddenly you were confronted by still other
dramatic possibilities. United States Secretary of State William Rogers' peace plan had brought out in the two obstreperous lands a new hope for that elusive creature, peace.
Egyptian President Nasser died and the new president,
Anwar Sadat, advanced suggestions that no one would
have dreamed possible two years earlier. Those erratic
wills-o'-the-wisp, the Palestinian commandos, were momentarily put down by the brutal Bedouin troops of King
Hussein—but the Palestinians remained the core of the
problem, and few doubted they would rise again, perhaps
in a new form. The Israelis hardened their position toward
the Arabs, despite Sadat, and were at the same time beset
by disturbing new problems within.

Still, despite these new elements, few were, at heart,
optimistic. Not if they knew the Middle East well enough,
for all they had to do was look back at the history of the
last twenty-five years (not to speak of the homicidal five
thousand years leading up to it) to see what they were up
against.

From the bitter days of the 1948 Palestine war, when
the surrounding Arab states fell upon the newborn State
of Israel—brought into existence by the fighting of mas-
sively outnumbered Jews and the decision of the world
community in the UN—the situation had steadily wors-
ened. The Arab states, though stricken by their demeaning
loss in the '48 war, never accepted the presence of Israel;
neither could they do anything about it, so they smoldered
and plotted. Worse, the approximately one million Palestinian Arabs who fled the fighting in Israel in 1948 were
kept as pawns in miserable refugee camps on the borders
of what had been their homeland.

From the Israeli-French-British attack on Suez in 1956,
after Egyptian President Nasser closed the canal, to the
lightning Israeli victory in the 1967 war—when Israel
pre-empted an Arab attack and approximately thirty thou-

sand Arabs lost their lives in the "six-day" war—the situation grew more and more bitter. And the "six-day" war stretched on and on, into years that seemed without end.

After 1967, the major front was along Suez, where some two thousand highly trained and motivated Israeli soldiers faced approximately sixty thousand Egyptians in an uneven but implacable standoff. The escalation was clear. In 1968, there were twenty-two hundred exchanges of fire along Suez; in 1969, there were two thousand every month.

The Israelis were losing approximately three hundred men a year, while the United Arab Republic or Egypt was losing about a thousand. Moreover, in July 1969, the entire character of the war changed. It was then that the United States began giving Phantom jets to Israel— aircraft which made it possible for Israel to strike deep into the Arab land mass, thus enlarging the already deadly conflict.

Meanwhile, not only the shores of Suez had become an empty wasteland but the entire Jordan Valley had also been emptied of humanity under threat of the growing holocaust, as guerrillas struck across the biblical river at the increasingly dense Israeli defenses.

But even when the conflict was at its height—and this was strange—it was often hard to find the war. It struck suddenly, in flashes, here and there, and then it was gone again. So even for those of us who were in the midst of it, it was often a fleeting thing. One moment we felt the dread of the war; the next moment the valley was sunny and quiet.

The conflict *seemed* at its height—it seemed headed toward an inevitable doomsday—when, suddenly in the summer of 1970, the United States presented the "Rogers plan" for peace. There was momentary quiet and momentary hope, as the guns stopped in a cease-fire along Suez, as the new Egyptian President Anwar Sadat offered to recognize Israel in exchange for Israeli-occupied Arab territories and as plans were afoot to open Suez.

But few who knew the area felt that peace was coming soon, for the roots of the conflict were so deep, so dementedly twisted, so darkly colored by ancient religious and racial hatreds that any small rebuff or oversight on either side could start the entire dismal thing up again.

In describing all of this, I have tried, too, to share *my* feelings—my anger, my delight, my disgust, my moments of personal defeat and my times of exaltation. But none of these feelings is evoked by only one country, one religion, or one outlook toward life. If they were, I would feel that I was less than human, for each people and each country in the Middle East is acting according to its own rationale; it is proceeding according to the only set of circumstances, the only thought pattern and the only memory that history has granted to it.

Therefore, it is perhaps well for me to state now, since this is a part of the world where every people *demands* that you be totally on its side and in contemptuous hatred of the other side, that I am neither pro-Israeli nor anti-Arab. Nor am I pro-Arab and anti-Israeli. On the other hand, I'm not pro-Kurd, anti-Afghan; pro-Dinka, anti-Berber; pro-Somali, anti-Eritrean; a Mahdist, a Gordonite, a Nasserist, a Golda-ite or a follower of King Hassan.

That is precisely what is so wrong about the Middle East and the way most people there look at it: they see only their prejudices and their own beliefs; they have put all their perceptions in one closed basket. I have tried here to carry a big inclusive basket, instead of a small exclusive one. I have tried to say simply that it is incumbent upon us as human beings to try to understand. Everything.

GEORGIE ANNE GEYER
CHICAGO, ILLINOIS

CHAPTER I

The Quiet Arabs?

▼▼▼

Cairo, a city at war?

It seemed impossible. The dusky gold city sat languidly
—indeed, it was almost limpid—along the Nile. Butterfly-
winged felucca boats crossed and crisscrossed the Nile,
sailing first in one direction, then in another, as they
meandered their paths back and forth across the great
river like drifting moths. The elegant university bridge was
guarded timelessly by its couchant lions, and the city
looked as though it was covered with a golden film as it
stretched out toward the pyramids, three triangles of mystery barely seen in the dusty distance.

As I sat in my window at the Nile Hilton that first
morning in Cairo, I thought about the "old Cairo" that
many Arab-lovers still dream about: how the sensual,
bloated King Farouk's mother had debased him with women
and dope in order to control him . . . how family assassins
had tried to kill his sister in the United States when she
married a Copt and not a Moslem . . . how Cairo and

Alexandria had been cities where a ten-year-old prostitute
was acceptable so long as she didn't look over eight.

I knew that Nasser, at heart a puritanical reformer, had
taken care of all that, even to the degree of putting body
stockings on the belly dancers. Yet the miasmic mood of it
lingered on, like an aphrodisiac scent long after the passion
was gone.

When I walked down into the lobby, I was caught up
in the expectant Levantine scene. The sloe eyes of the men
of the Levant wandered languidly from woman to woman
or, if they happened to belong to somebody's secret police,
from man to man and then from woman to woman. You
were likely to see a sheikh from Tunisia, looking like a
dark, animated barber's pole in his black-and-white-
striped robes, sitting soberly next to an Egyptian playboy
in pointed shoes. The whole scene had the sweet, smooth,
dark flavor of Egyptian coffee, sipped between the voluptuous rumors which elbowed their way genteelly in through
the tourists and hangers-on and floated from ear to ear.

I early dubbed this indolent waiting scene the "Lurk on
the Nile." Indeed, the texture was so sleek and velvety
that after a while I almost expected one of the smooth,
dark-eyed men to curl around one of the marble pillars
like an oriental snake bracelet and for his tongue to sweep
out and snap me up.

When I sat down for a few minutes to absorb the scene,
I could not help overhearing a sleek young Egyptian sitting
next to me whispering to a blond, miniskirted tourist
whose hand he held with the same limp spirit that seemed
to inform everything, "For a woman like you, there are
several levels. One is water, where there are many men.
The second is mud, where there will be eight or ten. The
third is quicksand, and this is obsession. . . ."

I got up and walked out to my luncheon, wondering
to myself: is the Arab world really going to turn out to

be as sad, as absurd, as tragicomic as most Westerners
think it is?

Within an hour I was sitting in the large wild garden
of an elegant villa shadowed by the pyramids. Through
the invitation of one of the editors of the semiofficial
newspaper, *Al Ahram,* Kemal Al Mallakh, a writer and
the Egyptologist who had discovered Cheop's boat, I was,
on my first day, catapulted into the educated world of
Cairo.

Next to me, a short, heavy-set, intense Lebanese with
devilishly sharp eyes that stared bemusedly—very nearly
insolently—from behind heavy glasses glared at me in a
friendly manner. "What we have with Israel is an advanced
technology at the service of a primitive ideology," he was
telling me, lecturing me really. "The commando movement is an advanced ideology at the service of a primitive
technology. We must humanize the Jews. We must have
a state where Jews are welcome. Jews are the final intrusion
of Westernization, your illegitimate child. You can't take
it back." He paused. "Jews look at us not as human
beings," he went on, "but as obstacles, so just remove us."

That was my first meeting with the fascinating Clovis
Maksuud, specialist on the Palestinian commandos, political columnist for *Al Ahram* and guru of many young
militant Arabs.

A few minutes later, a highly cultured doctor was telling
me from the other side, "Oh yes, we all support the Palestinians. But we don't necessarily support all their actions.
Plastiques, for instance—they can be counterproductive."

"War seems very far away," an architect chimed in,
whispering in my ear. "Maybe in five years it will come,
maybe not."

That night, Kemal invited me to another party, at
which I met many of the top writers and journalists of
Cairo. It was a beautiful apartment, filled with European

antiques, and everyone was terribly scotch-drinking European, except for those moments when an Eastern sensuality suddenly asserted itself.

At one point, as I talked and flirted a little with some of the Egyptian men, a beautiful woman journalist named Maha, who had been watching the scene as from afar but with feline discernment, said to me with a pointedly wicked smile, "You Western women all like Egyptian men, don't you? You think they're brutes."

Soon after dinner, which came at midnight, Kemal said to me, "Let's go now," and despite my protestations, we faded away without saying anything to anybody. That was the way things seemed to happen in Egypt—they came and went almost imperceptibly, faded mistily in and out, were there one moment and dissolved into the golden dust the next.

As I sat down in my room late that night to write down everything I could remember about the people I had met—their looks, attitudes, expressions, words—I realized that I had been surprised by what I had seen. And if I was surprised, then many American readers would be surprised, because I share their questions and concerns. But why?

I realized I had expected some sort of monolithic spirit among the Arabs. This is always foolish, of course—very few societies are truly unitary in spirit, certainly not Russia and probably not even China—and I should have known better. But the portrait of the Arabs in the United States was one of single-minded *fanatics;* the portrait even in my mind of Egypt was one of street mobs swearing allegiance as one writhing creature to a Nasseristic holy war. It would certainly be a sloppy holy war! I thought to myself at one point.

Was my gut feeling true of this day that this was probably a very stricken and fragmented society?

In the next week, I found that feeling, like most of my instinctive and visceral feelings, turned out to be very true. A week later, I started my first article on Egypt, an article totally different from most of the stories I had read about the Arabs, with:

> "There is a telling juxtaposition of tattered posters that seem to overlap on the walls of downtown Cairo.
>
> "One has a bitter-eyed, masked Arab throwing a bomb at what can only be a synagogue within Israel. The other is a swinging ad for the Go-Gos band— 'straight from Italy.'
>
> "And that's about the way it is these days.
>
> "Behind the violent posters, behind the headlines of war and turmoil in the Middle East, there lies a deeply divided and schizophrenic society: this one.
>
> "Fanatic but diffuse strains of Arab unity and hate for Israel vie with a still deep yearning for the Western Goodlife. It is, too, a society suspended between an ancient, sustaining lassitude and a new, abrasive militance.
>
> "And this is, from the Arab side, perhaps the main problem in trying to win the war. The United Arab Republic or Egypt, despite many and real revolutionary changes in the last seventeen years, remains a disunited and uncertain society fighting the fanatically certain and united society of Israel."

I found too, for instance, something that no one ever writes about—that the Egyptians have a superbly ironic sense of humor. I was walking one day near the Nile with an Egyptian friend and he gestured toward the brick barriers blocking the doors to apartment buildings. They had been built before the 1967 war as a protection of some sort. "If there were fighting those would just crumble and hurt somebody," he remarked.

Another night, I was dancing on the roof of the Hotel Semiramis, and a young actor told me with a wry and skeptical smile, "You flew United Arab Airlines—U.A.A.? We call it, 'Use Another Airline.'" The students had a slogan, too: "Make war, make peace, but do something." And they constantly told jokes about themselves: "If the Israelis had only pushed us a little harder," one 1967 joke went, "we would have invaded Libya for them." Another had Nasser going out in the dark of night to the Sphinx after the humiliating defeats of the 1967 war. "Oh, Sphinx," he intoned, "I need you now as never before. Please, in this moment of our greatest need, give me some advice." The Sphinx was silent and motionless, as it has been for so many centuries. Nasser tried again, pleading, "Oh, great Sphinx, please say just a word." Still the Sphinx was silent. "Oh, please, Sphinx, how I need you now. I beg of you . . . speak to me." Just then, the great Sphinx creakily turned its head toward Nasser. The great, battered lips began to move. And he spoke. He said, "Give me . . . an exit visa."

Sometimes the Egyptians did not really *mean* to be funny. I was driving through downtown Cairo one day with a talkative cabdriver who spoke good English and I asked him, for some reason or another, whether the young men were eager to go into the army.

"Not now," he answered unsmiling, looking straight ahead like a lion.

I asked him why and he roared. "It's dangerous now," he said. "There's fighting."

Did they mind going when there wasn't fighting?

"Not if there's no fighting," he said, with a sidewise glance which indicated that any fool would know that.

With this cynical, sometimes almost gallows humor, there was a bittersweet, autumnal sadness about the Egyptians I came to know and like. This group, admittedly,

was exceptional; they were the intelligentsia, the Westernized, educated Egyptians, the quiet Arabs who had constructed a place, albeit always an insecure, lonely place, for
themselves outside the puritanical strait jacket of traditional
Moslem society.

Evenings, we often met at the Gezira Club located on
the exquisite expanse of acres and acres of land on an
island in the Nile. In British colonial days, barely two
generations off, it had been the privileged watering place
for British authorities and no soft Egyptian voice, no matter how Oxfordian, was heard there. Now the Egyptian intelligentsia clung to the club, with its broad low trees, its
circular bar, its parquet floors and once-upon-a-time
wicker chairs, with the passion of a man who has finally
been permitted to marry a woman far, far above him. My
Egyptian friends gathered there early in the evening to
play (of all things!) croquet, and the war seemed a desert
apparition or a sudden dangerous sandstorm that smote
only those who wandered outside the manicured confines of
Gezira.

One night I was sitting there talking to a nice
Egyptian business couple, and the man was saying, "We
have a feeling of unreality about the war, as though it does
not exist. I only have one son, so he will not have to go
to the army. My brother has three—he has already sent two
to Canada, and the other will probably go soon. Nobody
likes this war." Another time, I was sitting there in the
genteel quiet, the only sounds the soothing swish of the
fellahin waiters' slippers and the tempered buzz of the
conversation, and suddenly I flushed in anger. It was
another Cercle Sportif in Saigon, the plushy old French
club, where no murmur of the war ever penetrated . . . until one day a bullet hit a wall and hit a tree and hit a
man innocently swimming in the balmy pool. One has,
occasionally, to get angry at the Gezira Clubs and the

Cercle Sportifs of the world, where war is simply a noisy beggar grappling at the gates.

Everyone warned me about the police, and about talking too freely, and yet everyone talked, albeit carefully. Even in that shady underworld of black-market money and a number of other things, there were certain warnings. After I had refused to change money on the black market one day, a Lebanese "businessman" commented wryly as he disappointedly conducted me from his shop out to the street, "You're wise not to. There are a lot of people around here . . . they'll tell you they're Boy Scouts, but they're not." I knew of a group of Egyptians who certainly were *not* Boy Scouts—those of the "city eye" system who watched every movement of foreigners within the city through the spying collaboration of doormen, cabdrivers, beggars and others.

But I was in the Middle East on a special assignment from my newspaper, the Chicago *Daily News,* to write a special type of article for it and for the hundred papers on our news wire. My foreign editor, Nicholas Shuman, thought that not nearly enough was written about the people enmeshed in this ugly conflict, about the mentalities at work and about the personal feelings and sufferings. This is what I was to get at—to (forgive the expression!) make the war come alive.

So in between these welcome diversions, there was the much more serious business of building up contacts one could trust, of getting information and then collating it in such a way as to make sense to the reader. The first problem was that Egypt was a mystery to most observers—its inner political workings were unknown even to foreign diplomats and to analysts who were on good terms with the regime. Nobody knew who was close to Nasser at any one moment or, indeed, even where certain people were or whether they were alive.

In most countries, I would start out with briefings at the American and other embassies, moving then to local journalists, to politicians, to intellectuals and to anyone who knew anything about the society. But here there was no American embassy. Relations had been broken off after the 1967 war with Israel, and the American "representative," Donald Bergus, a fine diplomat, could be found by going up the back stairs of the Spanish embassy, which is where he "hid out." As to the government, the Information Ministry, which would be the place to start for contacts in a country one did not know, was so afraid for its own positions that it helped only in requests like, "Where is the water fountain?"

Little insights, however, came, as always, from unexpected sources. There were—one of the endless anomalies of this peculiar war—a good number of American oilmen operating without a single problem in Egypt, many of them with installations right on the Red Sea staring across at Israeli-held Sinai. In the bar of the Hilton one evening, one of these men told us how two of their oilmen had gone swimming one day, only to find themselves staring into Egyptian rifles when they clamored back up the beach. "Those soldiers had lived next door to us for months," he said, shrugging because anger was too good an emotion for the situation. "They knew these men well. Nevertheless, they kept them for three hours and grilled them, saying they might be spies." That was one reason why Egypt couldn't win a war.

Contacts among the Arabs, however, came in unexpected and usually unstructured ways. Clovis Maksuud, whom I had met the first day at lunch, called me suddenly early one evening and said, "Can you come over immediately? I have the second to Arafat here."

It was certainly worth it to see anyone close to Yasir Arafat, the leader of the Palestinian Commandos, so I

rushed across the Nile by taxi to Clovis' beautiful apartment and found him sitting with a stocky, swarthy, taciturn
man who was indeed the notorious Abu Iad. Clovis
launched into a little lecture in his peculiar Indian English
(he had served in the diplomatic corps in India for many
years) while Abu Iad sat looking distrustfully at me.
"Fatah," Clovis was saying, "supports a central vision of
man, a humanistic nationalism that is neither racist nor
theocratic nationalism. It is in contradistinction to the
Zionist concept of nationalism." Then, "As in the Algerian
revolution, the nature of the confrontation determines the
outcome. . . ." He went on and on and finished up with
what seemed to be a ringing benediction, "The injection
of Israel in our midst has made every Arab a Palestinian."

I stayed only briefly because Abu Iad seemed intent
upon discussing some eerie business that was clearly not
mine, but I was equally intent upon establishing how I
might contact him in Amman. "Ask for Abu Lutuf at
30331," he said, "or call 39490 and ask for me." He
paused. "Or if none of that works, just go to the Fatah
Information Office." The Fatah Information Office? For a
moment I thought I was dreaming. What kind of mystery-
filled underground business was *this*? I left, feeling for the
first time the Arab world of illusions closing in on me.

In addition to seeing the commandos, I was desperately
eager to get close to the government itself, but this turned
out to be nearly impossible. President Nasser was out completely—he had been very ill at this time and after his
death it was admitted he had had a heart attack. The
Ministry of Information would not even arrange an interview with a street sweeper, its collective teeth set to chattering so every time I made a request. No one, but no one,
could get interviews with anyone in the army—which had
become Nasser's real power base—or with the technocrats

around him or even with members of the Arab Socialist Union, which was to have been Nasser's political party. However, finally, as always, through indirect channels, I did get an interview with Hassan Sabry El Kholy, Nasser's personal "representative" and as such one of the top handful of men in the government. It came accidentally through Dr. Hekmat Azouzeid, the highest-placed woman in the government. I had gone to see her about the birth-control program and she arranged the interview.

El Kholy, like most important men, didn't really say much. But he seemed such a nice man, such a charming man, I found it disturbing when, weeks later in Tel Aviv, I was shown a speech he had given to Egyptian troops telling them how Israeli soldiers raped Arab women during the war, something patently untrue. But then, I was just beginning to enter, not only the obvious Arab world, but the second world of illusion that all Arabs also live in.

At about this time, a friend of mine, Pamela Painter de Maigret, arrived unexpectedly in Cairo and, like many journalists, we decided to team up to do some traveling together. We decided to go to Aswan.

Pamela was free-lancing for several newspapers while her French husband was on an exploring expedition in New Guinea, but she had not been a journalist for long. Indeed, we had met and become friends originally in a Stanley-and-Livingstone way. She was, that year of 1964, notorious up and down the Brazilian Amazon as "that American girl" who was gold-mining, with a motley crew of Brazilians working for her, in a remote contraband gold camp called Cuiu Cuiu. Having a broken arm and several broken ribs suffered in a traffic accident in Rio de Janeiro, I was about as enthusiastic about going to a mosquito-infested jungle outpost pronounced Coo-yoo Coo-yoo as I was about going to hell. But the story was too good, and soon I was walking through the jungle pathways toward a town of fifty and past cemeteries of two hundred.

"I would have let you know I was coming," I said, when I finally found Pamela and her workmen standing knee-deep in the river water, "but I didn't know how." She has never forgotten those opening words.

At any rate, Pamela turned out to be an unexpected surprise. She was tall, beautiful and aristocratic-looking. She was fun. She just didn't like the ordinary life and neither did I. So we decided to go to Upper Egypt to see how they were "transforming" this ancient country.

Aswan. The High Dam. Around Aswan, which Lady Duff-Gordon had called "that most poetically, melancholy spot," the landscape was unreal. It was a huge rock pile, a fantasy place that looked as though some angry volcano god had thrust rocks in fits of fury to pit the earth. Across this, the Egyptians and the Russians had cut roads and . . . they had cut the High Dam.

Once, Aswan was the southernmost outpost of the Roman empire. Once, Egyptians sent honey, unguents, beads and cloths in exchange for the ivory, skins, gold and exotic feathers of the Sudan. Even today the Bisharin tribesmen from the Red Sea hills—those lean warriors that Kipling immortalized as the "Fuzzie Wuzzies"—still lope up the desert caravan routes to trade henna leaves.

But the peasants down the river now plowed with transistor radios hung around their cows' necks. In ten years, the population of Aswan had soared from 28,000 to more than 50,000. Handsome, pastel-colored new buildings lined the corniche drive along the Nile across the river from the caves in the sand cliffs where the early Christians once lived. The outdoor cafés were filled in the evening with engineers and other modern types talking in English,

Russian, Arabic and French. And the once-Edwardian Cataracts Hotel had an unseemly sign over the entrance to the lounge which read, "Drinking is compulsory."

The next morning they came from the Ministry of Information to take us to the dam and the dam was precisely what we saw; it was also just about all we saw. Let me admit that the Aswan dam is a stunningly beautiful thing. You would have to be a very myopic or politically small person not to be moved by it. The pale blue water of Lake Nasser stretches out on one side fingering its way into a thousand crannies in the rock-strewn landscape. In the middle is the huge pyramidal cement structure that is the dam itself. From this, sprays of water gush and plunge into the river which flows hundreds of feet farther down, creating rainbows across the length of the dam.

My assignment in the Middle East was to cover the important breaking news when it was breaking, and when it was not breaking, to do stories about the people. And what people were more interesting than the 35,000 workers who were uprooted from their tribal villages and transported to Aswan, where they were paid 80 per cent more than they earned as village fellahin. When their work was done they were given the choice of going anywhere in Egypt to work—few went back to the village, having seen the "high life" at Aswan.

As we stood at the top of the dam, with the blue water of Lake Nasser spreading languidly out across the sand clefts of the Nubian moonscape, I started toward an Egyptian workman who was scratching away at the dam. He looked like a harmless chap, standing there, dressed in his long white robe, and all I really wanted to ask him were some innocuous questions about how his family life had changed, how much he earned—things like that.

Before I got six feet, the Egyptian dam official, one Jehia Bashier, came after me in horror. "Even Egyptians are not allowed to talk to the workers," he warned me. The typical xenophobia again.

"Look, I came here to write about the dam," I said. "I can't write about concrete. I have to talk to people. All I wanted was to find out what they think about their work."

"The workmen know everything," he insisted. Then I may have dreamed it but I think I discerned a small wicked shadow of a smile. "They even know where the guns are hidden in the dam," he said.

Later we sat with Bashier, a charming lawyer originally from the Sudan, in his office. "It is very difficult," he said. "When we dedicated Abu Simbel [the ruins of Ramses II which were lifted up from under the water of the dam], our foreign minister brought many foreign ministers and ambassadors here. We have a fast rule that no one can take pictures of the dam, and I told our minister that the visitors could not take pictures. He said to me, 'But I cannot tell them that, they are ministers.' I said that I could." His lean brown face lit up in a smile. "I took them there at night," he finished up wryly.

Security at the dam, we soon found out, was intense. The Egyptians greatly feared an Israeli strike on the precious High Dam, the symbol and social and economic transformer of modern Egypt, so the windows of the town were painted with a midnight blue paint and at night, next to the dam that was to flood the entire Nile valley with the blinding light of electricity, the streets were mysteriously pitch black. Here we again ran head on into the cement wall that the Arabs, all the while insisting that they were deliberately not covered by the American press, constantly constructed against even the most desirable of coverage. Both of us wanted to see the nearby modern villages at Kom Omba, an area to which some 34,000 Nubians displaced by the dam had been moved. For me, it was a particularly interesting story because it was right in line with my particular interest in social change, an interest I had pursued in many countries.

But, no, we could not go to Kom Omba! Yes, it had been originally okayed in Cairo but just today the military commander of the region had de-okayed it. They were having military maneuvers along the way ("Two men on a camel," Pamela said to me at one point) and we might see them. No. No. And no. All right, then, show us something, you got us here, you want press coverage, damn it, show us something!

What?

A village—a villager whose life had been changed by the dam. Damn it, why'd you build the dam?

All right. Go home for lunch and we'll find a village for the afternoon.

Pamela and I were walking disconsolately home along the corniche when we saw a beautiful white cruise ship floating innocently along the quay. We looked at each other. It was a floating Hilton called the *Osiris* and to our ecstatic reaction, we found it was leaving, only a quarter full, that night for Luxor, where we had planned to touch down by plane anyway. We reserved staterooms and for the first time felt downright kindly toward the Egyptian government for not being able to show us any more Nubians.

From 1952 until his death, most foreigners tended to see in Gamal Abdel Nasser only the Nasser of "rivers of blood" and "volcanoes of war." But to be fair about this unusual man and thus to understand him and Egypt, one must look at what he and the "Nasserist revolution" did to and for his country. It was Nasser who gave the masses of poor Egyptians dignity when he spoke (the first leader to do so) publicly in the local Arabic dialect; Nasser who started

the schoolchildren painting the human form, thus breaking
the Moslem ban of centuries; Nasser who introduced on a
workable scale "Arab Socialism," which means simply
social justice, education for all, state ownership blended
with some private industry.

I was to come out of Egypt with as deep a respect for
what Nasser had done inside Egypt as I had a deep concern for what he was doing to Egypt and the whole Arab
world with his policy toward Israel. For I had seen revolutions before. I'd seen the Castro revolution in Cuba. I'd
seen the creative part—the schools, the social and economic
raising of the poor classes, the hospitals, the economic
development. But I'd also seen the hundreds of thousands
of destroyed lives—decent people who had simply said,
"But . . ."

I'd seen the young men who fought with him in the
Sierra Maestra destroyed, their illusions ruthlessly plucked
like ripe fruit when they couldn't take the step to Marxism.
I'd seen the Russian Revolution—such a cost—and Vietnam—such a cost—and I'd come fairly close to ending up
like one of the eyeless, earless, armless, legless Guatemalan
guerrillas who became mutilated corpses at the hands of
the rightist colonels.

It seemed to me that Nasser had carried through the
single most effective and least brutal revolution in an underdeveloped country that I had ever seen or read of. It
was very nearly bloodless, and even that ballooning syba-
ritic sodomite, King Farouk, had been permitted simply to
leave . . . and with fifty trunks filled with belongings.

Most objective students of Nasser's revolution agree that
in the beginning Nasser had not wanted absolute power.
Nor had he hated Israel or considered the Palestine question to be central. Rather, he looked upon the 1948 war
as a means of enhancing the reputations of his "new
officers" . . . a way of bringing them to higher positions

and thus to power. It is important to realize that, right up to the bitter Palestine war of 1948—all during the time when Israeli Jew was fighting Palestinian Arab throughout the bitter days of the thirties and early forties—the Egyptians took no part in the conflict. While Arabs were rioting against the Jews in 1936 and in 1939 in Palestine, Egypt was playing host to Jewish and Zionist organizations from Palestine. While Arabs in Jaffa killed their Jewish neighbors, the Zionist Maccabi basketball team was playing against the Egyptian Army team (for once, the Egyptians even won). The Tel Aviv Philharmonic Orchestra played under Arturo Toscanini in Egypt during this period and in June 1945, when two young Palestinian Jews were sentenced to death for assassinating Lord Moyne, the British High Commissioner, young Egyptians staged spontaneous demonstrations on their behalf.

It was only in 1948, when King Farouk ordered his army to grab part of Palestine that the entire picture changed. But this was done more out of intra-Arab rivalry than anything else. It is well to remember all this, for it is one of many signs that points to the hope that Arab and Jew have indeed lived together peacefully and therefore might be able to do so again, if there were only prerequisites for guarding the dignity of each.

It was not surprising, of course, that Nasser's revolution was carried through in Egypt by the Army, or that it is the Army's younger officers who are carrying on the same pattern in the other Arab countries, and even in Latin America, Greece and Asia. As William Polk, the knowledgeable Middle Eastern specialist at the University of Chicago wrote in his paper, "The Middle East: Analyzing Social Change":

> "The armies alone among the institutions of the underdeveloped societies were organized along nationalist,

modern lines without commitments to the past. The
military alone had a defined code, a clear line of command, lines of communications, mobility, force, and,
ultimately, will. The better it became as a modern
instrument of the state, the less committed it was to the
traditional state. In Egypt today the army is not only
a 'school' in civic virtues, but is in addition a school
to impart modern skills, a hospital to cure the ills of
society by turning out healthier men, and a source of
discipline."

My own personal journey into the internal part of
Nasser's revolution began that afternoon in Aswan when,
after pushing and pulling the ministry officials, we finally
got one of them to take us across the river to visit the
ancient Pharaonic town of Elephantine Island. The strange
rotund rock structures on which the island seems to sit
balanced gave it its name; actually, they look immensely
and immodestly like the ample rumps of the elephants
which used to be brought from the Sudan.

We crossed the Nile at three o'clock, a time when the
still oppressive afternoon heat seemed to form a film between us and the rest of the world, which now had turned
a dazed white. Our felucca waved back and forth, back
and forth, as it zigzagged its way sleepily across the Nile.
We sat under a colored awning as the white-robed, white-
turbaned boatman guided the boat, its twin sails like a
butterfly's wings, with a wooden steering rod as old as
time. To enter the village, we climbed up through a tunnel
of high stone steps built by the Pharaohs, and in the steps
were white marble measurement panels which have shown
the rise of the Nile for three thousand years. Only now, for
the first time in history, because of the dam the river no
longer rises.

The town was stark whiteness on stark whiteness; one

was grandly blinded; stone paths curved and lurched between the old houses; women giggled at strangers from behind the black folds that hid them like bats' wings; faces changed suddenly into harsh, suspicious masks.

We strolled through the village. There was a new community house on the outskirts—a fruit of the revolution. I paused suddenly to drink in the silence of the town, a silence broken at that moment by the pleasant, droning sound of the muezzin's call to prayer. We were standing just before the mosque, I suddenly realized, and there were two elderly, white-robed village men sitting and leaning against the building and observing us with intense interest.

Sixty-two-year-old Abdel Shukur turned out to be a retired schoolteacher. He was a big man, with a round mischievous face, and he was obviously much amused at two young *sleeveless* American women passing through his town. I began to speak to him through our guide, and he turned out to be a splendidly amusing man.

"The dam has very much changed my life," he mused, as the town stagnated around him in the unseemly heat. Pamela and I sat down facing him. "My children remember their lessons with no difficulty because they study now with electricity from the dam. We were not in a good light before. When I was young, I had to study by an old lantern, and when I would bring it outside to get some air, it would go out with the breeze.

"Electricity is very necessary in hot countries," he summed up, in words evincing a stunning new expectation that no former generation would have dared consider. "My children remember easily in the light." One of his children, it turned out, was studying mechanical engineering; another was in the cultural faculty and two were in the primary school. He did, indeed, have such a charming and slightly pleasant bantering manner, that I was enjoying sitting there.

"Now look," I said, after we'd chatted about fifteen minutes, "what do you think is bad about what's happening today."

Still with his mischievous look, he glanced very obviously at my bare arms. "I do not like to see women wearing short sleeves," he said, but with an abundant smile. "I ordered my children that I do not like to see their wives wearing short sleeves. It is necessary for the women, as we say in Islam, to have only their faces seen."

And, yes, as I had walked around Elephantine Island I had seen only the shadowy faces of the women inside the windows. If they went out, they placed those hideous black robes like Greek death masks between them and the world. And Abdel Shukur, who liked electricity, applauded this darkness.

Before we left, I asked him about "the war." For here was a man of the people—not a true member of the fellahin, for he was too well-educated, but still a man whose life swayed to the rhythms of the river. He gave me almost exactly the answer that I was to hear over and over whenever I asked the simple people of Egypt this question. It was in no way a propaganda answer—these people had certainly not been "briefed" in any way. Rather, it was that the people of the Nile share an ancient submission to the river and to its imperatives; they accept, they obey. "Every day I hear about the war from the radio," he said. "Im not afraid. We must succeed. My children will go . . . and I will go if necessary." He had resigned himself to the war as five thousand years of Egyptian fellahin had resigned themselves to the river.

The floating Hilton left that night for Luxor, and we were on it. And in the morning, like the historic people of Egypt, we were in the gentle clutches of the river, being

carried along on its sluggish, gently churning currents. It
is difficult to describe the beauty of the Nile. It is rap-
turous.

The predominant color, which seems to hang over everything like a fine veil, is a melodic rose. The landscape
changes constantly; gives way from high sand cliffs to low
deserts and then again to gentle green hills. One is constantly surprised at the astonishingly bright belt of green
fields that edge the river like an emerald necklace. These
fields are, for the most part, fifteen or twenty feet above
the river today. The river used to rise three times a year,
flooding the fields, already inseminated, and bringing forth
the harvests which then were heralded in the stylized gray
granite carvings of the Pharaonic temples.

From time to time, the ship stopped in the river, hauled
to shore to be tied up like a pet by barefoot boys with
strong brown arms. Then the entire contingent of tourists
would line up on board, straw hats and all, waiting duti-
fully to disembark to see still another dark temple.

As I watched and explored some of the temples, I was
struck by the fatalism of them. The dark fatalism born
of that dependence on the Nile was mirrored in the temples
dedicated to death that the Pharaohs built on its banks. In
death, they had then carried themselves in legend to the
rivers of the underworld in black boats. But today the
monuments of the river were built not to death but to life
—to such homey, unromantic things as power stations
and fertilizer plants. Industries were being built with the
two million new kilowatts of electricity, and two million
acres of land were being reclaimed with the water, which
now could be released as the nation needed it.

In the past, on the Nile, when drought came, fear came
with it. When the floods came, the joy of the people
erupted in a wild baccanalia. The Nile was a young lover
taking physical possession of his mistress, the dry earth.

What would the new rhythms do? What would they do
to the spirit of the people?

But at the same time, still underneath, drawing out the
lifeblood like evil bloodsuckers in an unfinished process
of evolution, were the nagging fears. The river could be
harnessed, yes; its waters could be channeled into irrigation
ditches and dams, so the floods were no longer needed;
three crops could be grown a year instead of one; man
could develop new balances with natural elements like
the water, the sand and the trees. But could he do it with
himself?

I knew that by 1971 the dam would be finished. But
that year all of its contributions, for which the country
and the people had sacrificed so much, would be wholly
neutralized by the steady, inexorable, primeval growth of
the population. There were other disadvantages: silt would
back up behind the dam; fish in the delta were dying
because the nitrates and phosphates that formerly washed
down from the highlands would come no more; malaria
and schistosomiasis were being spread by the dam. But
nothing was as fatally perverse as the population growth.
You can control the womb of a river or a seedling far
easier than the superstition-ridden womb of a woman;
and I, a woman, resented this. I resented it for myself,
and I resented it for these other women and I resented
it for all women. All of which changed not a damned
thing.

As we sat on the deck that day, drinking in the scene
and slightly dazed by the soft white heat, almost silken
as it brushed and enclosed you in its texture, the assistant
manager of the boat came up and sat with us. We were
talking when suddenly we saw a sign by the river: Kom
Ombo. That was where we had wanted to go to see the

villages where the Nubians had been resettled from their former villages under the dam. Seeing a good story drifting by on the river, Pamela asked the young man innocently: "Couldn't we stop here?"

He looked slightly dazed. "Why . . . no . . . you know, we can't hook the boat up simply anywhere." The other tourists aboard might be dull and grouchy, but we were clearly mad. When we explained that we had wanted to interview the villagers, however, he immediately fell into the spirit of the thing. "But we have Nubians on the boat," he said eagerly. "All our help is Nubian. They're from this village. You can interview all you want."

Much of the history of Nubia, which lies south of Aswan in Egypt and flows into the north of the Sudan, is lost in time. But what is left is a fascinating tale. Nubia was the trade route to the Mediterranean from the land of Punt, now Somaliland, where many historians think the ancient Egyptians originated. Pharaohs talked about the "wretched Kushites" in the kingdom of Kush, the southern part of Nubia, now in the Sudan, and, as Pharaohs will, were always crushing them. Under the Roman empire, the Nubians became Christians, and it was in the solitary deserts of Nubia that the lone anchorites and desert fathers originated. During the Christian period from A.D. 600 to 1323, the Nubians used Greek letters to write their own language.

Nearly a thousand years later than the rest of the Arab world, Nubia became Moslem only in the sixteenth century, but then remained so.

In looks, as in everything, the Nubians are distinctive. With rich coffee-colored skins, they have fine features and heavy-lidded, often very sensitive and expressive eyes. Though dark-skinned, they are not pure Negroid but a mixture of Hamitic and Negroid. They have always been distinguished by their honesty, cleanliness and reliability. They address each other with formal grace and, though they make excellent servants, do not like to be called servants.

Dejab Mahmoud, a big handsome Nubian, dressed in typical long dress and turban, sat beside us on the deck. He had so much dignity that it seemed obvious it was he who was doing us a favor. Only six years ago, his village of Kalapsha was flooded by the dam. The villagers had got on ships, many crying and moaning at having to leave their dogs behind, and sailed away to the new Nubian villages down the Nile. "But they had built the houses in blocks right next to each other," Dejab related, in the honest, straightforward way of the Nubians. "When you talk in one, you hear the voices in the other. Many did not like this at all. Before, each one had a yard. But that is the only reason we did not like it."

I had seen pictures of the romantic Nubian villages which had lined the hilltops on both sides of the Nile south of Aswan. They were sparkling white houses, often domed and often trimmed with exquisite hand paintings. All of Nubia, in fact, had a pristine whiteness about it, a whiteness now dimly reflected from underneath the blue waters of Lake Nasser.

Dejab, whose name means "gold" from the ancient Nubian gold mines, sat easily and talked, not even embarrassed by two Western women in bathing suits. A pink sandstone cliff reflected in the creeping water, and a white felucca boat sailed through the reflection like a flying moth, leaving soft ripples in its gentle wake.

"There is one other problem," he went on. "Some men had three or four wives, and before they had different houses. Now all the wives are in one house. Some have gone out and built additional houses themselves. But the young men—they have only one wife. They have more education . . . and life is too expensive."

This, in effect, was what had happened to some 34,000

Nubians in the villages that were flooded. They were resettled in thirty-three villages on 75,000 acres of reclaimed
land. The government had built new villages of red stone,
with houses in cubes, in place of the bulbous houses seen
now only by the staring fish of the lake. There was no
question that the government had done good things for
them, like building schools and hospitals. "Before, there
was a doctor each month," he said. "And now the government gives money to the people who are old and cannot
work."

"What other changes has the new village made in your
lives?" I asked Dejab.

"The little girls used to make holes in their lips and
put in different colors," he said slowly. "Now they go to
schools away from the village. They think this is no longer
so pretty, and they just stopped doing it."

For the first time, as they now were integrated into the
society, Nubians were being drafted into the army. And
the war? Dejab sat there stolidly, unperturbedly. "We must
go," he said stoically. "It is the law. It is for the country."

Another Nubian, a young man of twenty-two, was torn
still further—not between Kalapsha and Kom Omba, not
between wives on different sides of the river and wives
in one house, but between Cairo and his village. Cultural
schizophrenia is so common in the underdeveloped world
as it starts to develop that it barely needs mention. Ahmed
was a typical example. He had lived in Cairo with his
family and loved it. But if he married, he said, he would
insist his wife wear Nubian robes, at least while in the
village. "In Cairo, it would not matter," he said. "But
in the village it would be disrespectful to wear Western
dress." We all make our little compromises with life.

That night we had a "party" on the boat. Ahmed led
the Nubian dancers who entertained, dancing with great
dignity to the Nubian music which sounded so much like

some of the Negro music from the United States. I
wondered—had it come from Nubia to the States three
hundred years ago, or had it come up the Nile the year
before via Cairo from the United States?

We sat that night, at the "party," with the assistant
manager and Hessam Sadek, the big, handsome Egyptian
manager of the boat. At the next table was a rather weary-
looking young man—his expression was most jaded for
his age, which could not have been much more than thirty
—whom Sadek explained was from the Greek Alexandrian
family which had owned the largest whiskey factory in
Egypt before the revolution. At one point, Sadek picked
up the bottle we were drinking from and held it up to
the young man. "It still has your name," he called to him.

"But it isn't ours," the tired young man called back
in the exhausted way of Egyptians of his diminished class.

"Their business was nationalized after 1952," Sadek
explained. "He lives in Switzerland now. He's a millionaire."
He laughed slightly, but it was more like a muffled snort.
"This is the first time he's ever been up the Nile," he
said pointedly.

Sadek was a handsome, sensuous man with, one felt,
probably voracious appetites. For an Arab, he talked with
an unusual freeness and humor. "The women look shy,"
he said that night, smiling. "But the way they behave . . .
Once I was in Kuwait at a minister's party and one of the
wives had a long black robe with her face covered except
for the eyes, which had network over them. This woman
was going up the stairs, and she suddenly winked at me
from behind the network. Then she just happened to open
her robe in front and underneath . . . she had on a mini-
skirt."

The two men began a good-natured banter about women
and the ship. "Thursday night is the best time," Sadek
said, "because Friday is the Moslem holy day. So Thursday

afternoon the women go down to the river to bathe . . .
in little nooks and corners. . . ."

"He's out there with the glasses," the assistant manager
volunteered.

"The crew comes from these villages, and they like to
warn the women," Sadek continued, a big smile. "So when
we come close to the places where they bathe, they blow
the ship's whistle." He paused. "It's funny . . . so many
of them don't leave."

The next day we arrived in Luxor, halfway down the
river from between Aswan and Cairo. Luxor, where the
famous temple of Karnak stands. Luxor, where the valleys
of the Kings and Queens lie. Luxor, where the system of
vendetta, vengeance and revenge, which came to be the
evil backbone of the Sicilian Mafia, grew like a stunted
but persistent weed.

Among the Egyptian fellahin townspeople around Luxor,
the system of revenge—for a family death, premarital sex
or other insults—had become so refined that if, for instance,
a man of one family was killed by a man of another, the
first family would not wash nor its members engage in
marital relations or mourn until revenge had been taken.
A young boy would be told from the time he was five
that he was duty-bound to take revenge if, say, his father
had been killed. Nor could he marry until he had taken
revenge. Sometimes when ten had been killed on each side,
the feud would end; it would never end with nine on one
side and ten on the other. The Egyptian police were trying
very hard to deal with this. "We cannot punish people
like this as we would for other murders," a police official
in Cairo told me. "It is too ingrained in the culture. We
are educating them, and punishing them, too."

That afternoon in Luxor, sleepy, hot, dazed town on

the Nile, we went to visit a sheikh: one of the wise men
who thrive in the Middle East and who was supposed
to have supernatural powers of foretelling the future. We
passed through a narrow passageway into one of the old
houses on a narrow, babbling street. Inside there was a
small L-shaped room with hard couches. A cock posed in
a small aperture on the wall, and the light sifted in, in
strange patterns through the open roof.

A tiny, unshaved man, wizened and grisled, in white
robe and the wound headpiece of a sheikh or wise man,
crept out carrying a large, handwritten book and a shoebox
with little pots of red ink and pens. A tired-looking
peasant woman crept in. Dressed all in black like a frightened black moth, she glanced with hostile suspicion at
the foreigners there. Then, disregarding them, she sat
down at the "sheikh's" feet, sipping mint tea and murmur-
ing her troubles to him.

The old man took her mother's and husband's names,
wrote them down, mumbled to himself in a singsong as
he crossed and recrossed the letters with connecting lines.
Then he used new letters he got that way to look up pages
in the book and to give her advice—it was good, she
would have a baby. All the things she wanted to hear. He
wrote out three pages in Arabic in red ink and told her,
"Put these in lizard-covered boxes, burn one each night
for three nights with myrrh and stand over the smoke."

Just before we left, Pamela looked at me very seriously
and asked, "Don't you want to have yours told?"

"Those sheikhs . . ." the sacrilegious Hessam Sadek
said angrily as we got back to the boat. "They are considered holy men—good men by the villagers. Some of
them are. But the majority are phoney. They take advantage of the poor people." He scoffed. "We have put a lot of
them in prison. The young girls just married come to them

to ask for a baby. They're thirteen–fourteen. They think they are great men. First time, they pat the girls' hands. Pretty soon they are taking advantage of them. Then . . . the girls *do* have babies."

Sadek, with his cynicism and wit, seemed to me to represent the new generation of Egyptians. He was a lawyer; obviously, he was extremely bright. He was cynical about the past, hopeful about the present. He thought it was good that doctors now had to spend four years working in the villages after they were graduated. He wanted Egypt changed, and he, like so many, was depending upon the High Dam to change not only the farmland but also to change the man.

Over and over during the times I was in Egypt, I was surprised—no, surprised is not the word—stunned— to find so little relationship between the "fanatic Arabs" I had so constantly read about and the thoughtful, troubled, hopeful Egyptians I met. I found, among the average persons, no enthusiasms for war whatsoever. There was resignation, at best a sorrowful acceptance. In some rural settlements, families went into mourning when a son went north to enlist, to "play the fool." They never heard if he died—they only knew if he came home. Nearer the front, villagers felt more concerned, but also more helpless.

There is something softer, something strangely less hysterical about Nasser's *internal* revolution—something very rational about the reordering of society—and something that contrasts to a nearly unbelievable extent with the *external* hysteria. I kept asking myself how it could be? how to explain it? And it took a while before I could.

What seemed most sad in all of this was that Nasser, by his obsessive war with Israel, seemed to be destroying not only peace in the world but also his own revolution with his passion to be leader of the whole Arab world— and to gain this through vanquishing Israel.

"He never talks about the New Man any more," one Western diplomat in Cairo said, almost sadly. "Now it's just a desperate struggle to hang on." His earlier efforts to build a viable political system, through the Arab Socialist Union, for instance, had largely failed, leaving him, Nasser, the man, the heir of the Pharaohs, alone at the top, surrounded no longer by the craftful politicians who had helped him establish his new state in the early days, but by the military men, futilely eager for another "try," and by the technocrats, who always propose economic solutions to political and social problems.

Once Nasser died in that tortured fall of 1970, and Anwar Sadat became president, most analysts saw a new period of administrative efficiency coming in—the post-charisma period. But above all, no matter who ruled Egypt, lay the power of tradition, the instinct, nurtured over five thousand years of living by the river, to "do it" through the family structure and not through the impersonal institutions that typify a modern society. Egypt, despite everything, remained one enormous "clan" of 33 million people in which almost everyone, through some modest connection, had entry to someone important who could help him.

I was sitting in the Gezira Club one night, listening to the rather sad companion clicks of the cocktail glasses and the croquet balls of Egypt's new class, when Yusif Shaheen, Egypt's most talented movie director, sat down beside me at our table. I knew that Shaheen had produced a famous film, *Bab Al Hadeed,* about the Cairo train station of that name. The film was noted for its unusually realistic approach. In the film, Kinawi, a crippled waif who sells newspapers in the station, falls in love with a girl who takes the pendant he inherited from his mother and then mocks him cruelly. As the cripple turns from a gentle soul to the type of sex murderer whose headlined crimes he had shouted to the passengers, one is not incorrectly supposed to see in him symbolically all those who suffer from inborn defects . . . and something of the Arab character, switching so swiftly from openness to violence when provoked.

Sitting there talking that night, I felt I had known Shaheen for years. We were immediately friends. "I am writing a story now about two brothers," he was telling me. "One compromises and compromises for success and finally finds nothing left. It is the same theme of alienation I have dealt with before." He paused. "Here . . . nobody takes part. The peasants live with the closed eyes of centuries, but the ruling circles want us to romanticize them."

"You're talking about a form of schizophrenia," I said.

The handsome young man, wiry, with large piercing eyes, looked at me intensely. "Exactly," he said. "That ought to be the title of a book about this country."

Two days later, in the elegant, Frenchified, gilded, Nile-view apartment of Muhammed Abd El Wahab, the country's most famous composer, he explained the lassitudinous militance that is Egypt today in these artistic terms. "We haven't yet the forms of foreign music, like ballet and jazz," he said. "Here, the mentality still follows the melody. Why? It is a quiet landscape—the Nile, the desert, the sands. There is no thunder, no high mountains, no contrasts."

This man is a millionaire on anyone's terms, and he complains bitterly about the government's income taxes. But soon after lunch, a feast of sixteen platters piled with delectable dishes, he had to leave. He was going to record some Palestinian guerrilla hymns.

And that—Palestinianism—is what took me eventually from the Egyptian contradictions to those parts of the

world where there are no "contradictions" at all, where
Arabs are not quiet like the Egyptians but quite "mad,"
like the Iraqis and Syrians, and blastingly loud, like the
Palestinians. But not yet.

CHAPTER II

Of Russians and Poets and, Latterly, Us

The building of *Al Ahram,* the semiofficial newspaper of Egypt, is a spectacular new building filled with sometimes self-consciously ultramodern equipment, beautiful tapestries and an employee "cafeteria" on the roof that is perhaps the finest restaurant in Cairo. The director of *Al Ahram* is the handsome Mohammed Hassenein Heikal, a mysterious comrade of Nasser's from the early days of the revolution who, before the President's death, sat at the right hand of the throne. Heikal spoke for Nasser, and *Al Ahram* spoke for Nasser. But from time to time, Heikal went through periods of depression and didn't want to talk to anybody, particularly visiting newsmen.

One week he had a problem. He confided to a Western diplomat—and, curiously enough, he was generally on the best of terms with Western diplomats—that he didn't know what he was going to do; he was in one of his periodic withdrawal moods, and the New York *Times'* influential and important Cy Sulzberger was coming through the next day. *That* is very Egyptian.

I came to spend a lot of time at *Al Ahram* because in the very beginning I had met so many of their writers and they were so helpful. It was an excellent way to tunnel and burrow into the society. One day I was eating lunch there with Kemal Al Mallakh in the cafeteria when a slim, wiry, strikingly handsome young man came up to talk to him.

The man's appearance was arresting. It was not just that he was "handsome"—most Arabs are rather or quite handsome, but this man was not handsome in the traditional Arab-in-the-desert sense. He had large glowing eyes, and there was a gaunt, haunted beauty about him. It seemed that everything inconsequential was peeled away from him—and only something very simple and pure was left. When Kemal introduced us, the man looked at me with a long, searching look and said, "Yes, she is all right. She has a good face."

The haunted, spiritual-looking young man turned out to be *the* young poet in the Arab world, and as such was the equivalent of a Frank Sinatra in his time. He gave poetry readings for thousands of swooning young people in Cairo, and embodied in himself the traditional role of the Arab poet, whose words "flew across the desert faster than arrows."

Though only in his thirties, he was the father of the literary movement of the Palestinian resistance.

Always, poets had been specially honored in this part of the world, not only because the Koran is God's poetry but because in ancient times the poet was conceived to be a person endowed with supernatural knowledge and magic power, a defender of the tribe and its honor and a means of perpetuating its glorious deeds.

His name was Muin Besieso and he came from Gaza.

The next time I came to Cairo, I ran into Muin again at *Al Ahram* and we got together that evening to talk.

His poetry was very modern and skeptical—flowing and beautiful like the Arab poems of old but with none of that poetry's open-ended faith in God and fate. Muin saw the world in very stark, cynical terms, and in part this was because he was a Palestinian Arab, with all their opportunities for solidly based lack of faith.

His father had been a rich man in Gaza, one of the most awful places on earth—"We owned thirteen villages," he told me once—and in those days Muin liked to throw money around in Cairo night clubs. Later he became caught up in the "cause"—he identified strongly with Fatah— and now, in his late thirties, he wanted "only to go somewhere and write my poems and plays."

For a long time, he had had political problems with Egypt. When he was still in Gaza, which from 1948 to 1967 was under a harsh and corrupt Egyptian military administration, United States Secretary of State John Foster Dulles visited Egypt. Muin wrote a bitter poem about how Dulles could go to Cairo but he—a Palestinian supposedly being "protected" by the Egyptians—could not. It was the first instance that I had seen of the strong Palestinian feeling against the Arab governments. Apparently he, like many of the commandos and their higher-placed sympathizers, was carefully watched by the vigilant Egyptian secret police.

Inside Muin Besieso, as in so many of the men I met in the Middle East, lived a tortured human being. Brilliant; but with not enough psychic room for the free exercise of his brilliance. Ambitious; but, at the same time that he strove so much, feeling that all was somehow hopeless and abortive. And as with so many Arabs, at the end of gigantic outpourings of talent and energy, one seemed to come to a final point of weakness, a point at which everything came to nothing.

The Fates? Islamic fatalism? Palestinian bitterness? What was it?

Muin, likely nearly all the Palestinians I met, was intensely interested in analyzing the Israelis; but he did not take the closed position that the more fanaticized, less objective ones took. He was doing a book on Israeli novelists—comparing them to Arab novelists—and he told me he found that "all their heroes have this tremendous restlessness. It is a little like the rest of the world, but it is also different. At the end of their strivings, they come up against an invisible wall, where there is no future, no place to go in the world. It is easy to build tuna-fish plants; it is not easy to build a nation plant."

It struck me as so strange, for this is almost exactly what the Israelis would say about the Arabs, except it was *not* easy for them to build tuna plants.

Was it another example of the mutual projection of spirit these two peoples have toward each other? Of their strange identification with each other?

Muin, a graduate of the American University of Cairo, was bitter about the United States. Typically, he saw us as having a "tremendous technology, being able to put a man on the moon, but having no social and human development." "Where is your humanity?" he used to ask me, so accusingly that I started looking over my shoulder.

But despite this melancholy and bitterness, Muin could be very funny. He had a mischievous smile and a slightly fey sense of humor. I have never met anyone so totally the poet in terms of being traditionally, absent-mindedly, creatively engrossed in his work and thought.

One day I was to meet him at *Al Ahram* for lunch in the roof cafeteria, and I was about fifteen minutes late. When I walked into his office, he was standing by his desk fiddling with some papers and looking stricken. "Where have you been?" he demanded. "I was so worried."

"But, Muin," I remonstrated, "I'm only fifteen minutes late. It's only . . ."

"Thank God," he said, in obvious relief. "I thought you had gone to the Al Ahram out by the pyramids."

Apparently there is a business with the same name out by the pyramids at Gizeh, just on the outskirts of Cairo —a trip which would take about forty-five minutes from downtown. "Why," I demanded, "would I go to the pyramids, when I know very well that your office is only a mile from the Hilton?"

"Because it happens to me all the time," he answered, still slightly upset. "Every once in a while, I get in a cab and tell them 'Al Ahram,' and then I sit there thinking and composing and before I know it I'm out at the pyramids." That was Muin.

One evening Muin, by this time a good friend, invited me to have dinner with his "Russian publisher" and another Russian writer. I was delighted. Russia had long been one of my interests. I had spent three months in the country in 1967, and I spoke enough Russian to get by. I knew that Muin had been to the Soviet Union several times, that he was a personal friend of the famous Russian poet, Yevgeny Yevtushenko, and that he depended financially on the foreign exchange he could earn from his Russian sales; it was his financial passport to weeks of freedom, ironically, in the West. It was that breath of fresh air that the hungering, creative spirit in him needed so much.

When I saw the two Russians, I immediately had a strange feeling of "I've known you before . . ." One, Anatoly Safonov, was the famous editor of *Ogonyok*, the *Life* of Russian magazines; a hard-liner, he was heartily disliked by liberal Russian writers. He was huge—one of those bears of Russian men—and so was his companion, the far more ebullient and relaxed, Yuri Rumyantsev, the Soviet Writers Union man for Africa and the Middle East.

"But we've met before," I said to Safonov, hesitantly, a little unsure of myself, but still with the distinct feeling that I *know* this man . . . We exchanged dates in various places when we could have met, but none of them matched, so I soon gave up the game and we all went to supper.

We sat in an attractive outdoor restaurant on an arm of the Nile—it was already fall, and evenings were growing cool—and there developed, to my initial astonishment, a "big power" group of the Russians and me, the American, and a lone "group" of Muin, the brilliant Third Worlder.

Muin was playing the perfect host, trying hard to order things the Russians liked and even—the perfect Arab host —being slightly subservient to them. They, in turn, very nearly ignored him; they pounded the table, as Russians are wont to do with proletarians like waiters (particularly in underdeveloped countries, for their own waiters are more arrogant than the Central Committee), and demanded "more whiskey." They voraciously wolfed down all the hors d'oeuvres of cheese and sausage and demanded: "Is that all?" They talked to *me*—not because I was a woman, but because I was an American, and they put Americans in their same class. Once one of them said to me, in Russian so Muin could not understand, "These countries . . . these countries . . ." He shook his head. "You Americans and we Russians . . . we understand each other." Yes, we certainly had the world divided up neatly.

I was more sympathetic when, after Muin had elaborated the usual tiresome Arab rhetoric about war, one of them said, now very soberly, "They . . . they don't know what war is."

Safonov and Rumyantsev invited us back to the "Neel" Hotel for some Armenian brandy and we sat in their room drinking until well past four in the morning. As we approached the hotel, Safonov and I had been talking about Russian literature and I told him how much I loved Turgenev, that magnificent nineteenth-century Russian writer who so beautifully blended the facts of journalism and the truths of literature. "Turgenev," Safonov said, turning his huge hulk toward me. "That's strange for an American girl. You know, it's funny, but I was at a party in Chicago some years ago and I met a girl who loved Turgenev."

I started to laugh.

"It was you!" he cried.

And indeed it had been me! The slight redolence of remembrance that I had felt upon seeing Safonov had been accurate; we *had* met at a cocktail party for a visiting Russian delegation around 1961, when I was still reporting in Chicago. And we had argued about Turgenev!

The night was strange. Riddle piled upon riddle. As we talked, nothing was said directly, everything was slightly veiled. Very Russian. If anyone had been listening in, nothing could have been blamed on anyone, and yet—and yet, we all understood everything. Once, when Yuri spoke vehemently about intellectuals being free in Russia, I broke into laughter and fell over on the bed, holding my stomach. They understood perfectly. Muin was the only one who was more direct; he felt obliged, for matters of pride and conviction, I suppose, to say he was very distressed with the treatment of Yevtushenko. Yevtushenko had been scheduled to translate his poems into the Russian edition, but at the last moment was forced to withdraw from the project because of political pressures.

The evening ended, after all that whiskey, wine and Armenian brandy, with Safonov silently stalking off to sleep like a great bear going into hibernation and with Yuri and me arguing. Finally I got up and left, and Muin followed behind, for some reason very angry with *me* for insulting his Russian friends. Actually, by that time, neither of his friends had the faintest idea what we were doing. I had certainly not insulted them . . . and they understood this, for after all, didn't we run the world together?

Later, in the late fall and early winter of 1970, when I was back in the States for a while before returning to Russia and the Middle East, Muin went back to Russia with another famous Palestinian poet, Mahmoud Darwisch, who lives in the West Bank of Israeli-occupied territory. And Muin wrote a curious allegory for *Al Ahram:*

> One day in Russia, Darwisch was trying to fix the handle on his suitcase, which had broken in New Delhi. When he failed to do so, I said: "Look at the country without arms!" And when a hotel becomes a suitcase and when a necktie becomes a river and a shirt becomes a meadow and a coat a mountain and when all that can be stuffed into a suitcase whose arms fall off in New Delhi and whose body stays in Moscow without arms, the responsibility of the poet intensifies and under such circumstances the poet would want to tie his homeland with ropes over his shoulders and walk to safety.

I thought a good deal about the Muins of the Arab world. "He is a genius," Yuri had said, and doubtless in poetry he is, but the Russians didn't really respect him because they didn't really respect the Arabs. Moreover, he was a Palestinian born in Gaza, forced to live in Egypt and write, not for the Western world where his cultural roots lay, but for the Eastern Slavic world, never greatly admired in the Arab milieu. That unfamiliar world ironically became his means—through convertible currency—to return on rare, desperate flights, to the West. If one grasps the significance of that sad paradox, one grasps the type of conflicts that many Arabs live under.

Most of the Arab "geniuses," moreover, abhor the lack of intellectual freedom in Russia and find most Russians too heavy a people to really like. Some of them sorrow over the persecution of Russian intellectuals, just as they sorrow over the increasingly closed sound box their own searchings must be bound by. But to me one of the many great tragedies of the Middle East today is the way in which Arab intellectuals—all Western educated and oriented, remember!—have been spun around ideologically to find themselves facing the Orient they have always fled from instead of the Occident they have always craved.

After just a few weeks there, I could say without the slightest doubt that the Russians and the Arabs come very near to despising each other; this impression was strengthened even more in the months to come. At base, it is a question of temperamental incompatibility—they simply do not get along. The Arab intellectuals and leaders are Westernized and crave the Western good life. Deep inside themselves, there is an unconscious gut realization that everything good and modern and free in their lives came from the West, while from the East came the Mongols and the Dark Ages and superstition. As one of my Cairo friends spat out one day: "There are as many Russians here as there were British, but the British were gentlemen!" And another, one of those who inhabited the Gezira Club, sniffed: "Nobody would ever bring them to the club." Shopkeepers and cabdrivers complained about their being too cheap and one said wistfully, "They never smile. Never."

On another level, the pious Moslem of the traditional faith is a withdrawn, inward-looking man, stern with himself and private in converse with his God. He distrusts the Godlessness of the Communists and is temperamentally turned away by their arrogant assumptions that the world can and should be transformed in their image.

The English writer Harry Hopkins tells the story of the Egyptian man—a Moslem—who was told by a Russian colleague that the Russians do not encourage superstitions. "Now, one moment," said the Egyptian. "Remember you will not always be so young and strong as you are now. One day you will be old and you will need help and you will wonder about the meaning of it all. In what will you believe?"

"In the Leningrad Technological Institute," replied the Russian, without a second's hesitation.

One gets some idea of the chasm between the two peoples!

In another popular story in Cairo the Russians are telling the Egyptians over and over to retreat and "make a stand." But each time they make a stand they are defeated again. Finally, in desperation, the Egyptians ask once more what to do.

"Wait for winter," comes the Russian reply.

The Russians return the compliments a hundredfold. They find the Arabs dirty, unpredictable, neglectful of their children, dishonest, cowardly and unable to work together. They are impatient and infuriated by them, as they are with most underdeveloped peoples. But since they have to be in these "funny lands" for some reason, they create their own little Russia, complete with Soviet PXs and their own blocks of buildings.

One evening in Aswan, we went with our two Egyptian guides from the Information Ministry to the Russian Club. Just as in Cuba, the Soviets were living by themselves in air-conditioned compounds with their own club. It might have been as remote from the Egyptians of Aswan as was Milwaukee. Walking in the front door was like walking into an American clubhouse of some sort—a YMCA or an Elks Club. And indeed, both Russians and Americans are very much alike in their predisposition for joining and working

doggedly together on community betterment and amusement. Some were painting signs for the next musicale. A
jazz band was practicing. Some were drinking Coca-Cola
while playing billiards. It was a den of busyness, so different from the Egyptians' accustomed lassitude.

The two Egyptians with us, friendly fellows with whom
we had been having a fine chat, seemed suddenly to feel
terribly out of place. They hung back, afraid or wary of
going in, standing first on one foot, then on another.
Pamela and I walked into a side room and began to talk
to a charming young couple, both of whom were English
teachers, and an engineer.

"The Egyptians think now that they will be able to build
dams in other countries," Pamela said, in passing.

The engineer nearly exploded in laughter.

Then he said, pointedly, in a manner that I cannot imagine the most arrogant American ever assuming in a
"comradely" country, "When you travel around this country looking at what it was in ancient days and you look at it
now . . ." He arched his eyebrows, with unmistakable
meaning. By now our two Egyptian friends had moved
just inside the door to the room and were beginning to
look decidedly unhappy, so we soon left.

Another time, in Cairo, a Western diplomat told me of a
joke a Soviet diplomat told him that reminded him of what
Arabs were like. It seemed that there were three animals—a donkey, a rabbit and a fox—who came to a river.
They were trying to think of how to get across it. The fox
looked at it and said they must build a road that was
zigzagged, for that was how he ran. The rabbit looked at
it and said No, it would have to be built in islands, for
he hopped from island to island. But the donkey thought
and thought, then he said, "But no, first we must decide
whether we're going to build it up the river or across the
river." Later, in 1970, *Al Ahram* quoted Alexei Kosygin,

the Soviet Premier, as telling the Iraqi Deputy Premier: "You confuse us. We beg you for your own sake and for the sake of your friends to agree on one thing—agree on the maximum or minimum, it does not matter which, but agree. For heaven's sake, agree on something."

But it is too easy to look only at all these very obvious and true examples of Russian-Arab incompatibility; it is too simplistic to look at the Russian Club in Cairo with its sign over the door to "Russian-Arab Friendship" and to note that no Arab ever crosses its sill; it is too misleading to suppose these things are really important. On a human level, yes, they are. But on a political level they are not.

In the Moslem world, incompatibility is no grounds for divorce, but barrenness is—and it is the relations with the West that the Arabs see as having been barren.

Let us look very briefly at Russian expansion in the Arab world, if only to get some of the confusing facts straight. The Soviet Union immediately recognized the State of Israel after its creation in 1948, but by 1956 it had set about single-mindedly to increase its hold on the Arab world. From the mid-1950s to 1970, Russia invested $5 billion in economic and military aid in the area, 2.6 billion of which went to Egypt (compared to American grants of $795 million, loans of $583 million and military equipment grants of $88 million to all Arab states since 1945). They deliberately ignored the fact that their own Communist Party members were imprisoned by the Nasserites—they were looking at the bigger picture and thinking in the long run. By 1971, there were at least 10,000 Russians in Egypt alone, an approximate 6000 of these being military advisors who had penetrated all the way down to the battalion level. In the military schools, these

Russians decided who passed and who didn't. The Russians had indeed installed SAM-3 missiles along the canal and there were Russians—and only Russians—manning them, as well as flying certain planes. Russian pilots had come close to clashing with Israeli pilots. They had jet bases in Syria and Iraq as well, and their constantly expanding fleet in the Mediterranean, where the Sixth Fleet formerly reigned supreme, was backing up all the other military activity.

The Russians had moved carefully and intelligently, losing only a handful of men, craftfully expanding their influence in a gigantic area which controlled many of the waterways and much of the oil of the world. It was not an obsessive, mythological diplomacy, like the American diplomacy in Vietnam—it was a cool, calculated diplomacy, backed by military might and real interests. And it had totally destroyed whatever Western influence was still left in the area that the West had not destroyed itself. Of course the Russians were mightily unhappy with their protégé's lack of military prowess—they certainly did not want a repeat of 1967.

What struck me as most sad about all this was that none of it *had* to happen; the Arabs were the most pro-Western of peoples, and Nasser was until the late fifties the most pro-Western of leaders. It was the sudden switch—made more poignant and bitter by the feeling among the Arabs that they had been deserted and rejected by a West they adored—that led to the frustration and the fanaticism.

"It's such an awful thing," the young man named Soleiman, who was music editor of *Al Ahram* and shared an office with Muin, expressed to me one day. "We are being pushed into something we don't want. The way the Egyptians were toward the West—they were absolutely crazy for it. You can't imagine how they were. Then to

have the powerful turn against us. It's something more
than we can bear. I feel that if this is power, then I don't
want power, I don't want to be strong. You are telling us,
'You deserve nothing, you are nobody.' There [Israel] is
technology and here [the Arab world] is nothing. You
are forcing us to choose between this ideology and that,
and we don't want to do this. It is not in tune with what
we are. Moslem people are very religious. We just want to
be ourselves, and we can't be because of this. Sometimes it
makes us crazy."

As I traveled through and lived in the Middle East, I
came to realize, initially to my surprise, that, as one of the
few remaining American diplomats put it, not only every
cultured Egyptian but "Almost every single leader of the
Palestinian movement was trained in an American university. And so they're doubly bitter about American support
of Israel. They took the Declaration of Independence seriously."

Over and over to me, Arab leaders pleaded that the
United States simply "equalize" the situation somewhat—
make some "gesture" toward them, as they feel the French
and British have done recently. "Love us just a little,"
they seemed to be saying. They also felt that the 1967 war,
after which most of the Arab states broke relations with
the United States for its support of Israel, was the turning
point. "It is just impossible now to deal with the United
States," Omar el Hadj Musa, minister of national guidance
in the Sudan, told me. "Before 1967, Israel was a bother,
but it was something we could live with. Now, no. It is
not just Israel now but Egyptian land that is being held.
The United States gives us nothing, not even a gesture. At
least the British now say that there *is* an 'Arab side' and
this makes a great deal of difference. Even gestures would
help, if they were continuous."

Others saw the young Arabs turning away from the West and toward the East because of "moral revulsion with Western policies." "There is a feeling that the Western world has turned a blind eye to the massive injustice the Arabs feel was perpetrated in Palestine," said Walid Khalidi, professor of political science at the American University of Beirut. "The utter moral indifference of the West on this issue acted as a great emotional incentive in accentuating the leftward radical trend."

And, oh, the expressions of unrequited love. "The Russians . . ." an Egyptian woman journalist said, her mouth set bitterly. "They would, as we say in Arabic, burn all their fingers like candles for us. In effect, do anything for us. But we just don't like them. We still adore the West . . . and the West despises us."

At times, I had to ask myself: Were we, in our well-justified horror at ourselves for the horrible fate of the Jews under Hitler, now promulgating out of our unquenchable guilt a second wrong which could cause still another conflagration?

All of this leads directly to another Arab complex which is directly involved with this rationale. This is the "desert-bloom complex." The Arabs cannot bear to hear about how Israel "made the desert bloom" because it touches such deep chords of insecurity about Arab technological inferiority. The idea that those who "made the desert bloom" somehow have a greater right to the land—that with advanced technology there accrues also a moral right —is abhorrent and absolutely unacceptable to them.

Much of this feeling was expressed in the words of a Syrian chauffeur I had met later in Damascus who suddenly cried out, "There are ninety million of us and we have oil. Why do you stand behind one million Jews?" Implicit in that piteous outcry was the feeling that even ninety to one, with fountains of bubbling oil thrown in to boot, the West didn't think the Arabs were worth anything.

But if these traumatized attitudes dominated the thinking of the middle generation, I was soon to find that they very clearly did not dominate the thinking of the younger one. This generation was Cubanized. It was locked in an implacable, cold rejection of the West and all it stood for. The woman scorned now had a knife in her teeth.

The politicians of this group had simple answers—"Imperialist" answers. "The United States created a foreign entity in my homeland after my people were forced out," fedayeen leader Yasir Arafat said. "You can compare Israel to the East India Company from which England was able to expand and dominate all of India."

Dr. Khalidi of A.U.B. took the (in his words) "less vulgar" position that the "natural American system of checks and balances—in ideas as well as politics—had broken down as regards the Palestine question. "I'm not asking American public opinion to decide my way," he said. "I'm asking them to know what it is." He talks about the "Gentile Zionists" whose "attitude toward Zionism is an extraordinary mixture of latent anti-Semitism compensated for by Zionism . . . Christian guilt feelings . . . a very complicated story . . . in which they are fighting the Arabs by proxy."

And while it was still the rule and not the exception that Americans were treated with enormous friendliness and generosity in the Arab world, and particularly in Egypt, I could not but wonder how long this would last. While I was in Cairo, for instance, an American tourist was out walking, when suddenly a group of poor Egyptians around him began to shout and spit at him. A policeman led him out of the angry crowd, but not before he saw the

cart going by with the bodies of five dead Egyptian soldiers
from the fighting in Sinai. There were going to be many
more carts.

And then there were the American diplomats . . .

By the time I got to the Middle East, being an American
diplomat there was one of the hardest jobs in the world.
And one of the hardest jobs for a journalist was finding an
American diplomat. Since 1967, seven Arab countries had
broken relations with the United States, so the American
diplomats in these countries were hidden in peculiar "Ameri-
can-interests sections" of other embassies. "It's a little like
living in sin without the benefit of clergy," one American
chargé d'affaires, who acts as the senior American official
in one Arab country, said. "You don't know if you'll
be chucked out in the street the next day or what. You
only know what rights you don't have."

The American diplomats encompassed every type from
well-educated Arabists greatly bereaved over the loss of the
Arab countries to the United States to peevish men who
thought it was just as well to be rid of them. Many of
them were envious of us correspondents and in particular
of our contacts with the Palestinians, because it had got to a
point where almost no one would talk to them.

Here, as in most of the world, American diplomats
tended to swing between two equally unacceptable ex-
tremes of the pendulum—between identifying too totally
and too emotionally with the Arabs and despising them
too fully. There were few who looked fairly and non-emo-
tionally at simply what our interests were in this vast area.
Few seemed to be secure enough as men to be objective as
diplomats. Few were men who understood that big, secure
countries can and should do magnanimous things that little,
insecure, tormented countries simply cannot do.

And few who really studied the area were optimistic.
Some American Arabists like William Polk, the knowledge-

able director of the Adlai Stevenson Institute in Chicago, fear that the growing trends could eventually lead to total and anti-American militarization of the Arab world; of "Protorevolutionary war societies" and of societies which "will be politicized and revolutionized along the Algerian if not along the Vietnamese or Cuban models."

But how, I kept asking myself, did things get to this point? Where along the way did we, the Americans, do things wrong? Most important, was there at any point a chance of avoiding this outcome without selling out Israel to destruction?

It seems clear today that the United States could have helped both to keep the Arab world in the Western camp and to make Israel much more secure than it is today. Nasser was not temperamentally anti-Jewish or anti-Israel; history shows quite clearly he was not. Rather, he looked at Israel pragmatically, in terms of his own personal ends. And he was certainly pro-American.

The problem, rather, was on another level completely: the level of a great nation showing respect for a budding new nation and being willing, in its greatness and strength, to show a little patience. At heart, it was a question of how to deal with national humiliation. This, John Foster Dulles, the big-stick man of the 1950s, which were the key years for our relations with the underdeveloped world, could not—would not—understand. Dulles only wanted to talk to the Arabs about the "Communist menace," when their only interest was in ridding themselves of colonialism and regaining some of their long-lost dignity.

Here, as in so many areas, we made the crucial error of believing everything would be all right if we only gave technical aid. We did not understand that what the poor, rising peoples want is recognition, and aid only when it is symbolic of that recognition of their general use and value in the world. Had we given them this recognition,

it would have drained much of the psychic poison out of
their relations with Israel and staved off Russian hegemony.

From the period of the mid-fifties, when relations between the United States and Egypt were fairly good, we
went to the late fifties, when, step by miserable step,
they fell painfully apart. When the United States turned
down Egypt's requests for military aid, Nasser announced
in September 1955 that Czechoslovakia would supply
the arms. This was followed by Dulles' announcement on
July 20, 1956, along with a statement that the Egyptians
were not capable of building the dam, that the United
States would not lend Egypt the $200 million for Aswan.
On July 26, Nasser nationalized the Suez Canal. This was
followed by the Israel-French-British invasion of Suez, the
UN cease-fire, increasing Arab terrorism against Israel, and
finally the 1967 war, when U Thant removed the UN force
that was between Egypt and Israel, thus allowing Israel to
strike first in response to Arab armies massing menacingly
on her borders. It was a tit-for-tat progression worthy of
five-year-olds but not grown men.

The devastatingly quick Israel victory in the 1967 war
traumatized the Arabs, who only a week before had been
ghoulishly eloquent with the most earth-shaking threats of
destruction. As William Polk has written in a Chicago
newspaper of all the abundant Arab defeats: "The governments of the Arabs who created Islam, who conquered
half the world, whose caliphate shone with the bright
glow of civilization while Europe slept in the ignorance of
the Dark Ages and whose vast corpus of literature and
rich language were admired all over the world, were spot-
lighted as impotent, backward, corrupt bombasts."

One does not have to excuse the many vulgar stupidities
of the Arabs during this period to see that the United
States, too, was flagrantly wrong and shortsighted on many
points. If they were to play the immature game of tit for tat,

it could at least be blamed on the fact they were a new, only recently colonized, and extremely touchy nation. What about us?

Again, one does not have to excuse the pathological hysteria of the Arab governments to see that many of the things we did to them were humanly intolerable. American diplomats who were in Cairo at the time of Nasser's rise recall that one of the things that most infuriated him was, after his debut as Third World leader at the Bandung Conference in 1956, American embassy personnel in Cairo were referring to it as the "Darktown Strutters' Ball." Nasser has got sorely blamed for the "Nazi agents" he brought to Cairo after World War II—but Miles Copeland, the American intelligence agent who with the CIA's Kermit Roosevelt was perhaps the American closest to Nasser at that time, has told how it was the United States who pushed these German agents off on Nasser. They were agents who had co-operated with us and we needed a secure niche where they could fade away after the war. Copeland says the Egyptians made little use of them, mistrusted them and paid them far less than other advisors.

But what about the Arab absurdities that turned the civilized world off the Arab world? Why this consuming hatred for this tiny country in their midst? Why the martial bombast?

There are many answers, but they can all be distilled into one important but usually missed point. It is a conclusion I came to only slowly, and then with surprise, as I traveled through the Arab world.

It soon struck me that the war "between the Arabs and the Israelis" is not a war between Arabs and Israelis at all. It is a war between the Arabs and the West—or, if you want to be very, very metaphysical, between the Arabs and their own tormented vision of themselves.

It is not Israel that the Arabs hate so much, and far less the Jews because they are "Jews," but the fact that they think the West, acting on its own guilt, "imposed" Israel on them and then abandoned them in admiration for Israel. What the Jews brought to Israel that was offensive to the Arabs was not their Jewishness, it was their Westernization and their ability to succeed . . . and it is this that affronts and infuriates and drives the Arabs. Their pride has been destroyed, and the webs of their pride are as thin as those that spiders weave. Pride dominates Arab culture.

Unless we understand all this, we miss the entire core of the reality of the conflict. We have not a collision of two peoples and certainly not two religions or even—though this is closer—two rights; we have a conflict of two epochs, of two dialectics, of two ways of looking at man. As they grapple in their blindness, they comprehend even less of each other. This is why everything in the Middle East is so oblique and apparently unfathomable; that is why, so much of the time, so little makes any sense.

I liked all of Muin's poems that I read—they had a ringing, thoroughly original cynical lyricism about them—but the one I liked best had to do with the famous *"Murad, the Bear."* Muin, with his still slightly accented English, always called it "Murad, ze beer."

It seemed that the Russians had sent the Egyptians a circus bear, whom they christened with the noble old Arab name of Murad. But Murad didn't like dancing in captivity to the caprices of his trainer, and one night in Cairo he attacked and killed the man. Soon, with the help of Muin's poem, Murad became famous. He was moved to the Cairo zoo, which is a lovely zoo, and the Sunday I strolled over to see Murad his keeper proudly told me: "Murad is very happy now that he is in the zoo and not in the circus. He has his own room. He is very gentle and we have no trouble with him." Just then Murad roared and nearly bit his lady bear's ear off. "He did not like to dance," the keeper, really now more of a guide to Murad, finished. I almost said that I wouldn't have liked to dance with him either, but I restrained myself.

In the poem, Murad comes before the judge, charged with the murder of his trainer.

"What is your name?" the judge asks.

"My name is Murad, and I am a bear," the animal answers respectfully.

"What was your business?"

"I danced in the circus," Murad answers.

"And now you are charged with killing your trainer," the judge continues in the poem. "Why did you do that?"

"I am really very sorry," Murad answers. "I didn't mean to do it."

He pauses, then continues sadly: "But I am a bear. Are bears supposed to dance? And there are other animals in the circus. Are they supposed to walk on their hind legs and jump through hoops? Is that what animals are for?"

It struck me that Murad had become so popular because there are so many people, Arabs like anyone else, who do not like to dance. Now they are unhappily dancing to a Russian tune, but it never had to be that way.

CHAPTER III

Hello, Miss Smith

▼▼▼

The Jordan Intercontinental Hotel in the Jordanian capital of Amman has a pleasant, if slightly packaged, supper club on its roof. With its padded booths and pseudochic *décor,* it reminds you a little of one of the "better rooms" in one of the "better, bigger, newer motels" around the big American cities.

When one or another of us journalists were not out with the Arab commandos, listening to them curse the Balfour resolution, we would meet there in the evening for dinner and listen to the excellent little band. From the roof of the Intercontinental, there are no lights of Amman. This city is a true desert city. The houses are squat and of sand-colored stone and seem to rise simply as a natural extension of the seven sandy hills on which Amman, like so many other historic cities, is at least in legend built. Except for those weeks which came with dreary regularity about every six months, when Jordan erupted briefly into civil war between the fedayeen and the Jordanian Army,

Amman could seem as removed from the war as Egypt.
Only a few valleys away, Bedouins, those classic rootless
Arabs, were calmly keeping their flocks.

This night, a Saturday, we happened to have a large
and unusually gay group. It was said at times that there
were more foreign journalists in the Intercontinental watching for commandos than there were commandos watching
for correspondents; but this night there were only six of us
watching each other. In addition, there was David Sisson,
head of the United Nations Relief and Works Agency or
UNRWA camps in Jordan, and his Palestinian wife, and
in the midst of our party, if that is what it may be called,
there suddenly appeared another—a tiny, dark-haired
specter.

She was a little frail woman, probably in her fifties but
with dark stringy hair. She wore a matted fur coat that
matched her hair. But the thing that struck my attention—
and I think I was the first person she spoke to, as I was
sitting on the outside—was her almost fearfully bright,
slightly hysterical eyes.

"You all looked as if you were having so much fun."
She said this, and then she just stood there. It was a
plaintive sentence, plaintively spoken and plaintively meant,
and it came as such a sudden shock that it seemed to hang
there in the empty air above our cluttered table for a full,
breathless minute. "I'm sorry to disturb you," she went on,
more commandingly now, "but there's something I think
you should know."

At this point, David, a husky, dark-haired American
with sad eyes and a gravely courteous manner, rose and
pulled up a chair for the uninvited intruder. "Please sit
down," he said, and suddenly everybody was saying, "Oh,
yes, do . . ." and "Please do . . ."

I had not been mistaken in those eyes. "I have just
come from two days in Marka Camp," she began, in a

heavy stage whisper, referring to one of the scattered
UNRWA camps around Amman which house the 600,000
Palestinian refugees, "and I am the last person to get in
there." She sat back, looking both martyred and trium-
phant.

David leaned forward with an almost imperceptible
movement. "How would you like a drink?" he asked her.

She soon told her name, but here we shall simply call
her Miss Smith. She said she would certainly like a brandy.
When it came, she drank the whole thing down in one
gulp and asked for another. I smiled to myself. Things
were moving.

"Oh, it was awful," she went on. "You can't imagine.
The family I stayed with were so clean—and yet they
still had two rats and a cockroach in their house. And the
toilets . . . you can't imagine. Nobody in the camp uses
them."

At this, wondering glances passed from eye to eye.

"And what did *you* do, Miss Smith?" David asked with
just the suggestion of amusement playing about his lips.

"I didn't go." Said stalwartly.

"In two whole days?" someone asked in amazement.
"What did you do?"

"I prayed," she said. "And when I got back to the
hotel . . . it was like a flood." She laughed, a good-natured
laugh. Indeed, since she had made it back to the hotel,
she had something to laugh about.

Finally someone asked her how she spoke to the people
in her camp—did she have an interpreter? "I brought a
copy of the Koran, in English and Arabic, and showed
them verses to show what I meant."

A kind of helpless mirth had engulfed the entire table
by this time. Miss Smith, having had three more brandies,
finally thought to ask David whether he knew anything
about the camps, to which he answered, "I run them."

This type of sentimentally outraged reaction, I found, was—unfortunately—about the only one we had gotten on the Palestinian refugees. That and total disregard on the part of most of the world. But now the story was no longer simply that of misery—the bad-toilets syndrome—and I was determined to report it in a new way. For out of these camps had come the Palestinian commando groups, numbering probably fifty thousand men at this time and unquestionably the most smashingly successful phenomenon in the Arab world.

I was tired of the "miserable refugee" story because I thought it no longer was true. It was a cliché, and clichés are made to be broken by journalists. The very commandos who told you, "We have nothing to lose but our tents," likely as not were doctors, lawyers or poets and graduates of Cairo University, Harvard or the American University of Beirut—and the only tents they were likely to see were on their camping trips to France.

In a moment of whimsy—of sheer perversity—it struck me on one of the first nights in Amman, when I was getting ready for bed: Wasn't it possible that the camps had operated in just the opposite way from what is generally assumed? Wasn't it possible that the camps had actually *bettered* the level of the refugees?

At the time, it was a piece of black humor of the kind we correspondents use to relieve our tensions. I had no idea—or perhaps I did have a strange, unconscious premonition—that this would really prove to be so.

After I put in a request at the Ministry of Information to stay overnight in one of the camps, à la Miss Smith, I began going about Amman, making my contacts with the Arab Palestinian commandos. I knew that it would take a little time, for guerrillas are notorious for "testing" would-be observers with little periods of waiting in which these "friends of the cause" show their faithfulness by infinite, slavish periods of hanging around. It is part of a certain arrogance—you must know when to go along with it and when, frankly, to tell them to go to hell.

I had been among guerrillas before, most notably in Guatemala, where I stayed with them for several days in the mountains after having waited more than a month to get up there with them. But they were, like most respectable guerrillas, totally underground—fighting in their own country against an incumbent rightist government.

In Amman it was completely different. Here the guerrillas—or commandos, as they liked to call themselves; or terrorists, as the Israelis liked to call them—were in a more or less friendly country. Three-quarters of the neat little country, which was artificially created by the British after World War I, was now actually made up of Palestinians, and 600,000 still lived in the camps. In addition to them, there were 300,000 in the Gaza Strip, 140,000 in Syria and 160,000 in Lebanon—most to one extent or another being supported by UNRWA.

Before the traumatized Palestinians swept over Jordan like a wailing wave, the nice little country was largely a land of Bedouins, those original Arabs from the Arabian peninsula who lived in tents of goats' hair and roved the deserts on their camels, raiding other weaker tribes and using the system of vengeance as a means of control in a nomadic society that had no external institutions. They were organized into clans, with every "tent" representing a family. The Bedouins revered the Hashimite kings—first King Abdullah and then King Hussein—because they were descended from Mohammed, and they were most definitely *not* pleased at the invasion by the Palestinians. For one thing, the Bedouins despised city Arabs, saying, in their delicate way, that Allah made the Bedouin and the

camel and then made the town Arab out of the camel's
droppings. It wasn't long before it dawned upon them
that the Palestinians took to the cities with much the same
alacrity as had the Jewish people in medieval Europe. For
this and many reasons, a bitter conflict developed between
the Palestinian newcomers and the Bedouin old-timers,
one that came to a head in the fierce civil war of October
1970.

But Jordan had sustained an even greater blow than the
original emigration of the Palestinians when, in 1967, the
most fertile part of the country—the West Bank of the
Jordan River—and half its people were taken under Israeli
occupation after the six-day war. In tourist revenues from
Jerusalem alone (the old city of Jerusalem had been under
Jordanian administration), they lost $35 million a year.
Jordan had been developing nicely before this, despite its
strange truncation, and was a prosperous and largely
rational little land.

But now . . . Jordan had become the country of the
fedayeen. Amman had become their capital—the "Arab
Hanoi," they called it—and King Hussein, the one leader
who had helped them, taken them into his country and
even given them citizenship, had largely become their prisoner.

At times, Amman seemed like a never-never world, and
not only on the roof of the Intercontinental. At night, the
streets were taken over by the commandos, who rode
freely about in their jeeps with submachine guns sticking
out the windows like unwieldy stalks of corn. Every night
during cocktail hour on the balcony of the Intercontinental,
the commandos came around, looking terribly neatly
pressed and soft-spoken polite, and collected money for
their groups. If you donated, they gave you pastel-colored
tickets denoting the organization; the next night you could

put the tickets on the table, and they wouldn't bother you.

Getting through to the fedayeen can be a lengthy and frustrating process or it can be relatively simple, depending upon whom you know and where and when. The night I arrived in Amman, I found myself getting my visa at the airport along with the two leading Italian journalists from *Corriere della Sera,* Vittorio Lojacono and Gillo Faedi. "Victor" wrote and Gillo photographed. What a team! They'd been through everything, including ferreting out a Mafia chieftain in his Sicilian hideaway and convincing him to make a deal with the authorities. Victor was a big, square man, completely honest and forthright and totally professional. Gillo was a will-o'-the-wisp, with big expressive ironic eyes and a headful of curls that made him look like a handsome Harpo Marx.

Victor and Gillo immediately included me in their already arranged meeting with one of the fedayeen leaders the first morning I was there, and after waiting for about half an hour at the home of the Associated Press correspondent John Halady, the leader suddenly appeared.

We knew he was a prominent surgeon, and we knew that his group wore unusual, even slightly comical, uniforms; they were khaki and covered with rows of variously colored fringes; on their heads they wore hoods with only eye openings. Later I found out that these curious uniforms represented still another example of something that penetrated the entire fedayeen movement, gave it shape, and informed it with a sense of historical ubiquity and inevitability—the uniforms were adapted from a historic Arab battle in Yemen in 2000 B.C., when the famous Queen Balquis adapted these camouflage suits from the Assyrians.

The doctor—or Abu Nidal, as they called him—marched in at the head of three other men. He was a good-looking man of medium height and he had a good sense of humor, which emerged in nervous, almost barklike laughs; he had, too, a distinctly pedantic side which at times bordered on the intensity of a fanatic. This day, he sat behind the desk and we sat in front of him—like students or acolytes—while he lectured us for three full hours.

"We believe Palestine can only be liberated through the armed struggle," he would say. "We have little faith in negotiations. We cannot negotiate the loss of our own country. There is nothing to negotiate. We have been forcibly ejected. Our property was confiscated and our country eliminated from the map."

At this point, Victor, a big, no-nonsense man who is one of Italy's most resourceful journalists, asked Abu Nidal, "What about civilian targets—it is your group, isn't it, which has attacked civilian targets?"

I thought I detected just a momentary contraction on the doctor's face. Then he answered with the same cool assurance he had shown before. "We believe that we Arabs are among the more humanitarian nations in the world," he said, delineating every word as though we were schoolchildren. "Our national history bears ample testimony to that fact. However, we've been subjected by Israeli forces to constant bombardment of our civilian populations. They have respected neither civilians nor hospitals.

"One act was unspeakable. On August 4, 1968, there was the attack on Salt. The Israeli Air Force raided the headquarters of Fatah, near Salt. This was a legitimate goal; I would even allow for a certain degree of miscalculation. What I will never forgive the so-called graduates of Dachau and Auschwitz for is the fact that after more than ninety minutes of constant bombardment, when the

whole area was leveled and when medical personnel and
ambulances had gathered the dead and the wounded, the
Israelis came back again and committed an atrocious mas-
sacre. They killed doctors and civilians. I cannot justify the
second raid. The Red Cross ambulances they bombed were
clearly marked. We call that murder."

I did not know at the time how traumatic that day had
been for him, but I was to find out.

"And so Israel has been warned that its civilians can't be
protected while ours are not," he went on. "Our first
warning was a bus station in Tel Aviv. The time of 6 A.M.
was chosen because there were few people there. Our
next explosion was in a well-populated spot where nobody
expected guerrillas to reach—the beach at Hercilia north
of Tel Aviv. Sixty were killed and injured."

I was interested in this man. Clearly, he was no ordinary man; his strange mixture of cool deliberation and
underlying passion presented a fascinating combination.

It turned out he was a highly skilled cardiac surgeon,
educated at Harvard, from a prominent Palestinian family
of eleven children, all of whom were expert professionals.
It also turned out that his brother Omar had been killed
in the raid on Salt.

Little by little we pieced together the story. At that
time Abu Nidal was a healer, not a killer, though the
two often turn out to be sides of the same coin. He was one
of those who went out to Salt after the Israeli air attack to
treat and evacuate the wounded. It was he who urged his
younger brother, his favorite, who was twenty-three at
that time, to come with him because medical help was
needed.

Two things happened that day. Abu Nidal, who, when
young, had had a special idealistic vision of a doctor staying with his patients under fire, had been wounded when
the planes dipped down to napalm the ambulances; he had

crawled away, momentarily overcome by fear. The second
thing was that his brother, whose presence there was his
responsibility, was incinerated with napalm.

Everything in this world of Palestinian commandoism
seemed to alternate back and forth, like some crazy-quilt
pattern, between tragedy and absurdity, and so the next day
we all went out with the Action Group to take pictures up
on a hill about midway between Amman and Jordan. It
was that way this day. We went from the strange but
serious talk with Abu Nidal to this empty golden hilltop
surrounded by other hilltops that rose like golden clouds
out of the valleys. The sky that day seemed to be foaming
into mountains of white clouds that then evaporated into a
classically clear blue sea of a desert sky.

For three or four hours, forty "Action" snipers, all
dressed in the enduring designs of Queen Balquis, posed
with guns raised, jumped over stone fences, crouched with
binoculars, climbed up into the trees, marched up a mountain, poised atop a mountain, marched down a mountain
and drank little cups of hot Arabian coffee for us. One
older commando, indeed, appeared to have no other job
but to serve the little cups of hot coffee from a pink
thermos bottle.

As we drove out the little road from the hilltop where
we had been photographing, I spotted at the entrance a
TV camera crew of unknown national vintage filming
some other guerrilla group "in action." The whole thing
was like a Hollywood scenario. I began to feel more and
more the unreality of the whole phenomenon. But then, it
was Sunday, and guerrillas need a day of fun too.

We ended the day by driving down to the Jordan Valley,
the magically golden valley. And suddenly it did not all
seem so ridiculous. The valley, with its gentle golden hills
on each side stretching their arms up into craggy, barren
cliffs, was ravaged. We drove through town after empty

town on the Jordanian side. Once thriving agricultural
centers now were ghost towns. The fields lay untilled because farmers were afraid to come down there, and eventually we came to Karameh, the site of the Israeli attack on
March 14, 1968.

Karameh had been founded in 1952 by a group of
refugees, and they gave it that name because in Arabic
Karameh means "dignity." They established houses, a
youth club, a mosque, civic center and electric plant. There
were 25,000 people originally and another 25,000 came
there after the 1967 war. Even from the dreary ruins,
one could see clearly that it had been a prosperous Arab
town, not one of the omnipresent scratching villages.

The Israelis had attacked because Karameh had had
Fatah members stationed there, but the unusual thing about
Karameh was that, despite a tally of 28 Israelis dead to
170 commandos, it was an Israeli defeat. The Israeli soldiers were forced back by the Jordanian Army, which
had two divisions and eight infantry brigades overlooking
the valley, and by the fedayeen—to the point where in
the withdrawal they left substantial amounts of equipment
behind.

But Karameh was completely destroyed. The "second
chance" for the refugees, who originally were driven out
of Palestine, was over. Now they moved up higher to the
camps around Amman, camps where there were no lands
for agricultural production such as there were in the valley
and where again they had no work.

That Sunday, as the afternoon grew late and the golden
sunlight turned to cold shadowy darkness, we roamed
through the blasted, shattered houses of Karameh. A door
kept slamming—why, in deserted towns, do doors always
keep slamming?—and I jumped each time. It was an
eerie business, and I felt a distinct sense of uneasiness
and a desire to be up and away. A gentle howl that started

deep down the long valley rent the silence on its way
toward us, seeming to increase in volume as it approached
the town. The wind. Now it was dancing wildly through
the empty houses, slamming more and more doors, blowing
plaster off into dizzy patterns, sweeping the darkening
town and riding confidently over us like an arrogant Arabian stallion.

Everyone seemed to feel it. "It's time we get back," the
Iraqi driver muttered.

But before we left, we walked quickly into the half-
destroyed mosque. Scrawled across the walls in Arabic
were the names of the fedayeen who had died in the battle
for Karameh. They were not written in any list or line,
like we used to have on the honor role on our corner of the
boys next door who died in World War II. They were
written in strange unpatterned circles . . . here and there
. . . as though the wind had scattered them.

So often in the Arab world I felt lost. I felt I was either
not catching up with things or I was one step ahead or I
was on another level so different in substance and in form
that our arms could never link. Moods changed from
moment to moment. One moment it was all death and
horror and the next it was bourgeois elegance, as though
there was nothing at all wrong. What confused and
troubled me, I guess, was that through all of this the
Arabs around me never changed—they never showed emotion, never wept and seldom seemed really joyous. I leapt
from feeling to feeling, from question to question, from
contradiction to contradiction—*I* was concerned, angered,
seeking, worrying, while they were like choruses of stone
watching wordlessly and almost lifelessly the life that was
their life and not mine.

That night was like that. From Karameh we went to
the home of a very prominent family. The wife was Abu
Nidal's sister, who was also a doctor; the husband was a
Supreme Court Justice and on the board of the Inter-

continental Hotel. Everything in the house was so golden,
it looked almost as if a pot of gilt from heaven had been
spilled over it, from faucet to couch. It was Frenchified
in that manner that French-oriented Arabs apparently
crave because "We are not barbarians."

The conversation was friendly and innocuous for an hour
or so, and the scotch glasses remained full. Then, suddenly, almost without warning, Abu Nidal turned from nationality to nationality, and the always latent hostility of
the Arab toward the West came out. For us Americans, the
attack was on the "Zionist-controlled American press" and
the "plots hatched between Jews in American society and
in Washington." Then he narrowed his eyes and focused
on Victor. "I always say about the Italians," he said, with
eyes slightly narrowed and a cold smile on his lips, "that
they can't make love and they can't fight."

I could not but think that this was just the sort of thing
Abu Nidal must have heard said dozens, perhaps hundreds,
of times by Westerners about the Arabs.

Victor smiled—a friendly smile—and said, "How are
things going, *Dr. Isam Sartawi?*" Sartawi's face dropped.
Then a dark look of anger passed over his face. None of us
had known his real name before this. We had known him
only as "Abu Nidal." He had tremendously enjoyed the
little deception—he had played with us over it, like a cat
with several rolling cotton balls. Victor had dissolved the
charade: a revenge that far overshadowed any talk about
virility and courage.

It was one of the first times that I observed, on my
own, the apparently immutable fact that the Arabs always
lose.

In the process of "getting to know" the commandos, I
started to make the rounds of the curious apparatus they
had set up in Amman. First I went to the Palestine Libera-

tion Organization, the umbrella group of all the commando units. I asked for Abu Iad, as he had told me to do, but he was out of town or something, so instead I found another man, Zuhdi Terrazzi, who became my helper. He, in turn, sent me to Ahmed, the official looker-over and a Marxist, at the Fatah Information Office. He looked me over dispassionately and made some suggestions.

I was ready to play their game, at least for a few days. So, yes, I would be happy to go to lunch with three of their men. And, yes, I could be counted on Tuesday to make the weekly visit to the Ashbal or Lion Cubs camp. And, damn it, why didn't you tell me sooner that yesterday was graduation day at the women commandos' camp because that was something I particularly wanted to see?

It struck me again that Fatah sometimes seemed to be one big public relations effort. The day I took the "tour" to the Lion Cubs—young boys from five on up who are training to be commandos—at the Baqua'a refugee camp outside Amman, we had in the group an English youth hosteler, a Welsh nationalist, two East German radio reporters, an Iraqi doctor and two Swiss tourists who went on to Petra the next day. I watched with a sort of grim horror, as these children leapt over barriers, learned to use guns and marched about wide-eyed. Soon they would be chanting, as they prepared to cross the Jordan mine fields, "Oh, Zionists, do not think you are safe! Drinking blood is a habit of our men."

The "tours" also took me to the Fatah convalescent home, where pathetically wounded young boys lay moaning, many of them unable even to turn themselves over; to the clinics Fatah had set up in the refugee camps; and to the schools for the orphans of the "martyrs" killed in battle. Fatah had developed a good social security system, and the Institute for Taking Care of the Families of the Martyrs was spending about $70,000 a month on all its social service activities. It was through these activities, Fatah leaders told me, that they were slowly showing what the future socialist society of Palestine would be like.

In between "tours," I began to send back to my office some simple stories about the general situation in Jordan. And in the censor's office (censorship in Jordan was a pleasant formality, not a pain-in-the-neck as in Egypt) I found Habeeb Husseiny.

Habeeb was the censor. He was also a gentle, well-educated Jordanian who had studied in England and spoke English exquisitely. He never questioned political judgments in the stories—indeed, he seemed to interpret his time in the censor's office as a means of bettering his own vocabulary and guarding the quality of journalism in the world.

"Opt?" he would say, raising his curious, questioning eyes to me. "Did you really mean to use 'opt'?"

Then I would start thinking about it and wondering whether I really *did* mean to use opt and sort of wishing that Habeeb Husseiny were more like other censors.

One evening, as we sat in the office with little cups of coffee, he talked to me very seriously and very intelligently about the growing atheism of the Arab youth. "We go to the mosques," he said, "but only occasionally. We believe in God in a generalized sense. The important thing, of course is to know thyself. Know thyself!" He stopped to savor the words. "I guess that is what you and I should know, too."

I had never had a censor tell me to know myself—not anywhere in the world. More often they told me things that were unprintable. And so I developed a liking for one Habeeb Husseiny.

The two East German journalists who were with me in the Lion Cubs camp deserve, I think, a special kindly note, too, since they once played the role of proxy targets for Americans. They were friendly to me, and I often spoke

to them in German in the dining room at the hotel. Then
one day, just as the Lebanese crisis began and the Lebanese began attacking the commandos in their country,
there were bitter demonstrations against Lebanon in Amman.

I, the (smart) American devil, happened to be drinking
coffee in the Ministry of Information at the moment when
the effervescent, youthful commando-led demonstrators,
having just divested the Lebanese embassy of its flag,
marched jubilantly past the Intercontinental. They saw the
two East Germans, actually their friends in ideology but
both blond and rather resembling Americans, and they
chased them and the Welsh nationalist, who was with them,
up to their rooms. The threesome barely saved themselves
by locking themselves in, as the demonstrators proceeded
very nearly to wreck the halls of the hotel in their revolutionary "enthusiasm."

"Why do people always think we're Americans?" one of
the East Germans remarked to the Welshman in helpless
anger. Sometimes ideology alone isn't enough. They should
have been wearing lederhosen.

But if *I* was having trouble, it was nothing compared
to my friends Victor and Gillo. They had been promised
an interview with Leila Khaled, the doe-eyed girl who
earlier that year had hijacked a TWA plane and was "hot
copy." Victor was close to the Popular Front for the Liberation of Palestine, which was about as easy to get close to
as to a cobra, and one day they would tell him to go to
Beirut for the story . . . and he would go. The next day
they would tell him, "Oh my! Leila just left for Amman"
. . . and they would come back. They never did find
Leila. "Slippery Arabs."

Meanwhile, while I was waiting, I decided to go out to a
refugee camp and stay with a refugee family—to see what
all those heart-rending pictures I'd seen all those years

(of gaunt Palestinian refugees, held in UN camps "on the borders of their homeland," with dark hollow eyes and holding empty supper dishes) really meant. I must admit that, even after everything had been arranged, I approached the whole thing with about the same enthusiasm with which I had originally approached Pamela in the Amazon or the guerrillas in the Guatemalan hills. Actually, this was worse; a story like this, was extremely painful to me because of the great formality and the number of rituals that went into it before you could actually get down to something of substance.

* * *

There is nothing to do at night in the camps. No electricity, no movies, no television. The desert darkness comes down suddenly and totally, like a shroud, and the little corrugated iron houses and the tents on the sand hills are lit only by eerie oil lamps. That night I sat on piled mats on the floor with Mr. and Mrs. Sadat Hussein Abdel Khader and their seven children. He was a square, strong man, built like a truck, and he was talking. . . .

"Jemsu." He spoke the name of his home town in what is now Israel and the eyes of their seven children shone like olives. He let the word hang magically in the air for a few seconds. "For twenty-two hundred years, my family lived in Jemsu," he began as his wife, Amienh Aiub, went quietly about in her long embroidered Palestinian dress, carrying little glasses of hot tea. "My family had many houses and many lands—olive trees, grapes and many other fruits."

Then he related the story his children have heard thousands of times—how they fled from partition in 1948, lived in a cave in Jericho, where there was "neither clouds nor sky," how UNRWA finally gave them a tent, how they settled then in Jericho. Every once in a while, he punctured his story with, "And I was angry!"

y I was working in the garden with many fruits
ning a salary," he went on, "and then the war came
in 1967. I *felt* the war coming—like 1948 or more.
w all the planes. . . ." He waved his arms toward the
y. "In forty-eight, there were not planes, now there was
bombing and napalm. . . ."

I soon would learn that every man in Marka Camp, just
like the Jewish people across the Jordan Valley, has scars
from the things that fear and uprooting and homelessness
do to men. Sadat, probably one of the best-balanced of
them all, had his. He displayed them simply, almost without embarrassment, as if they were just part of life. Forced
to move again, he said he took one small son down to
cross the Allenby Bridge into Jordan and then planned to
go back for more.

"But when I got to the bridge, the planes came over
and"—his voice faltered for a moment—"I left my little
son and hid myself in a sewer." Now his voice rose to an
almost desperate shrill sing-song. "I was very sad for myself," he went on. "Why did I leave my son? How could
I do that? Then I took his hand, and we walked across
the River Jordan."

What has hurt these people most, I soon came to realize,
was not Miss Smith's bad toilets but the stunting spiritual
deprivation. For whereas other people look both ways—
backward and forward—these refugees look only backward because there was no forward. The educated and
professional people were assimilated into many Arab
societies, but for the Palestinian masses there was no place
to run but Marka, kept alive on the UNRWA stipend of
$40 per person *per year* for food.

"If I were not a refugee, I would speak English with
you," Sadat told me once, through the interpreter. "Because
I was a refugee, I couldn't learn. No time, no school,
nothing, no life." This was probably not true—had he

stayed a peasant farmer in Palestine, he probably would
not have spoken English—but the important point was he
thought he would have. Like all the refugees, he blamed
every one of his failures as a man on Israel.

Another time, as we all sat around over tea, he burst
out suddenly, "This life is very bad. Very, very bad. Very
bad. I hope to return to Jemsu. Every hour, every time,
every day, I think about returning back. After three years,
after twenty years, you do not forget to return to Chicago;
I am like that, too."

When I came in—and I was wearing what I considered
a very conservative black cotton dress which was really
quite long—I sat down on a low stool with my knee showing only slightly from below the dress. There was a noticeable "stir"—a moment of discomfort on everybody's part
—and then one of the men who worked in the camp
found a towel and simply placed it over my legs. It was
one of my first experiences with the Arab attitude toward
sexuality; bare breasts meant very little, because Arab
women, even while they often covered their faces as
though they were leprous, would routinely bring out a
breast to feed a baby. But knees were titillating.

It struck me strangely too, when, late that night, after a
day of all this obsessive knee-covering, the mother took me
into the second room alone. She insisted that I undress and
wear one of her silk nightgowns underneath, and a heavy
nightgown over it. Then she led me, wearing the flannel
gown, back to the second room, where her husband and
several men were still sitting. No one even stirred. I was
about as covered up as a woman can be, but in my own
society I would have felt uncomfortable. It was the form
that was wrong. I felt uncomfortable about it, but they
most certainly did not. No knees were showing.

Reminders of the basic humiliation the Arabs feel in the
face of the United States come fast and furious. In the

afternoon, for instance, we had strolled over to the house next door. A commando in checkered Arab headdress and khaki uniform, machine gun in hand, welcomed me to a small room with commando posters on the walls. "Why are you helping Israel?" he asked immediately. "Israel is small, the Arab world is big."

It was the same everywhere. "You give us food, you Americans, to make us forget," Mosa Amer Jarbour, an UNRWA worker in the camps said later, sitting in "our" house. "But we don't forget. You give cans to us and guns to Israel."

Yet to me personally, their kindness knew no bounds. They gave me all their mattresses to sleep on, while they slept on the floor.

But the "rage" of these men and of Sadat—a poor man's rage, an inner anger that eats quietly and fatally at a man's dignity and honor until he is nothing but an empty hulk— is not the rage of the young Palestinians. When I asked his bright-eyed children what they wanted to be when they grew up, their eyes shone even brighter than when their father talked about Jemsu. With complete, innocent confidence, each one said, "A commando." "Now they go to school," Sadat said, "and later they become commandos." And this was natural. The commando rhetoric was the only rhetoric of any hope in the Palestinian world.

What continued to fascinate me was the substance of these curious people, these Palestinians, and the more I saw of them, the more I was convinced that my first guessed-at assumptions were terribly correct. The Palestinian Arabs—this ultimately fanaticized people—were not what they seemed to be. They were not all, as they had been widely pictured, poor. They were not, by and large, uneducated. They were not all a people without hope, and their cause was not a cause born primarily of depredation and poverty.

After many more weeks of investigation, I came to the carefully based conclusion that while some of the approximately 2.5 million Palestinians living today were poor, even in their poverty—even in the admittedly miserable refugee camps—they had the kind of education and the kind of peculiar historic experience that had made of them a rare "modern people" in the Arab world. Outside of those who still lived in the camps, there was a group of nearly 50,000 to 80,000 who were college graduates—one of the highest percentages of university people of any national group in the world and a number equal to the number trained by Israel in the same period of time. It was nearly impossible, among the 30,000 to 50,000 commandos to find a leader or subleader who was not a doctor, lawyer or literary person. There were 800 Palestinian teachers in Algeria, 150,000 Palestinians in Kuwait, and they owned the biggest bank in the Arab world.

In this apparent contradiction, almost unnoticed in the plethora of news coverage of this obstreperous revolutionary movement, lay the fascination of this curious people. They were a revolutionary force in the world *not* because they were poor and without hope but rather because they *were* the most advanced people in the Arab world. They were so advanced, in fact, that they called themselves, with an oil-and-water mixture of irony, pride and bitterness, "the Jews of the Arab world." It was equally strange that their furious need for retribution was in a style both biblical and postmodern.

I suppose what first gave me an uneasy clue that there was something odd about the picture we've had since 1948 of the hangdog Palestinian refugee, without land and without future, was the rarefied qualities of the commando movement's "goals." It came to me one of those first

nights in Cairo, as I sat sipping scotch with Clovis
Maksuud and he kept talking about their being a "primitive technology at the service of an advanced technology
and Israel being an advanced technology at the service of a
primitive ideology." These were not the plaints of people
who were hungry.

This same superintellectualization that informs the entire
Palestinian movement was present a few weeks later in
Beirut, in the handsome library of Walid Khalidi, the
Palestinian political scientist at the American University of
Beirut, and a prime guru of the fedayeen students. "Palestine," this unassuming man said in his Oxford accent, "was
always our historic crossroads. From our point of view, it's
the hub of our area. Our idea is that Zionism was allowed
to grow because of the rottenness of Arab society—from
that comes the importance of the revolutionary trend of
standing up to Israel."

This idea of "purification through confrontation" of the
enemy—a word grouping often used by Arabs, and
straight out of the Third World philosopher Frantz Fanon
—shows the extreme intellectualization of the entire matter. But why, I asked Khalidi, a brilliant man who refuses
to indulge in "vulgarizations" about his "Jewish cousins,"
of all the refugees in the modern world was it only these
Palestinian refugees who kept on with this insane insistence
upon a return?

"It was the wholeness," he said slowly, "the wholeness of
everybody being put across a frontier . . . and not on a
time scale to allow the great healer time to do his work.
You woke up and you said 'Am I not in Jaffa? Of course,
I must be.' Then, compounding injustice, plus insult,
there was the closeness of standing in Jerusalem and seeing
a Jewish family washing clothes on your balcony. And at
the same time, there was the din of applause for your
persecutors ringing constantly in your ears."

To another keen observer, *Time* magazine's John Scott, the reasons for the difference in *this* refugee situation lay in the fact that the world community did a halfway humanitarian job, thus upsetting the Darwinian pattern. "The UN stopped the conflict from being resolved in a Darwinian fashion," he has written, "so it should logically have enforced peace in the area. Instead, it stopped with a cease-fire. This was unfortunate, for if the UN was justified in stepping in to secure justice and the rule of law instead of the rule of might, it had the obligation to impose in fact the rule of law."

And Barbara Ward, the brilliant British economist, has warned that a number of situations are nearing the explosion point of the Palestinian commandos. "We see in the fedayeen what happens when you abandon people long enough," she said, "and we are near total explosions on a number of such situations in the world."

Now I was getting a little closer to the chorus of furies which sang and drove the Palestinians on. While stories were shamelessly distorted for propaganda by all sides, it is agreed by most historians that about one million Palestinian Arabs fled the tiny, crowded, imperfect triangle that had been Palestine when it was partitioned into Israel in 1948. Ardent Zionists, including Israeli Prime Minister Golda Meir, will assert that there never was a Palestine, using as their proof the fact that it was only a mandate under the British from 1917 to 1948, and that before that it was a backwater Syrian colony of Turkey. But the fact is that the Arabs who lived there, as feudal and fragmented as they were, had lived there for up to two thousand years.

The Palestinian Arabs base their claims on the fact that in 1918 the Jewish population of Palestine was 100,000; by 1948, it was 650,000 and today it is in excess of 2.5 million. In the early years, the Arabs were usually five or six times that many. The hundreds of thousands of Pales-

tinian Arabs at the beginning of the century had grown
to at least 1.5 million by 1948, but after *their* "Diaspora,"
there were only 200,000 left in Israel, where they have
remained as well-treated but not full citizens. The Arab
state which was also to be formed by partition was immediately sabotaged by the constituted Arab states, who
soon moved in and seized this territory, leaving the
Palestinians without a homeland, divided up like booty
among the Arab states and filled with nearly as much hate
for their Arab brothers as for the Israelis.

Where does the truth lie? To whom does this small bit
of land belong?

"Facts" are very hard to come by. Much of the land was
bought by Jews from the 1880s on, often at exorbitant
prices from greedy Arab landowners—but much of it was
taken over, without compensation, from Arabs who fled
during the war. Many of the refugees of 1948 were urged
by Jewish leaders to remain but were told to leave by their
own corrupt Arab leaders, who expected to destroy the
infant Israel in oncoming attacks, and many fled simply because of war—they feared the mortars and the holocaust.
But innumerable others were driven out by Jewish terrorists, and none has been permitted to return or has been
compensated.

There really is no one "just" claim to the land that was
Palestine. It was promised by the British to France under
the 1916 Sykes-Picot agreement; to the Jewish people under the 1917 Balfour Declaration; and to the Arabs in the
Husain-McMahon correspondence of 1915 and 1916. Con-
sequently, any absolute claims are simply nonsense.

The main and most important "fact" is that they were
two entirely different people, one which could cope and
one which could not. The Arabs were simply unable to
cope with the educated, able, flexible Jews, whose consist-
ent tactic was to create a reality—such as the reality of

Jewish settlement—and then to gain recognition of this established "fact." The Arabs, on the other hand, were more temperamentally suited to sulking when things did not go right or else going off into raving, massacring fits—*their* tactic was not to take part, to refuse to negotiate. They lost.

What most analysts have missed in interpreting the elusive but endlessly fascinating Palestinian phenomenon was that being driven out of Palestine by Jewish terrorist groups, or leaving under duress or out of desperation or on the orders of corrupt Arab leaders or for whichever of the many reasons they left, was what took the Palestinians out of feudalism and into modernism. Old Palestine, after all, had had a feudal leadership of landed Muslim and Christian Arab families, with 80 per cent of the populace rural peasantry. It was the very experience of *their* Diaspora that eventually forged the link between this people and the "scientific socialist ideologies of the Third World," something that would have been impossible back in the mud-hut, orange-groved, Moslem hierarchy-ruled villages of Palestine.

The new life in the camps, where at night only oil lamps flickered across the pristine desert all around, was brutal. It made vegetables of the fathers, living in memory, without hope, without work, without future, without the security of the timeless Moslem village hierarchy. But it made cosmopolites of the sons, educated in the far more sophisticated UN schools, given good medical care by UN doctors, given university scholarships *because* they were refugees, and exposed to the sophisticated influence of the educated Arabs, who came to them as political mentors and, for the first time, as equals. Men, who would have ritualistically obeyed the strict class system of their feudal past, now put this aside in the interest of the common cause and the common hatreds.

The commando groups started in the late fifties and
early sixties, when university students who had left the
camps to study on scholarships began to trickle back and
hold small group discussions in the camps and elsewhere.
By 1964, the militant young Palestinians had held a
Palestine National Assembly, which formed the Palestine
Liberation Organization, or PLO, to set up an army (the
Palestine Liberation Army, or PLA) to train Palestinians
in a form of guerrilla warfare to free their homeland.

It must be remembered, too, of course, that the late
fifties and early sixties was a "time of revolution." It was
the age of the Bandung Conference, the coming of Castro,
the Viet Cong; it would certainly have been unnatural if
the Palestinians had not awakened in much the same way
and had not gravitated toward, and grasped, the New
Marxist influences coming in through Russian-supported
Egypt and Syria, through China and through the whole
Third World.

In those days, the leader was a flamboyant Arab, Ahmed
Shukairy, now despised by the commandos as all flowery
rhetoric and little else. Like most Arab leaders of the more
traditional stripe, Shukairy was nothing if not adaptable
and, occasionally, ghoulishly amusing. After saying for
years that the Jews must be "thrown into the sea," when he
discovered this sounded "unpleasant" to many people, he
changed his mind and said, No, they must only "leave by
sea," that is in boats.

The young Palestinians—and the other Arabs who
flocked to their cause out of opportunism or belief or a
mixture of both—were not about to be caught in a trap
like this one. And so people like Clovis Maksuud, then a
diplomat in India but still closely working with the
Palestinians, came up with the idea of the "secular state"—
a new Palestine made up of the land of Israel in which
Jews, Moslems and Christians would live together in a re-

clining paradise of lions and lambs. The idea came to him,
Clovis told me once, out of a mixture of Nehruism,
Gandhism, Maoism and a few other things. Did they mean
it? I never thought so.

But it was only after the 1967 war that the dozen or so
commando groups (with the Arab propensity for prolifera-
tion and atomization, there were up to thirty-three commando organizations at one time or another) really thrived.
"The defeat of '67 obviously caused a tremendous disil-
lusionment with the constituted governments," Dr. Khalidi
said. "At one point, it was a feeling almost of trauma. The
Palestinians acted as the catalyst of hope, because at the
time when Moshe Dayan was waiting for the telephone to
ring to receive the surrender of this or that Arab leader, the
Palestinians took the initiative in standing up to them."

The fedayeen also attracted young men by their very un-
Arab insistence upon recognizing ability rather than family
background or wealth, and this very important factor is
shown by the fact that military ranks were not even marked
among the commandos—there were commanders and
there were soldiers and they were chosen on their ability,
an idea totally foreign even to the Egyptian Army, which
still suffers from severe social distinctions.

This "equalitarianism," so strange to the Arab world,
was not accidental. "The camps gave them a kind of education and demonstrated an upward mobility that might not
have occurred for years had they remained on their plots
of land in Palestine," Michael Hudson, associate professor
of political science at Brooklyn College of the City University of New York and one of the few academics to have
analyzed this phenomenon, has also written. "Precisely
because it was harsh, the disastrous confrontation with the
West and with Zionism tended to break up the traditional
parochial social structure that had inhibited effective political organization under the mandate."

Each country created its own commando group, but of all of them, Al Fatah was by far the most important; it had the broadest highly general socialist umbrella philosophy and practical guidelines. On the far left, the Popular Front for the Liberation of Palestine—the fanatics—stood alone most of the time; it became known for its Maoist philosophy and its indiscriminate hijackings, bomb throwings and terrorism.

All of the groups got scads of money out of the "bankers" of the Arab world—the rich, conservative "cousins" like Saudi Arabia and Kuwait, who "paid off," at least in part, to keep out of trouble—and from the many prosperous Palestinians abroad (a quarter of Kuwait is Palestinian) who "tithed" up to 20 per cent of their ample salaries to the movements. By two years after the 1967 war, when the fedayeen were a negligible force, they were getting approximately $44 million from the Arab governments and from Arab individuals.

Since Fatah is the major group and since Fatah's philosophy turned out to be for a long time the most arresting one for attracting young Arabs, let us look at what this broad-based ideology is. I judge Fatah certainly to be socialistic, but to be socialistic (at the moment!) in a very vague, amorphous and non-denominational way. Basically, its attraction lies on another level. They call their parents' generation "the generation of defeat" and they call themselves "the generation of resistance" or the "generation of revenge." The 1967 war is seen not as a political war but as a "clash between civilizations." This is heady stuff—ego-rescuing stuff—and it should be obvious why it would appeal to young people desperately in need of self-respect. But, at the same time, there is, in my opinion, also a curious similarity in the two generations. The Sadats will

blame all their failures as human beings . . . all their
weaknesses as men . . . on the Israelis. But the fedayeen
young show a weird dependence upon the Israelis, too, for
they are saying the Arab world cannot develop except by
using Israel as a ploy.

This is also straight out of Frantz Fanon, the black ide-
ologist of the Third World who argues (*The Wretched of
the Earth*) that the oppressed man can only rise by
destroying his oppressor. Violence not only destroys, it
has a therapeutic, saving effect on the destroyer. It liberates
him from his shortcomings and anxieties, inculcating in
him both courage and fearlessness concerning death.

Another important point revolved around the difference
between the beliefs of Nasser (whom the fedayeen greatly
admired but with whom they often disagreed) and the
ideas of Fatah. Nasser finally came to the idea that war
was inevitable, but he argued that the Arabs should prepare
themselves thoroughly first—that unity and strength would
lead to the "liberation" of Palestine.

Not at all, said the fedayeen. As they saw it, Nasser's
position was cursed with a fatal inner contradiction, for
the Arabs could not unite or set their own house in order
so long as Israel existed.

Fatah argued: "The Zionist existence is the root of all
our diseases and not one of their consequences. Disunity,
lack of national consciousness, backwardness—all are
psychological outcomes of Israel's existence." Why? Because Israel "aroused complexes, fears and irrational anxi-
ety among Arabs as to the anticipated danger of the hated
Zionist occupation.

Actually, "Palestinianism" was simply the newest symp-
tom—the newest expression—of Arab nationalism. In
style, it was a twentieth-century successor of the Moslem
insurgents like the mujtahid, the "sacred strugglers" of
Mohammed, or the hashish-smoking "assassins," who

struck terror in the ranks of the crusading knights. Even the word "fedayeen," meaning "those who sacrifice themselves," has come from historic root; it comes from the name given those twelfth-century Moslems selected to assassinate the enemies of the Isma'ili sect.

More recently, the Palestinian movement is a continuation of the Arab revolt which began earlier in this century against the Turks and which ended in the total frustration and the absolute desperation and a furious sense of having been victimized that characterized the Arab reaction to the English and French mandates.

Even though they themselves are not really Arabs but are a mixture of Greek, Turk, Phoenician, Babylonian and Crusader, the Palestinians considered themselves the vanguard and saviors and regenerators of the Arab world . . . the catalyst for social revolution . . . the bearers of a "scientific socialism" allied to the socialist countries of the Third World. And in many ways, until their at least temporary decimation by King Hussein in 1971, they were these things.

The radical Libyan coup of September 1969 could be traced directly to frustration over the 1967 war and to identification with the fedayeen (the prime minister was a Palestinian). So could the radical Sudan coup of the spring of 1969. King Faisal of Saudi Arabia lived in dread of a fedayeen-inspired coup, and so did Morocco's king.

Until the Jordanian Army took after them in the civil war of 1970, they were a radicalizing factor everywhere, a wild card in the wily game of Arab politics that must always be taken into consideration because any constituted Arab leader scorned or challenged their popularity only at his own risk. They were a force, like a psychiatric experience which brought all the contradictions in the Arab world to the surface.

Arrogant? Mad? Of course. They are the ultimate fanatics, people who feel no responsibility whatsoever to a
world they believe forsook them and are quite willing to exchange their rage for world holocaust, if that is necessary.

But though I was getting for myself some tentative
answers to my gnawing questions—and if I am to tell the
truth, I have to say that I do all of this basically to answer
my *own* questions—there were still many left unanswered.

Why, for instance, were the young people so obsessed
with the idea of a "return"? They had never seen Palestine.
For them, there were none of the memories of Sadat—
none of the emotional remembrances of a father's village,
of the shade of the orange trees and the view of the Mediterranean sands.

One day, for instance, I was down in the Jordan Valley,
talking to some of the PLO commandos in one of the eerie
ghost towns, its houses and stores with gaping holes in
them. They had taken up command posts in the now-
empty former homes only a few hundred yards across
now-dormant fields from the Jordan River. It was a beautiful late afternoon, with the sun shining its heart out and
the silence that stalked the valley more ominous than a
chattering machine gun.

In the dulling heat, we sat on one of the outside bal-
conies, the young commandos sprawling on their blankets,
and I asked them why they—so young, so inexperi-
enced—yearned as they did for a country they had never
seen.

"I know that Jaffa is there and that it belonged to my
ancestors," said Abu Naji, a twenty-two-year-old, who sat
leaning against the porch railing. "I always see it in my
mind. I don't really know what it looks like, except from
my parents' descriptions."

"I want to become a martyr," another boy said, speaking of the commandos who die fighting Israel. "It's become a sort of obsession. I know it's the best way to die."

"We live with a sentimental attachment," was the way Zuhdi explained it. "I was born in Jerusalem. I dream of going back because I was born there and spent the happiest years of my life there. But for the young Palestinians, it is quite different. They never knew Palestine; they never saw it. They know that geographically this part of the world that was usurped belongs to the rest of the Arab world. Legally, it belongs to their parents—less than 6 per cent was property of Jews in 1917. Their passion is a scientific one, an ideological one. They know that a terrible injustice was done, and they yearn to correct it."

This is what distinguishes the Palestinians so markedly from so many other earlier bread-and-butter revolutionary movements of the world and makes them, like their Jewish "cousins," with whom they share a certain cerebral view of life and against whom they are not accidentally pitting themselves to regain their own honor, such an equally interesting people.

CHAPTER IV

The War in Lebanon—The Story of a Week

There are those who say that when you pass the Syrian border you have entered a mad country. Asked why they believe this to be so, they whisper themselves in a circle and seem puzzled as to how to answer. It is the inherent madness of the Arab world, they say, the dream world in which all Arabs live, the distilled nightmare qualities of so much. There is something about the Syrians . . . the unrealistic and inappropriate Frenchification imposed under French colonialization upon an already schizophrenic and too intellectualized society. Or could it be that vast tract of barren desert sand that is Syria that twists the mind and cripples the human spirit?

And they mention other things about this closed and hermetic country that has come to represent the strange qualities of "madness" in the Arab world. The Syrians are not fighters . . . yet they start all the wars, and then leave the fighting to the others. They pride themselves on their learning, and yet it is so rarefied, so without humanistic leavening, that they have become barbarians, never taking prisoners and scarring and mutilating horribly the dead bodies before displaying them on the Israeli border.

Ethnically and racially, they are totally unrelated to the real Arabs of the Arabian peninsula—they are a Mediterranean people who supplied much of the intelligentsia of Rome. Yet they are the most wildly Arab nationalists. Perhaps they have been invaded too many times, for their whole history is a history of invasions and migrations. Perhaps it is their too-theoretical intellectuality, so completely removed from the practical realism of the true Arabian.

Whatever it is, I noticed nothing particularly different that day when I crossed over the border from Jordan to Syria, but all these considerations were on my mind. The teeming border post between open, spontaneous Jordan and closed, xenophobic Syria was a den of desert foxes, with Bedouins from Jordan in their long robes mingling noisily with Syrian guards displaying that peculiarly misleading Syrian martial bearing. Heroic commando posters covered the walls of the squat and squalid low stucco building and stood out like ugly billboards in the middle of the clean and beautiful desert all around them.

I strolled impatiently about the post, for we were in a hurry. At one point, I came upon a particularly prominent poster—a large one with a sketch of Sirhan Sirhan (big) and one of Robert Kennedy (small). It read, in English, "A tragic confrontation. One lies in his grave, the other faces the gas chamber. The real culprit, Zionism, is still at large." In the upper right-hand corner was a quote from Sirhan: "I did it for the sake of my country." I felt, suddenly, sick of heart and mind, remembering for the thousandth time that awful spring when my own country, too, had been quite mad.

Americans were getting few visas to Syria in those days—forty-eight-hour transit visas flatly were the only ones being given, and those rarely—and they wanted you out faster than that, if possible. But I had a special visa, a rare visa—a thing to behold! It had my picture stapled to it, and it had a great deal of detail in Arabic saying it was good for one trip to Syria and back, with precise dates. It also said my name was Fedowa Kouzy, which means in Arabic, "The treasure of Jerusalem." In short, I was a Palestinian commando.

Pamela and I had a guide, Muhammed, from Saiqa, the Syrian-sponsored commando group. He was a tall, lanky, eager-to-please young man and it was he who was in one of the squat little buildings negotiating our visas. It was only later I discovered that, with these visas, we had not crossed through regular immigration but through the special fedayeen border control. At this time, if you knew what to look for, on most Arab borders around Israel, there was a "fedayeen post" which stood out because it flew, not the flag of the country itself, but the flag of Palestine, a country which exists only in the metaphysical imagination of the Arab world. It was my first real taste of the strange extraterritoriality that the commandos were claiming for themselves—an extraterritoriality they claimed for the simple reason that they were stateless.

The trip had come about suddenly and providentially, and I was deeply excited about it. For at a time when no other correspondents could get anywhere near the area, we were on our way through Jordan and Syria into south Lebanon which now was on fire, with battling between Lebanese Army troops and the commandos.

Only two nights before, Saiqa had received us in their office in Amman. It was dusk, and the seven hills were darkening. We went up some back stairs, where commandos posed languidly against the railings. In the first room, a kitchen, one was making coffee in a little pot. The last

room was a kind of garden room, with big windows on
three sides overlooking the square.

The Saiqa commanders seemed much tougher and much
sturdier men than many of the other fedayeen commanders
I'd seen. They were much more soldierly, much more
martial and efficient—and, of course, many were not
Palestinian amateurs but had been detached from the
Syrian Army.

Not many of the fedayeen, despite their vaunted revolutionary propensities, are really very revolutionary about
women and their first response was a doubtful skepticism.
Every one of their first sentences started with a "But . . ."

I may be mistaken, but I think the change in their attitude came when after all their protestations about us being
too young, too feminine, too tender-hearted and too inex-
perienced, I said with a distinctly mischievous look, "Now,
look, we've both been through this before. We may look
nice, but we aren't."

They laughed good, broad, healthy laughs—one of my
continued surprises was the fact so many Arabs had senses
of humor—and began to nod instead of shaking their
heads.

And so, on October 26, 1969, we crossed into Syria, and
on that day Lebanon was very close to the edge of collapse.
Only the day before, in Amman, a Western diplomat had
read to me an official cable from his embassy in Beirut
which said of that lovely mercantile country: "The patient
is under the knife." As for the American embassy, it had
been expecting trouble for a long time. Even in Jordan,
hundreds of miles away from the main scene of the
Lebanese trouble, they had begun burning the embassy
files three months earlier. Meanwhile, in south Lebanon,
the Lebanese Army was moving in on the Arab commandos it had now vowed to "clean out" of the Lebanese
border areas. Arab was fighting Arab, and it was an im-

portant story—a story that was to tear the whole area apart over the next two years. There it was, laid out before me, the basic schizophrenia of the Arab world; guerrillas versus tradition.

That night we checked into the Hotel Semiramis in downtown Damascus, and everything seemed normal enough if you didn't notice that the first five floors had BOAC ads on the door keys and the rest had Interflug tags on them. It was simply a little bit of East-West segregation. Since Syria went fanatically anti-Israel and pro-Socialist bloc with its Neo-Ba'athist government in 1963, the Soviets and East Germans and Czechs had moved in en masse. It was to Damascus only recently that the myriad little African independence movements had come—to be closer to the Soviets. And so, to keep peace, the hotel, which still managed to serve good scotch, kept its Western guests on the first five floors (Fly BOAC, old chap!) and its Eastern guests on the remainder (*"Fliegen Sie, mein guter Kerl, mit Interflug!"*)

On Sunday I got a further sampling of what might be called the extraterritoriality or the lack of humility—call it what you will—on the part of the commandos.

We were sitting in the Saiqa command headquarters in a suburban housing project that looked as drab as 1956 East Germany, talking to Mahmoud Ma'ayta, a square, solid-looking Jordanian and commander-in-chief of Saiqa. He leaned forward, his strangely thoughtful eyes looking straight at me, and said, as if any fool would understand:

"Our simple demand is to be free to operate in any Arab land."

That was all they wanted. It only meant that the fedayeen considered themselves above the law, above national boundaries, beyond national differences. It also meant they were damnably clever, for in the next week they proved they knew how and when to fight, not fight, retreat, ma-

nipulate, sweet-talk, cajole, shout, refuse to talk to anybody anywhere, do nothing at all, kill, tell the other Arabs
they loved them and tell other Arabs they hated them, but
above all get what they wanted.

And in Lebanon that next week they got the right to go
anywhere in south Lebanon in order to attack Israel from
Lebanese territory, and they even got the recognition and
the best courting attentions of the Soviet Union, which
formerly had thought them a wild-eyed bunch of socially
undesirables.

Ma'ayta was not at all pleased to see us. He couldn't
understand why his office had sent us or why they had
even let us into Syria. When I explained that Saiqa in
Amman had promised we could go clandestinely into south
Lebanon to Magdal Selem to stay with his troops, his pleasant face paled. It was at Magdal Selem that the Lebanese
troops had moved against the commandos a week before,
deciding to end their control of the south once and for
all.

Ma'ayta sat there, looking alternately pained and puzzled, and then suddenly rubbing his head. "Magdal Selem
fell three days ago," he finally said. This had not been
known in Amman. "We lost twenty-five men killed and
twenty wounded. Fifty-five were captured." This was not
known either—indeed, it was thought there had been no
casualties. "I have given the order for our troops to withdraw, because we don't want Arab fighting Arab. Many
of these young Lebanese officers don't want to fight us, and
we don't want to fight them."

As we talked, dark young men in military khakis came
and went, bringing Ma'ayta messages and asking him advice. As I was to be many times, I was struck by their
lack of emotionalism. They were clearly under stress, and
there was something strangely unnatural about the quiet.

Once the initial hostility and shock had been broken by several small cups of hot black Turkish coffee, Ma'ayta leaned back and—again something totally inexplicable happened. In the midst of the "crisis" we talked for nearly two hours.

"It is not a battle in the real sense," he began. "The commandos are trying not to clash with the Lebanese Army. They've been told not to clash unless they are in a position to defend themselves. We don't want this to be a clash with the Lebanese. They're our cousins. We just want a route through Lebanon.

"We know the anti-revolutionary powers are interested in getting people inside the Arab world into a clash." Then, confidentially: "Seminegotiations are going on with the Lebanese, and we never negotiate from a position of weakness."

Then his voice hardened. "We insist upon a path through every Arab country. Lebanon is part of Palestine. It is not for any Arab regime to decide the future of Palestine."

Next to Ma'ayta, sitting hunched on a folding chair like a khaki bundle, was the bulky figure of Kemal Nasser, fortyish and good-looking in a slightly pasty way. A bachelor, attractive to women, it is said, Nasser was one of the top men in the fedayeen movement. As spokesman for the Palestine Liberation Organization, the central organization of all the major commando groups, it was he who made formal announcements to the world.

Nasser had a way about him, despite a considerable charm and a winning sincerity, that reminded one always of a man who had just been hit squarely on the head by an unexpected blessing from heaven. Perhaps it was because he spoke such perfectly enunciated Oxford English and had a slightly disrespectful wit. Perhaps it was because he was Anglican and a poet from the West Bank,

which came under Israeli occupation after the 1967 war.
But he fit the popular image of the fedayeen movement—
with its mud and its one eye showing above the draped
arab headdress and its clenched machine gun held dramat-
ically in hand—about as well as an Indian rajah might
have.

"We are a nation," he enunciated now, in his excellent
English. "We are not racists, not Nazis. Jews were cherished among us. We can coexist with all people. We were
driven out of our land, and others came to occupy it. It's
our right, our simplest right, to try to regain what we lost."

All of it seemed perfectly real, being there. But what
both of them were saying, I had to keep reminding myself,
could at the very least be described as peculiar. Ma'ayta was
saying that no Arab regime had any right to tell the commandos what to do anywhere—and yet it was the Arab
regimes which were the source of total financial support
for the commandos, and it might be remembered, too, that
they were after all still the governments more or less in
control of their countries. He even thought that Lebanon
was a part of Palestine. Nasser was saying the Palestinians
were "a nation," which they were only in a mystical, metaphysical sense, and had *all* right on their side.

Yet in the ensuing struggle in Lebanon, what the commandos had said about their movement being the catalyst
for revolutionary change in the traditional Arab countries
was uncannily coming to pass. The commandos needed
Lebanon—needed Lebanese border territory—from which
to attack Israel. But Lebanon is a beautiful, immensely
practical country which takes pleasure in buying and selling, and all this seemed outrageous to them, especially
since it meant Israel would strike back and close down
shops in Beirut. But when it moved its army against the
commandos in mid-October, it soon became clear that the

Lebanese government no longer understood the dangerously unstable makeup of its own country. The deep fissures in that society—always held together by the Scotch tape of self-interest and barter—widened disastrously. The Moslems tended to be with the commandos, the Christians with the army. The young were certainly with the commandos, the old were certainly with the army.

Lebanon was so different, so tolerant, so generally out of the radical mainstream of the Arab world that there were about 5000 Jews still living there, usually without any problems at all. They appeared determined to stay. How unusual this was could be seen from these numbers; before 1948 there were about 800,000 Jews living in the Arab countries, but by 1970 the number had declined to about 100,000. Many had left only at the constant urging of Israeli official bodies, and in other countries they were forced to leave or were squeezed out in the most brutal ways. In some, notably Syria, where there were still 3500 Jews (compared to 40,000 in 1948), they were no longer allowed to buy land, trade abroad or leave the country. The UAR and Iraq also had stopped granting departure permits to Jews, but Lebanese Jews could leave at will.

Suddenly Ma'ayta began talking in a sad vein. "There are better things in life than wearing battle dress," he was saying. "I do not know how you would explain the meaning of the Cross, but to the Arab world it means suffering, and now we are suffering. In the Koran, it says to love your neighbor, but it is our destiny that we have to fight. Over the last twenty years we tried to present our cause through the United Nations. Nobody heard our voice until we started fighting. Now we are more popular and more numerous than the Arab regimes."

"We must be humble," Nasser inserted. His voice was low, but even at that innocuous decibel he was somehow incapable of sounding really humble. "We believe the Palestinian movement can create a new human be-ing. . . ."

The trip from Damascus to the border with Lebanon and, very nearby, with Israel, is simple. We were there within an hour, traveling at an easy speed in a recent-make American car, as if headed for a Sunday picnic. Ma'ayta had given us no less an escort than his deputy commander, one Major Said, another soldier and a young teacher as in-terpreter.

Major Said (first names are hard to come by with the fedayeen) was, physically and in his bearing, one of the most impressive Arabs I had seen. Tall, straight, sure of himself without at all presuming upon your attention, he was one of those rare men—he was only thirty—who gave the impression of inner peace, security and self-confidence. He had—yes, that's the word—grace.

Born Palestinian, he had come as a child and refugee to Syria to live. He had joined first the Syrian diplomatic service and was posted in Morocco. Later he joined the Syrian Army, from which he was detached to Saiqa.

By this time, we had no idea what we would find at the border or how far we could go. Naturally, I was disap-pointed. They had promised me in Amman, that spare desert city of voluptuous and tropical—if often erring—rumors, that I would be "sleeping on the side of Mount Hermon" this night. Mount Hermon, the biblical mount. . . . At times, it all seemed slightly theatrical.

We crossed easily into south Lebanon and drove a few miles to the village of Orne. In this part of the Middle East, there are many beautiful valleys, but this was one of the very loveliest. The crease of the valley was filled with orchards. The hillsides were barren but golden. Druze

tribesmen, members of that strange Moslem sect whose beliefs are revealed to no one outside the religion, rode by
on their donkeys.

It was too quiet.

In an old shack, postered with pictures of Che Guevara
and heroic Palestinian commandos, we found the commandos. All young boys—all very, very young. Again, with
that strange and unnerving lack of emotion, they told us
that the Lebanese Army, the night before, had overrun the
next town and the commandos there had evacuated. The
town, Shab'a, was only two miles away. We had gone as
far as we could go.

A young Palestinian whose pseudonym was Abu Khali,
and whose home had been Jouna now in Israel, sat unemo-
tionally in the shack. He was one of those who had fled
Shab'a the night before. "We saw the army advance in
daylight and stop," he related, as he sat on a cot. "We
didn't know they were coming to bomb us. Then, about
11 P.M., they began mortaring the village. Helicopters and
a Mirage bombed the two houses where we had been, I
had just brought the orders for the fedayeen not to fight,
so we retreated."

How did a Mirage jet bomb a tiny village at night? I
asked.

Using flares, he answered.

His voice and manner were so calm that I asked him
with some puzzlement if he was not angry. The voice of
one of the other commandos hardened. "Of course, of
course he's angry," he said.

So instead of going forward to Magdal Selem or to
Shab'a, we drove back to Damascus, just in time for
supper. "We know this is a side battle," the teacher explained. "We know there is a whole plan to force us
into a battle between ourselves, and we do not want to

take part. We want to go directly to the battle and not sidewise."

Back in Damascus, that dusky capital that is supposed to be the city longest occupied by man (why man chose this one to start with boggles the imagination), the commandos did something they often did. They insisted upon taking us to the best restaurant in town.

In this case, it was an excellent French restaurant named Place Vendôme, situated on a small and stylish square that looked very Parisian and must have harkened back to the French occupation. I never refused these invitations. I knew that with Arabs such as these men, it was their way of showing Westerners they were "not barbarians, not savages." They were convinced we thought of them in this way.

Major Said was at his best. He kidded about being only thirty, "too young to get married." He said he would take as his nickname "Abu Gee Gee" because Gee Gee was my nickname.

He recalled how, when living in Morocco, a druggist he knew and patronized once asked him where he was from. He answered, "Palestine."

"Are you happy there?" the druggist asked him.

"Oh yes," he answered. "My mother and father were killed there."

Somehow, he said, they never talked much after that. It was clearly a bitter-sweet jibe at the peripheral, non-involved Arab countries—like Morocco—who knew and cared so little about Palestine.

Talking over dinner, with wine and excellent French food, the major tried to think of the name of a new French book he had just heard about. "I know that the author spoke a great deal about the Middle East," he said, trying hard to remember. "He said the Arab countries would become the greatest power . . . the first power . . . militar-

ily, in the world. Russia would be second and the United
States, third." He looked up, his handsome young face expectant.

Driving back to Amman that night through the desert
blackness, Muhammed, the guide, so quiet before, suddenly became talkative, just as I was dozing off. "I want
to tell you something about what I remember from
Palestine," he blurted out in a voice that grew more and
more demanding for attention.

"My uncle was killed in 1948 by the British and
another uncle was killed in 1956 by the Jews. I don't
remember anything about my grandfather except the day
I saw him lying dead in the war. My father was in prison
for resisting partition, and my mother had to leave with
four little children. She carried the baby out in her teeth
because she couldn't carry all four. The baby died along
the way."

Earlier that day, I recalled for no reason at all, Ma'ayta
had said, "As a responsible man, I am worried that our
people will become sick with hatred. We don't want them
to be sick with hatred. It is unhealthy for a nation."

Muhammed looked out the window at the darkness that
covered the barren sand hills of northern Jordan and
asked, "Now all we want to do is fight. Do you blame
us?" He asked the question again. Insistently. "Do you
blame us for hating?"

I don't know what happened to Muhammed, for I left
Jordan the next day. But several weeks later I was sitting
in the coffee shop of the Tel Aviv Hilton eating my
"sabra breakfast" of fish and cheese and green peppers
and cucumbers and reading the Jerusalem *Post*. "The
Lebanese crisis" was long over, and no one doubted that
the fedayeen, for the moment, had won everything they
wanted and wrapped it up in a secret agreement in Cairo.

But already the trouble was starting again. The paper

that morning carried a story about the Israelis bombing a
fedayeen base on the slopes of Mount Hermon in retaliation
for the Lebanese again allowing the fedayeen to operate
there.

Eight commandos had been killed, and one of them was
Major Said.

So much of the world of the Palestinian commandos is
show, so much is public relations' thunder and lightning,
and so much is shadowboxing and theater, that it is always shocking in this world to hear that someone has died.
It seems almost a vulgar intrusion, a grotesque incongruity.

The next morning after returning from Damascus to
Amman, I got up at 6 A.M., wrote two articles—one on
the commandos evacuating the south, and why, and one on
the possibility of co-operation between Israel and Lebanon.
I rushed them through my favorite censor, "Know thyself"
himself, and rushed them down to the cable office to be
filed. It would take several hours for them to get to Chicago; it was a beautiful day, and I felt wonderful. I also
felt it was time to get to Beirut, so I left that night by plane
for the center of the trouble.

The next morning, sitting at breakfast in the elegant
Rivieraesque St. Georges Hotel on the waterfront in Beirut,
I read in the Beirut *Star* that Yasir Arafat, *the* leader
of the commandos, was giving a press conference in
Damascus that afternoon. He was an extremely hard man
to catch, operating as he does out of everything from caves
to cocktail lounges, and clearly I had to go. I stopped by
the PLO office to get information on crossing the
Syrian border, which had been closed between Syria and
Lebanon since the trouble started. The man in charge,
when he saw my fedayeen visa, was astonished—he had
never seen one given to a foreigner, he said—and he

did something very curious: he in effect endorsed it, just like TWA or United, for further travel into Syria. "I'm writing on the back that you can go in again," he explained, "but be sure to show this at the fedayeen post and not the regular post."

All of this turned out to be unnecessary because Syria opened the border then, and carfuls of journalists crossed over. I hastily had a sole bonne femme for lunch in my room—a great mistake, it soon turned out—and took a rented taxi toward the border.

In Damascus that afternoon Fatah was at its public relations best. First we were ushered into the Fatah information office, where we were registered and given identification cards with our pictures on them and the words at the bottom: "Good only for Yasir Arafat press conference in Damascus, October 1969." We later simply cut this off and used these as press passes throughout Lebanon, but Fatah never found out.

I was, of course, interested in Arafat for he was not only the leader of Fatah, he was head of the PLO and therefore top man of all the groups. And he seemed such an unlikely leader. . . .

Arafat is short—about five foot four—and shaped much like an overripe pear. He always had precisely a five days' growth of beard, and he usually wore his traditional checkered Arab headdress draped in an insolently informal manner, flying behind him instead of formally draped around his shoulders. He always wore fatigues and dark glasses and he usually wore gray suede sneakers in which he sprang when he walks, a habit which caused his favorite "V for Victory" hand sign to bob up and down like a cork. He is a great admirer of Winston Churchill and often quotes him.

Though stories about Arafat's background differ somewhat, this much seems almost assuredly true. He was born

in Jerusalem in 1929 close to the Wailing Wall, an area
now partly flattened by Israeli bulldozers. His family was
a well-to-do, landed one and his father and elder brothers
had fought in early Palestinian causes against the British
mandate. After the 1948 war, the family moved to Gaza.
He became a civil engineer at Cairo University and soon
was very active in forming the Federation of Palestinian
Students, the group which later gave birth to the other
Palestinian military groups. For a while, he was a traveler
in Arab revolutions. He joined the Moslem Brotherhood,
that fanatically puritanical Moslem sect of revolutionaries
whose guerrillas tormented the British along the canal
during colonial days, but he separated from them. He
studied Cuban and Algerian revolutionary techniques and
met secretly with Ernesto "Che" Guevara and Cuban journalists in Algeria in 1964. An ardent seeker, he studied
explosives in West Germany, lived in Kuwait in 1956
doing nobody-knows-what, and in 1961 helped create
Fatah. He lived clandestinely in Israel after the 1967 war,
his followers say, though he is such a heavy, noticeable
man it is hard to imagine him crawling about under barbed
wire or making himself "invisible."

We found ourselves, identification cards held tightly
in hand, in the law school auditorium of Damascus University, waiting for the *líder maximo*. Young fedayeen with
machine guns stood around the balcony and once Arafat
came in, smiling broadly, five tough young men posed in
threatening positions behind him, machine guns always at
bay. I may, of course, have missed something, but I don't
believe they moved during the whole time.

I did, however. Though it was still unknown to me at
the moment, I was in the first stages of salmonella, a
nasty, typhoidlike, not very rare infection I apparently
got from the fish I had eaten at lunch that day. Right

in the middle of Arafat's learned discourse on the commandos' growing prowess, I suddenly became violently ill.
While the poised trigger-happy commandos threw nervous,
daggerlike looks at me, I moved as unobtrusively as possible
—and that was pretty obtrusively—out of the room and
asked for the bathroom. Once there—it was one of those
strange Old World toilets that was simply a cement hole
in the ground with two places for your feet that looked
like foot pedals—I vomited violently, with unladylike vol-
canic noises. And all the while I was hoping to myself
that none of the machine-gun-toting commandos thought
to question why an American correspondent found it necessary to throw up in the middle of his leader's speech.

Arafat didn't say much, really. In an effort to bait the
poor Lebanese, who already were waiting for him in Cairo
to make an agreement, he said he "wasn't sure" if he'd
go. He voiced some run-of-the-mill anti-Americanisms.

But what was interesting about him was that, when he
began to talk that day, the style of the new Arab leader
began to come through (even through the dark glasses).
He was humorous. He cajoled the audience. He smiled
sardonically. He indulged in no flights of flowery rhetoric,
half-answered most questions, appeared to be speaking
directly when he wasn't, and completely ignored questions like one about Fatah and Sartawi's Action Organization having at it the week before and killing a few of
each other—a question he didn't like.

At one point, I had to smile to myself (and here, if
you had any sense at all, you kept all your stupid smiles
to yourself) at how hard it was for the Arabs, like so many
formerly colonized people, to escape from the bloody British. "We have made the six-day battle part of a very
long war," Arafat said then, and his voice suddenly seemed
to take on that historic, ringing quality one hears on nar-

rative history records, "When the Allies were defeated at Dunkirk, I like to remind myself that fear could have made the Allies yield to the terms of the Nazis. But Churchill persevered and said there is nothing left for us except blood, tears and sweat. He insisted they were going to have victory and so do I now insist we are going to have victory." He gave the "V for Victory" sign.

What interested me, too, was his bemused attitude toward the things that he and his commandos could do. When asked that day whether Fatah was responsible for oil-tank explosions in Lebanon the night before, he commented wryly, "Now, we are not security forces for any of the Arab governments. We are revolutionaries, we are rebels. That question should be addressed to the Lebanese Minister of the Interior."

There was a pregnant pause. Then, referring to the fact that the poor Lebanese government, which the commandos had been shamelessly hounding, still was unable to form a cabinet, he added dryly, "If there is one."

Another time, referring to the acquisitive mercantile character of many of the Lebanese, he commented matter-of-factly, "They are going to find that despite everything, the Israelis will turn out to be better businessmen than they are."

Is Arafat really a new-style leader, a "new man"? The next day I was describing this performance in Damascus to an American who is considered one of the best Arabists in the business. He thought so. "The old Arab leader based his appeal on bravado and physical appeal," this man said. "His emotions were maudlin and—what is the word?—cloying. And the young Arab feels he suffered from such high-blown rhetoric and archaic qualities. The new-type leader bases his appeal on logic, he employs a sense of humor, he realizes that he needs a dash of dispassion and

a critical look. He is a more realistic leader. I think that
Arafat is this type of man."

A British Arabist put it in very simple terms: "The
Palestinians are simply men of their times."

The next few days were, for me, hellish. Salmonella set
in like an Israeli bombardment, and pains assaulted my
middle from back, front, top and bottom. I lay whimpering in my bed in the St. Georges—I have always found
that when one is sick and alone, whimpering is an enormous
help—trying alternately to do away with myself for having
eaten the damnable fish, to think of ways of poisoning
the whole bay, and to get up and write a story. Any
other time, it would not have mattered, but this was an
important, breaking story—the kind I would have usually
worked on eighteen hours a day . . . and I literally could
barely move.

Any direction you went you found a great story. Leftists
had taken over and were occupying the city of Tripoli in
the north. The commandos continued fighting the army in
the south. The students at the American University of
Beirut, a quarter of whom were Palestinians, were demonstrating for the commandos. Palestinian commandos had
taken over fourteen of the fifteen UNRWA camps in Lebanon (housing 86,000 persons) and were running them
with the government's helpless acquiescence.

It was clearly a fight between generations. One day at a
raucous demonstration at AUB, a bedraggled father was
bemoaning the state of things. I found his response touching. "When I was young, I was idealistic, too," he said. "In
the army, I defended our borders. Now the young people
want no borders. I'm glad my son believes in something . . . but I just want him to live."

This generational conflict was something new. Before,

the fight in Lebanon had been confessional—between Moslem and Christian. Now it was ideological, and the ideology split old and young, Lebanese nationalist and Arab nationalist, those who clung to the balances of the past and those who wanted a creative chaos in the present. Little, 2.2-million-person Lebanon, so long insulated from the passions of the Arab world, so long the Summer Paradise for the Arabian Sheikh and The Bank for the Solvent Saver, had come upon hard times—modern times.

And while all this was happening, I . . . *I* had salmonella. I managed to drag myself up at 6 A.M. every day to file my report by long distance phone calls, but it was simply impossible to get around as much as I wanted because I could not stand up. All of this was only slightly lessened by my foreign editor's cable the next day: EVEN GOD RESTED ON THE SEVENTH DAY. REGARDS TO SAL MONELLA.

It was during this time, however, that I began to lay out the structure for the series I was going to do on the Palestinian commandos. And gradually I got back to work.

One of the first questions that people usually ask me is how correspondents work. First there is my "blitzkrieg" approach to interviewing—I interview everyone possible who is related to the story, working often up to sixteen or eighteen hours a day. I take down everything—and I mean *everything*—they say.

Once I have done enough work and interviewed enough people and seen enough to satisfy myself about a story (and this point must remain very subjective), I am usually alive inside with ideas and strains of ideas fighting each other and struggling with each other. I try to let them stew a bit. Creatively. Then, nearly almost without any conscious effort on my part, the lines of thought seem to straighten themselves out (almost by themselves) and present themselves to me.

But far more important than these technical matters is
the overall commitment of the writer. I have always had
strong ideas about the type of dedication a journalist, and
in particular a foreign correspondent, must have. For at
best, he is a person living in a third world of critical
non-commitment, where there are no absolute truths, where
there are reasons for everything if you search long enough
and where total loyalty to anyone or anything is suspect
because total truth can never be known.

I have always felt that the primary job of the correspondent is to bring the consciousness of other peoples
to his readers. This means not being bounded by one's
own experience but breaking through it and going further
—to penetrating the memories and historic shadows of
another people.

While other people ask of strange and curious peoples
in the world: "Why are they not like me?" the good
journalist asks: "Why are they the way they are?"

There is a reason why every person and every people
acts as it does. Every human experience has its own rationale—it was formed by a real series of events, by a
complex of instincts, experience and fears which create
that unique consciousness. One has only to come to understand this complex of instincts, experience and fears.
Only . . . and that is the most difficult task in the world.

Actually, it was just the first few days that I rested.
The fourth day, we got a car and headed toward Yanta,
the town in the south where Fatah was holding out and
from which it was attacking the Lebanese fortress-town of
Rachaya. It was here that I gained a visceral understanding of something I had only understood intellectually before. This was the brutality and the tragedy of everything
that was sweeping and churning around me so often robed
in other, less frightful colors. This was the real thing.

The valley was so beautiful it took your breath away. It was all gold and gray, and the towns were so simple they looked like classic temples. This was the biblical land of milk and honey, and you can understand even today the historical passion for it. We stopped first at Rachaya, a lovely mountaintop town lying in the shadow of Mount Hermon, whose crown was a Crusader fortress. The beauty seemed torn asunder once, however, when we saw the body of a young commando lying bloated and dark and alone under a blooming bush.

They were so picturesque, the town and the fortress, that they looked almost like toys. The fortress, for instance, with its ancient crenelated walls and jagged stone parapets, was lined with brightly blooming flower boxes. At the peak, I talked to the colonel, who told us that the commandos had attacked the night before but that they could not see them now.

As we went down the walkway to head toward Yanta, we came upon a touching little scene. A beautiful Lebanese mother from the southern village of Ain Horsch was hugging her twenty-four-year-old son, who looked both moved and embarrassed by her tears and was using his dog tag as worry beads. A half circle of his friends stood around him smiling and watching the familial scene with obvious sympathy.

"Why do you worry, Ma? I'm all right," he kept saying.

Her handsome dark face, toughened by the wind, was covered with tears. Then she regained her spirit. "Don't worry, my son," she cried suddenly, slapping him on the shoulder. "Be good and strong, and if you're not a good soldier, I'll come and take your place."

"*Masbout,*" the soldiers cried, and they applauded, as they stood about sniffing marigolds. "That's right."

I spoke to the mother, who kept apologizing for her simple worn clothes—she had come directly from the orchard, she said, to see her only son. Asked about the com-

mandos, she was very direct. "They're Syrians," she said
with disgust, referring to Saiqa's birthplace. "We don't
like them." Yet she was afraid enough of them—and there
were now many near Ain Horsch, she said—that she did
not want her or her family's name to be used. That's the
way it is . . . once the lines start to be drawn.

And it was clear to me that day how deeply the lines
were being drawn in Lebanon, such a lovely, innocent
country. As I moved through that day, a pervading sense
of sadness overcame me. I was still a young journalist,
but I'd already seen too many lines. I remembered Santo
Domingo in 1965, when the rebels were finally encircled
in the small downtown section of the city with a wall
of American troops supposedly protecting them. Lines and
divisions—lines and divisions that finally were broken down
physically, but never spiritually, leaving the country still
sick, divided, fractured.

It brought to mind Vietnam. Only in Vietnam the lines
were largely invisible, like the real feelings on the faces
of the Vietnamese. There you could cross the line any
minute, anywhere, between the Viet Cong and "our side,"
and never know it, until you got your head shot off and
then, yes, you knew where the line was.

There was Berlin, of course, and all those other countries
and cities we've managed to cut and divide up like divisible
pies whose sides we had thought would stand alone and
straight once the wound was made. For people like me,
who've seen it before, who've seen these weird divisions
over and over again, who've played the observer at this
awful game of national jigsaw puzzles in four continents,
it all seemed bitterly familiar.

Now chalk up Yanta.

When you've done this a bit, you can sense the mood
of a town a mile away. That day, as we approached Yanta,
only five miles and a mountain and a terrace of golden
fig trees away from Rachaya, it was clear something was

wrong. Only four days earlier, the commandos had entered
this spare town atop a barren mountaintop to a welcome
of broad peasant smiles and Turkish coffee.

Today the streets were empty.

A strange and ominous quiet hung like a cloud over
the starkly beautiful countryside, whose mountains now
echoed spasmodically with the gruff shouts of the commandos and occasional gunshots.

Everything was so different. So different. Now there was
no dichotomous mood, but one clear mood—hatred and
war. Now there was no sense of the absurd about the
commandos, but one clear impression—a bullying tough-
ness. Now there was no sense of unreality, no untenable
shifting back and forth but a drear sense of reality—real
reality reality.

Some occupied towns are more occupied than others,
and when I visited Yanta that Friday afternoon, it was
clear that Yanta—the commandos' main headquarters in
south Lebanon—was very occupied indeed. The young
guerrillas with frightened brown faces, themselves dispossessed of a country, now were frightening and dispossess-
ing others with their Russian machine guns. Many had
been killed. The people were staying indoors and we were
told in the eerie stillness of the valley and mountaintop that
day, "Clear the town, get out or we'll shoot." The Lebanese flag had gone down Thursday and another stateless little no man's land was created in the world. The whole
southeast of the country, in fact, had been enclaved like
a badly blotched and fevered skin between them and the
Lebanese military, who only wanted to keep their country
for Lebanese.

The commandos drove us out that day. They even followed the car with their jeep. When our driver went to ask
them if we could drive out the other way, they threatened
to shoot him if we didn't leave at once.

The politicians, who never had to stand on these lines they drew, were far away in Cairo, dickering about the wording of an agreement that might just momentarily keep all these people from killing each other . . . or might not.

Arafat, who finally deigned to go to Cairo to negotiate, after keeping the Lebanese waiting for three days, met with them and with President Nasser in Clovis Maksuud's beautiful apartment to draw up an agreement for a cease-fire.

When I read this in Beirut, for some reason I remembered Clovis talking about the refugee waifs with their big questioning eyes and saying, in a rare moment of Arab fairness, "I suppose the Jews had boys like this, too." But this kind of moment was growing rarer and rarer. And within weeks the agreement would fail and everybody would be fighting again in Lebanon and then Jordan would fall apart into civil war, and . . .

As it turned out, it really didn't matter whether they agreed in Cairo or not, for the words would disappear into the air. The truths of the week were elsewhere than in Cairo—they were in Shabie with Major Said, in Damascus with Arafat and, most of all, in the golden fright of Yanta. The hatreds that drew the lines would not disappear and I wrote my closing story, in a style far more emotional than any I usually use:

> Here, the invisible and not so invisible dividing lines, with each small area held by a faction representing some undigested, unassimilated striving of mankind, were quite real. We used to have enclave nations—now we've enclaved up the nations. And in some form or another, here as in all those other lucky countries, the lines will probably last—like scars—for a long, long time.

CHAPTER V

The World of Illusion?

▼▼▼

I have been rather frequently in situations which demanded
swift decisions and the application of difficult judgments.
I have been on breaking news stories where, no matter
how hard you worked, you couldn't get the one piece
of information you needed to complete that day's story.
I have been in areas, like Latin America, where people
tell you what you want to hear, simply because they are
kindly people; and I have been in countries, like Russia,
where before your eyes an almost visible psychic curtain
closed on people's faces when you asked them too much.

But before I went to the Arab countries, I was never
faced with the real possibility that much or all of what
people were telling you belonged not to the real world but
to a world of illusion which they had built up around
themselves.

The ideological lies of Russia, Cuba and North Vietnam,
the political lies of Washington, the social lies of upward-
striving, angry minorities—all of these are easy to spot

and easy, eventually, to ferret out. But after coming to
the Middle East, I soon realized I was up against something else. Was it actually possible, as many contended,
that the Arabs lied about *everything?* And if they lied,
was it deliberate, conscious? Or was it even correct, in this
instance, to use the word "lie"? Was it not, perhaps, something far more subtle, far more on a psychic level than a
political one? Certainly there is a metaphysical "otherness"
about the Arabs and about many underdeveloped peoples:
They are "not there" much of the time in our terms; but
since so many of them *are* this way, should we not then
assume that this outlook is at least as "normal" a human
one as ours?

What first leads most journalists, scholars and diplomats
—including those friendly to the Arabs—to doubt the
veracity of the Arab claims are the clear discrepancies in
obvious things like military figures and statistics. The Egyptian claims on losses at Suez are often palpably ridiculous.
If Egypt had shot down all the Israeli planes it claims,
Israel would be a couple of hundred aircraft in the red.
If Egypt had had all the victories it claims, there would
indeed be no Israel.

But it is not only in the formal military statistics that
there is such an enormous difference in what the Arabs
say and in what the Israelis say, and in what neutral sources
say—it is in everything. And all of this is what a correspondent must deal with. What is he supposed to do?
Qualify every quote he uses with, "Of course, he may
well be lying?" Or footnote every story with, "Of course,
none of this may be true at all?"

I came headlong up against the whole "world of illusion"
syndrome while dealing with a particularly emotional question—the Arab allegations that Israel was torturing Arab
prisoners.

I came upon this indirectly while waiting around in Amman for Fatah or anybody to take me on a raid.

"Look," Zuhdi Terrazzi at the PLO said to me one day, "while you're waiting, why don't you talk with some of the deportees from the West Bank. There are some interesting people here—the Arab mayor of Jerusalem, this Anglican priest, a number of women's leaders. . . ."

I wasn't, frankly, enthusiastic; I was concentrating single-mindedly on the commandos, I was leaving time open to meet with them. Besides, I can only stand so much propaganda in one day. But in order not to waste time, I finally agreed to talk to these deportees, and in five minutes on the phone Zuhdi had all the arrangements made, leaving me slightly suspicious.

The first contact was with the General Union of Palestinian Women, many of whom were deportees from the West Bank of Jordan that was occupied by Israel after the 1967 war. I sat down in a big, rather untidy room, and eight women marched in, in a line. They were, for the most part, good-looking women; they were all, like most Palestinian women, extremely bright and quick; they wanted very much to tell their story, and they were quite systematic about it.

The commandos were training women "to play their role in the liberation movement." The work began in 1965, but really got its impetus only after the six-day war. Women were in many ways "leading the fight in the occupied territories," with strikes and leaflets and helping prisoners' families. . . .

"The Palestinians do not want to kick the Jews out," one attractive young woman said, with assurance. "We lived a long time together. As we say, we are cousins. They say we want to push them into the sea, but they are the ones who are pushing us into the desert." The usual.

Then came the first, first-person account I had heard of

the torture and maltreatment of Arabs by Israeli officials in the occupied territories. "They have humiliated men in the villages by gathering everyone and making them kneel all day in the sun with their hands raised. In one town there was a curfew for thirty-two days; a four-year-old went out to get water and they shot him. In court, a young girl from Nablus showed how her chest was covered with cigarette burns."

"We are asking to be equal with men, so we must suffer the same punishments," another young woman interjected here.

"They beat men and women with rubber ropes, with steel inside. One man couldn't walk for seven days. In another case, three sisters were arrested for helping fighters. One sent out a secret message in which she said she did not confess because of torture, but because of 'something that was unbearable.'" The women glanced hesitantly at each other. Then one said, "They used a large rod. . . . Many girls have lost their virginity in this way."

I looked at the women carefully. Virginity is such a primevally emotional thing in the Arab world, guarded by so many atavistic dragons, that it was quite natural and possible that they would use a purported loss of virginity as an excuse for perhaps a ready confession—and might even believe it themselves. And who was going to check it when they came out?

I asked them, "Have any of you actually been tortured in Israel?"

The forceful woman who was sitting next to me—a hefty woman with an obviously strong personality—leaned forward, and the room quieted. "I am Mrs. Abdul Hadi from Nablus," she said. "I was imprisoned for forty-five days—from March 13 to April 25, with my daughter, who is seventeen. Then we were put on the bridge. My daughter was tortured in front of my eyes. She was whipped

with rubber whips. But you know, many were tortured,
and they are all alike. You did not feel whether it is your
sister or daughter. The Israeli soldiers told me, 'You are
not a mother. How can you endure this, when you see
your daughter tortured?' I wanted to take the whip out
of his hand, but he was a big man. Then he told me,
'If you don't tell us, we'll send her to Jerusalem to the
soldiers.' I could do nothing but spit at him."

Mrs. Hadi had been arrested on suspicion of helping
the commandos in the occupied territories through the
Arab women's organizations; eventually no charges were
brought against her, and she and her daughter were "put
on the Allenby Bridge." In effect, they were deported into
Jordan.

As we left the women's meeting that day, I asked Mrs.
Hadi, "And did you help the commandos?"

She turned toward me with a smile indicating a clear
degree of intimacy in the understanding between us. "Of
course," she said slowly, "we all sympathize with the
commandos."

The next day I religiously persevered on my researches
and went to see the Reverend Elia Khoury, the Anglican
priest who had been deported from Ramallah on the occupied West Bank and who was then in charge of the
Near East Council of Churches in Amman. He turned
out to be a tall, arrowlike man, angular and direct, with
a certain sad gentleness about him. He was also the brother-
in-law of Kemal Nasser, the bachelor poet.

"They are right to be concerned with security," he said,
sitting in his little office, "because they waged a war to
get peace, and they didn't get it. You can't have peace
and land too."

I found Reverend Khoury to be an interesting man,
because he was one of those men in whose person is
exemplified—as in so many Jewish people too—a deeply

metaphysical battleground for good and evil. Most important for an Arab, everything must be qualified; the
Westerner must be convinced that he, the Arab, was telling
the whole truth, was not living in the "world of illusion"
so often attributed to him, and was aware to the tips of
his tingling nerve endings where not only beauty but, most
important, reality and truth lay.

He began his deposition by completely denying that he
took any part in any commando activities against the Israelis. But he said clearly, "I certainly refused occupation
—as a principle and as a way of life for myself and for my
people. Occupation is pretty grim sometimes. There are
curfews and they try to terrorize the people through shooting. We have an evangelical school for girls which was
hit by a bomb during the war and two girls were killed.
Afterward, the girls demonstrated against the occupation
in the schoolyard and the Israeli soldiers dashed in and
beat the girls and teachers and sent them home."

He paused and accentuated the following sentence: *"I
want to be very careful and tell you only the truth, what
I have seen myself."*

Then he painted what was to me a fascinating picture
and one which was to reoccur in the stories I was to hear
later on the West Bank: a confrontation between the Arabs
and the Israeli military government, which became in the
Arab mind a clear confrontation between good and evil.

"I used to take Christian clergy to the military governor
to protest," he went on. "I used to talk to him of good
and evil. I said that good was original in man and that
evil was accidental, that man has a value given to him by
God and that no one on earth has the right to rob any
man of this value. I talked to him on the highest level.
He said, 'I don't know.' That means he apparently didn't
agree with me. I said I had seen his men beating girls
of twelve and thirteen on the streets because they were

demonstrating in the school. I told him, 'I can tell you
frankly that we are all against occupation.' He said, 'Where
were you when your girls threw stones at our car?' I said,
'Maybe that is a mistake, but the greater mistake was that
of your men, because the wrong of the strong was greater
than that of the weak.'"

On March 2, 1969, at 1:30 A.M. that Sunday morning,
he was picked up in his home. He was held forty-eight
days in Ramallah prison in solitary confinement, he said,
"completely cut off from the world."

Then came another footnote. "I want to emphasize one
fact," he said, "for all through my life I have been just
and fair. I was not badly treated. I was not beaten. I was
not exposed to torture, although spiritually I was badly
treated. But I used to hear them beating other men and
women. I heard crying and screaming. It was a common
thing. One guard said to me, 'What forbids us from treating you the same as those dogs?' I said, 'I beg your
pardon—those are not dogs, they are human beings.'

"I had discussions with them in prison about the suffering of the Jews. And I had one discussion with a representative of the prime minister in East Jerusalem. I
told him, 'We Semites, our fate is to live together in this
part of the world. You received your religion here and
Our Lord was incarnated here. You have technical abilities,
we have natural resources. Why can't we live together and
stop these hostilities? But peace is given by the strong,
not by the weak. Zionism is hostile even to Judaism. If
you take that thing away, Jew and Arab will meet.'"

Finally, Reverend Khoury was given the choice of staying in jail or going "across the bridge." He decided to
leave. In words that seemed slightly fulsome to me, he
ended up with, "Spiritually, I suffered so. Do all people
who stand for truth and justice suffer? I said, yes, but it

was too much for me to accept. Now my family has joined
me here."

The next evening, on the glassed-in porch of a handsome house on the top of Jebel Lwebdeih, across the street
from an attractive modern mosque, I spent two hours talking with Rohi Khatib, the Arab mayor of Jerusalem until
the Israelis abolished the job and deported him. It was
more of the same. . . .

Now, these men and women were not Arab peasants,
they were not workingmen. They were in every way people
who should, by education and by experience, know truth
from falsehood and reality from illusion. They were the
leaders of the Palestinian Arab world, the cream off the
top. If even they were lying about all of this, it certainly
made a difference in the righteousness of their cause.

And so, suddenly, I was faced with a vexing task. I had
to try to decide, after applying all my powers of judgment
and all my abilities as a reporter, whether these stories of
mistreatment and even torture of Arabs under Israeli occupation were true, in whole or in part. Some journalists
would simply throw away testimonies like this, bringing to
bear their own traditional ideas, commitments, and, perhaps, prejudices. I was tempted to do this, for it was very
difficult for me, having been as idealistic about Israel as
I had always been, to believe that Jews themselves could,
even under extreme provocation, do unto others a small
part of what others had done unto them.

We knew, of course, that the Arabs—in particular the
Syrians and the Iraquis—were barbarous in their treatment of prisoners. And yet—and perhaps this is not fair—
it seemed worse when the Israelis did it, and we were simply bound to judge them more harshly because we expected so much more from them.

So, as much as it troubled me, I could not throw away

these charges. I had seen too many people fool themselves too often—and I was not personally immune to this. I had seen my own people, the Americans, tell themselves over and over that we were not mistreating people in Vietnam. And then came My Lai and all the rest. . . .

I had learned, the hard way perhaps, that there is more than one kind of a world of illusion. As much as I liked and respected Israel, I could not look less critically at another country—or believe it more intrinsically irreproachable—than I had looked at my own country.

So I wrote a story—an extremely cautious and carefully worded story—about the accounts of Israeli torture that were floating around Jordan. But I also asked the paper to get a response from the Israeli government.

The response bordered on the irresponsible. I was sure the Israelis could have carefully documented these cases, citing details to prove their points and calmly refuting the allegations. Instead, the government spokesman highhandedly rejected everything . . . across the board. All the accusations were "utter nonsense." It was an insult to the Israelis. They did admit privately that Mrs. Hadi, who happened to be one of the leading Arab women on the West Bank and, in the words of one American diplomat "a stellar woman," had been "mistakenly" put in with Israeli prostitutes. I was depressed with this answer; indeed, I didn't consider it an answer.

I was perhaps most disturbed by the problem of telling this story. Here you were not dealing with fact, which is what we journalists are theoretically supposed to deal with. Nor were you dealing, to put it less simplistically, with attitudes or feelings. You might well be dealing with psychic forces, with mental sets, with illusions and disillusions—in short, with things that would be more properly dealt with in psychiatry, anthropology or sociology.

Yet I was as convinced as always that there was simply

no way of telling *what is actually happening* on the deepest levels in situations as fraught with complexities as the Middle East—as opposed to dealing with *straight breaking news*—without bringing an awareness and an understanding and an interpretation of these factors into account. This is what foreign reporting comes down to today . . . or what it has to come up to.

And so I began to delve into the whole question of what can perhaps best be called the world-of-illusion syndrome in the Arab world.

I found that the great Arab philosopher al-Ghazali, several centuries ago in his book *The Revival of Religious Studies,* had said: "Know that a lie is not *haram* (wrong) in itself but only because of the evil conclusion to which it leads the hearer, making him believe something that is really not the case. If a lie is the only way to reach a good, it is *halal* (permitted)." In effect, truth and falsehood are of instrumental value only. The lie is not wrong per se —only the result is important.

Another prominent line of thought has it that it is the beautiful Arab language that leads to the exaggeration of reality; that Arabs become bewitched by the preponderant beauty of expression in their language.

The man whom I found to be unquestionably the most brilliant interpreter of the Arab personality—and the man with the most insight into these questions—turned out to be, ironically, an Israeli. He had also been the head of military intelligence from 1955 to 1959, when he began his studies to become the foremost Israeli Arabist. He was Yehosophat Harkabi, of the University of Tel Aviv, and he was a charming man. His friends occasionally called him Yehosophatah, after Al Fatah, whose papers he endlessly pores over. That bit of humor in itself sets the

Israelis apart from their Fatah "cousins." So does the way in which I talked to Yehosophatah.

It was a cold January morning, and my interview with Dr. Harkabi had been arranged for ten o'clock. It was pouring down a cold, almost glittering icy rain. I climbed the four floors to his apartment in a nice but by no means ostentatious building in downtown Tel Aviv. When I rang the bell a voice called down the stairs from the fifth floor, saying, "Would you please come up here?" I trudged up still another floor, dripping rainwater into little puddles on every step, and found the short, attractive Dr. Harkabi standing in the door of what had been the laundry room.

"This is my study," he said, with the engaging smile that usually animates his intelligent features. The "study," a bare and simple room except for the hundreds and hundreds of books on the shelves, was perhaps five by nine feet. It was a cell, a cold cell, and he was bundled up in a heavy sweater.

Here were all the differences between the Israelis and the Arabs distilled into one single frame of the film. I could think of no Arab leader—particularly a general and a scholar—who would proudly, even humorously, have his study in a laundry room and receive foreigners there.

I *try* to be simply a finely tuned receiving instrument, forsaking personal likes or dislikes, but I must admit un-journalistically that I liked Dr. Harkabi better than anyone I had met in the Middle East.

Here was a man, a devoted and dedicated Israeli, a man who had served in one of the highest positions of his country, yet a man who could humorously and critically look at his own country at the same time that he was looking fairly and justly at the Arab world.

We sat up in his cold laundry room, both of us bundled up in sweaters and coats, and talked about the Arab world-of-illusion syndrome. "Psychologically, they have less of a feeling for consistency," he said slowly. "They don't feel cognitive dissonance as we do. If we express ourselves differently in a different position, we feel inconsistent, uneasy. They are not uneasy. Some say they are hypocritical, I don't think so. But when people express things in different ways, you must ask, where do they expose their genuine attitudes? I think it is within the collective and not when they are alone. This is very different from American culture."

He did not embrace the idea that the language somehow misleads the Arab into excessive thoughts he would not otherwise express. "Many say it is more important to listen to what they say than note what they do. But they are not victims of their beautiful language. Language is an instrument." And in one of his excellent papers on Arab psychology, Dr. Harkabi wrote: "Perhaps one can relate the frequency of falsehood to the phenomenon of hostility between Arab men. The closer a man is to his fellow, the more loyal he will be and the harder it will be to lie to him, and vice versa. Yet all these explanations are not wholly satisfactory. The problem is still perplexing."

In this paper, which was on "Basic Factors in Arab Collapse During the Six-day War," Dr. Harkabi went on to warn that "The habit of not relating to reality results in the development of an inflated personality, a glorified image of the Arab as the product of an illustrious history. An inflated image of oneself is likely to interfere with a correct estimation of one's strength, and this no doubt was a factor in the Arabs' inaccurate evaluation of their own military preparedness—for which the Egyptian military command became the scapegoat."

The entire question of reality and unreality in the Middle East, more than in any other single area in the world, soon becomes a predominant factor which fractures all

of the serious student's or journalist's thinking. It has
been historically, after all, *the* area of religious passion
and torment. In it lie Mecca, to which the Moslems face
six times a day, and Jerusalem, to which Jews throughout
the centuries have dreamed of returning. It is the "land
of milk and honey," the "Holy Land," the "Promised
Land." It was in these deserts that the prophets of all
the religions, with their slightly mad eyes and their holy
dreams, arose, shaking off the constricting sands of the past
and shaking the future like earthquakes with their ideas.

Once in Jerusalem, the city which even today exudes
myth and remembrance, an American diplomat said to me,
almost in a whisper, "In Jerusalem, it is not too good to
breathe too deeply. This is the country where myths are
made. Just as today it is not good to breathe too deeply
of the Palestinian thing. . . ."

Very well, if you are a mystic and can afford to sit
about inhaling and exhaling legends! But what if you are
a diplomat or a journalist who must make judgments on
what is real and what is not real?

I was lunching one day in Chicago, in the fall of 1970,
with Clovis Maksuud, my foreign editor, Nicholas Shuman,
and Hassan Abdallah, head of the Arab Information Service
there. Nick gently chided Clovis about the commandos
that day saying, after a single Marine Corps identification
card was found in Amman, that Marines had taken part
in the Jordan civil war a few weeks before. Hassan, who
had been living in the States for several years and had
arrived at a keen sense of the importance of accuracy in
dealing with the finicky Yankees, agreed that it was bad
for the cause. But Clovis angrily, even pettishly, disagreed.

"But even if it is wrong," he cried, "it *could* be right.
It is plausible. We may be wrong on small things. . . ." He
looked directly at Nick and at me. "But you . . . you
are wrong on your whole basic proposition."

Here again I felt the inability to reach an instinctive level of understanding with another people. It gnawed at me, it deeply disturbed me. And I knew that I would probably never reach it, not if I lived in the Arab world the rest of my life. To us, it is a twilight and dawn world—half Occident and half Orient—whose lips are sealed in eternal secrets.

Let us take a few very practical and, in the light of the entire Middle Eastern conflict, highly important areas where the whole question of reality or illusion can and does make the difference between war and peace, life and death, progress and regression. Take, for instance, the case of the late Gamal Abdel Nasser.

The Israelis believed that Nasser was a totally insincere man; they believed that all he told the Americans about how he wanted peace was simply part of his world of illusion, while what he really wanted—the destruction of Israel—was what he showed he wanted on a working level, in his ranting speeches. As an American diplomat in Tel Aviv told me one day, "The Israelis think that what the Arabs say in public is the most important. They think that the Arabs say in private what the Americans want to hear and that publicly they say what they mean. The Israelis believe one way, we believe the other. They say to me, 'If you're right, it's fine, if you're wrong, *we're* dead.' They can show other precedents where leaders stood up and said what they were going to do—and did it."

Or consider how you might attempt to deal with the statistics on the dead and wounded. The Arabs give out extremely inflated figures on the numbers of Israelis killed and ridiculously deflated figures on their own losses (which the Israelis claim to be about 80 per cent among those who cross the Jordan River). On a journalistic and historic

level, we *know* the Syrians lied when, just before the 1967
war, they claimed the Israelis were "massing on their
borders."

Nor is this the simple lie of the Pentagon excuse-maker.
It is something far different and far deeper—it involves a
total change of personality, to the point where what the
Arab is at one moment, he is not the next.

"It is very strange," Professor Amnon Rubinstein, the
youthful and energetic dean of the Law School at Tel
Aviv University, told me one evening when we were discussing this subject. "I have seen it myself. The commandos
will do extremely courageous things—in crossing the
Jordan, for instance. Then, when a terrorist is captured,
he becomes totally obsequious to his captors. He will point
out the caves where his friends are. Then when he is put
in prison, he reverts to his first stage and stages strikes
with his fellow commandos and throws things around."

To the Israelis and to many Arabists, this means they
live in a "dream world" that changes according to outer
experience and is not formed by any hard reality within
the man. So the reality they see about them can change
from moment to moment. To Harkabi, the problem with
the Arab fighting man is that he is an atomized man. He
has no bonds of trust tying him to his fellow man. And
so, in battle, "Instead of becoming part of a team and
deriving confidence from it, the Arab soldier turns into a
lonely and isolated individual."

There is the question, too, as to how you interpret
people like the Egyptians. Such quiet, nice, gentle people,
as I have said. And yet, even while they are like this,
you know from history that they can turn into a raging
mob, unequalled for mass savagery, which in the early days
in the fight against colonialism used to literally tear
foreigners limb from limb.

And how do you explain, as you chat with these charming people, the brutal teaching of the most vicious types of hatred which they write into even their schoolbooks for children? When Jordanian children are asked in school to develop the theme: "Israel was born to die. Prove it!" And when the Syrian Minister of Education in 1968, Suleyman al-Khash, writes in a letter to M. René Maheu, Director General of UNESCO, "The hatred which we indoctrinate into the minds of our children from their birth is sacred." How do you explain the horribly irresponsible way in which the Egyptians still teach their children about the "Protocols of Zion" and the "ritual killing of the Gentiles by Jews"—both unquestionable medieval hoaxes that led to pogroms and insufferable brutalities?

There *are* answers, at least partial ones.

—It seems obvious to many Arabists that the modern Arab is a person fraught with feelings of insecurity. He is the dregs of a once great empire, a man who despite his enormous numbers is as nothing in the world.

—Arabs distrust everyone, particularly each other, and even children in school say not "That's interesting" but "Why would he say that?"

—He is forever marked by the fact that Islam rose so suddenly and grew with such fantastic rapidity—within one hundred years, it had taken over nearly half of the known world—that the Arabs never learned the art of patient, long-range application of talents.

—His tendency is not to see the whole but to weave shiny theories often about unrelated details. Appearance is everything. Appearance and the escape provided by the demands of "honor."

—Perhaps, too, no "world" in the world resists change so fiercely as the Arab world. Indeed, even the Arabic word for change, *ghaiyara* carries the implication of "to corrupt" or "to change for the worst."

—Dr. Sania Hamady, the perceptive Lebanese sociolo-

gist, notes how the Arab is totally enmeshed psychically
and socially in his family group, to the extent to which
"it may be said that the Arab has not attained full in-
dividuation as a person. He is still a non-differentiated part
of his family." And only a secure individual can give
loyalty on a larger scale—to a nation.

—This drowning of the individual in the familial sea is
due to the importance of shame as *the* social pressure in
Arab society—in contrast to guilt pressure in Western
society. Sin consists only in the outward act and not in
the inward inclination. (What a contrast to the demanding
morality of the Jews, which is so highly internalized!)

—Harkabi believes:

> "Among the Egyptian people there was a consensus of
> admiration for Nasser, but this did not create real cohe-
> siveness. The applause for his speeches demonstrated
> public enthusiasm for, and approval of, the leader with-
> out necessarily signifying readiness to act. This enthusi-
> asm may well be a kind of escape through public ecstasy
> from the sadness and loneliness of the individual in a
> society lacking in cohesion and rife with internal hostil-
> ity. Modern Arab literature is stamped with the sadness
> of the isolated individual."
>
> The flaw does not appear in the Arab as an individual,
> Harkabi points out, "since he is gifted with the same
> abilities and talents as other men. It is a collective or
> cultural weakness, rooted in the relationship of the indi-
> vidual toward his fellow men and toward society."

One must understand, of course, that there are many,
many types of "Arabs." There is the desert Arab—mystical, aggressive, saint-worshiping. The zealot. And there is
the Levantine Arab—the city man who exults in buying
and selling and looks toward the exciting scents and freedom of the open sea. And one must understand, when we

talk about the fiery individualism of the early Bedouin Arabs that this individualism gave way in the cities to the passive and anonymous attitudes that are part of a shame culture.

Under no circumstances is the Arab world fixed in its present state of idiosyncrasies and eccentricities forever. In my own experience, over and over the Arabs told me things like, "I want to be very careful . . . very careful . . . to tell you only what I know" and "We are trying to remove any exaggeration" and "We want to be very careful with the truth." This is a characteristic of the "New Arabs," this attempt to deal with truth and reality. It comes from a deep awareness that the outer world is critical of and contemptuous of their former exaggerations and that to join the modern world they must somehow learn to deal less cavalierly with truth. They are growingly conscious and self-conscious, and a "new man," often technically trained, is emerging.

Nevertheless, looking at all the tendencies in the Arab world—the reformist, like Nasser; the Islamic purists, like the Moslem Brotherhood; the radicals, like most of the commandos—Harkabi came to the conclusion (as did I) that the radical tendency would prevail, at least in the short run. But he pointed out that this does not necessarily mean more danger for Israel.

"It sometimes means simply more fragmentation and inner disruption," he said, "like Iraq and Syria. There is no institutionalization of politics, and every change is violent. What happens with radicals is that the university levels go down. They become obsessed with radicalization. Conflict is salient in their minds. Frustration becomes much greater. But you don't learn science. You can curse Israel a million times, but you don't learn calculus."

In effect, you don't learn how to be a developed people—and, as many Arabs know, only a developed people can purge itself from the mistakes of the past and the fatal weaknesses and propensities for illusion that are holding the Arab world back.

But what about the "torture" of Arabs by Israelis? Did it really occur? Or was it, too, part of the illusory world? It wasn't until I got to Israel that I was able to clear this up, and even then only more or less so. But I will say one thing. In today's world, it is not only the Arabs who live in worlds of illusion.

CHAPTER VI

A Tale of Two Desert Kingdoms
or
The New Arabs Take Over

When the Coptic anchorite monks go to the deserts to live in solitary caves and commune with the shifting sands, they go, they say, to listen to the "voices of silence." Great empty vistas of sand do things to people. They impart a feeling of peace, a sense of wonder, and the stylized security of outer serenity.

But the desert kingdoms of the Middle East are not, today, hearing many voices of silence. The predominant voices are strident and harsh, calling for revolution in the name of historic hatreds and a new-found social justice, as a new generation of desert Arabs takes over. In particular, this is what has been happening on the oases and in the cities of Libya and the Sudan.

Libya had always rather fascinated me, it was such an enormous mass of sand on the map to have only 1,750,000 people. It was here that the Phoenicians had founded the great Tripolitania that blossomed between 700 and 146 B.C.; here that the Arab invasion had submerged the

native Berber culture; here that Thomas Jefferson had sent
a squadron of three frigates and a sloop to meet in battle
the Barbary pirates to whom he already had paid two
million dollars in tribute.

Libya was half the size of India, eight times as large as
the British Isles and the fourth largest country in Africa;
but to what avail, when as late as 1951, 90 per cent of the
people were illiterate and—to give just *one* measurement
of misery out of so many possible ones—three-quarters of
the people were infected with trachoma?

For some reason, the Italians were always mystically
drawn to Libya, where the great Roman cities of Lepis
Magna and Sabratha lay in magnificent ruins. It was here
that Mussolini had come before World War II, telling his
people as he invaded that these ruins, which are strung
like rare gems along the Libyan Mediterranean, were proof
that the Italians "belonged" in Libya.

But these were not the only strange things about Libya,
I found when I arrived there. Here were, in the mass, the
least attractive people, physically, I had ever seen in the
Arab world—but with the most handsome young president.
Here was the country that had been closest to the West—
and was now the most hostile to it. And here was the
country most neutral in the Israeli conflict—and now the
most passionately radical in it.

No one had expected the coup of the twenty-year-old
lieutenants and captains in Libya. No one was prepared
for it. One day in August 1969, Libya was ruled by one
of the last remaining monarchies in the Arab world, that
of the hoary King Idriss. The next day, a group of
"children," whom nobody had ever heard of, had taken
over the country, proclaimed it a Nasserite "socialistic"
republic, and started a series of events that could only be
described as zany were they not so dead serious.

I was in Cairo at that time, and I immediately tried to

get a visa to Libya to cover the new "revolution." But it was impossible. The Libyan embassy was crowded with people, mostly Libyans wanting to go home to see what had happened; the same principle being in operation, apparently, as when the Israelis bomb Arab capitals and everyone goes out on the rooftops.

Everyone was very polite, and appropriate telegrams were sent, but somehow my visa never seemed to come through. One day, sitting in the embassy, the consul thoughtfully went through all the permissions he had got from Tripoli. "Here's Tass," he said, leafing through the cables, "and *Pravda* . . . and *Tribuny Ludy* from Poland." He looked up. "But not yours." Imagine!

After a couple of months, however, I did get a visa, and my plane was setting down at Benghazi to go through customs before we went on to Tripoli. Here I got my first impressions of the new revolution . . . and of the Libyans, too. Strict prohibition had been announced from the start, and they dedicatedly searched every suitcase for alcohol. This customs agent didn't even notice the long misleading leatherette case I always carry which contains two plastic flasks, so I got in easily with a little treasured scotch.

But he did notice—indeed, he became quite fascinated with—one of my more intimate belongings—my Tampaxes. He removed the outer paper, pulled the cotton out by the string and held the circular part up to his eye like a telescope. When he had taken the whole thing apart, slowly and analytically, he put all the pieces back. I've gotten over being embarrassed by things like this, but I was afraid he might take it up to the top customs man, make me tell a translater what it was or some damned thing. It's at moments like this that I wonder what a nice girl like me is doing in a place like Benghazi, where you can't even get a drink.

A colleague of mine, Nazir Jwehdah, of Iraqi ancestry

and long working for the Chicago *Sun-Times,* happened to
arrive the same weekend, and his problem was with a
bottle of scotch whiskey he had in his suitcase. They took
it away from him, with reproachful looks, and told him he
could have it when he left. He looked at it as it marched
away from him in the arms of a young soldier with about
the sentiments of a father seeing his son march off to the
Thirty Years' War. Then he started arguing with them in
Arabic—the new regime was making a big, big thing out
of everybody speaking Arabic—and they got angry.

"They want you to speak Arabic," he told me later in
exasperation, "and when you do, they get mad!"

Never before—not in Cuba, Guatemala, Vietnam or
Russia—had I ever been bodily searched when entering a
country; never until Libya. They took me to a barren little
room where a very hostile-looking policewoman proceeded
to search me. Her expression was extremely unpleasant and
surly until she suddenly spotted, on the gold charm bracelet which I always wear, a long gold fish from Brazil whose
fins flex engagingly. "Ooooh," she said, turning it over and
over in her fingers like a little child caressing a furry new
animal. She smiled broadly, and I was permitted to leave.

Before taking off for Tripoli, where we were subjected to
still another baggage search, an oilman and I stopped to
have coffee in the airport lounge. I have never in my life
tasted anything quite like it. We looked at each other with
weak smiles. I had almost had enough of Libya already and
I hadn't even been there yet.

But it was only beginning. I checked in that night to
the Uaddan Hotel, a handsome Italianate hotel that had,
until the revolution, a thriving casino, bars, swimming pool
and night club. Now, in the evenings, the poor (spiritually
poor) oilmen, who spent months drying out in the desert
and came to Tripoli on leave to undo the drying out,
were reduced to sitting around disconsolately drinking

Coca-Cola and exchanging stories about what the "new nationalism" was doing to their psyches and livers. They couldn't even find their way around the streets any more, because all the Roman lettering had been taken down. But I, at least, had a lovely room. It was done all in bright, blood-red satins and plushes and looked much like the intimate sanctuary of a high-class courtesan. But despite the possibilities for psychic escape and the dreams that a room like this offered, the hotel was only a third full. Indeed, who was coming to Libya, with its dry sands and its dry bars, these days—besides Tass men and me? Moreover, the Uaddan had problems in communicating with its clientele.

While I was there one 2 A.M., several soldiers barged into the hotel and searched the offices. In line with the dictums of the revolution, they proceeded to destroy everything with Roman lettering on it, for Western lettering reminded them of the Italian days, when the camel trains ran on time. This included such unimportant things as an Alitalia note pad and such important things as the hotel's correspondence with Europe and the United States.

"How can we go on like this?" one of the Italian-born clerks asked me with a distraught cry. "They have made all the hotels charge one price, even though *we* are a deluxe hotel. Now they are demanding we fire all foreign employees . . . but what Libyans can run this hotel? And the menus have to be in Arabic . . . and all our guests are European or American. . . ."

The next day I set out innocently to see the city and to find some of the leaders of the revolution. Despite the presence of the wizened, pock-marked little Libyans, who are tribespeople of North Africa and not really Arabs in anything except their language and their futile passions, the city was quite lovely. It lay along the blue Mediterranean like a long, chalk-white summer necklace in the stunning

heat. I could see that it could have been an attractive
place for Europeans in its "day," for it had a pleasant
beachwalk, some nice apartment buildings and a beautiful
sea. Even today, 30,000 Italians remained, but their days
were numbered under the "new nationalism," and soon
they all were to be expelled.

The idea of finding the leaders of the revolution turned
out to be naïvely quixotic. "This country," a British diplomat remarked to me at one point that day, "must be one
of the very few in history run by a secret society."

He was referring, of course, to the top-secret group of
seven—or was it twelve or fifteen?—young lieutenants and
captains in their twenties who were running the country.
They raced around from Benghazi to Tripoli, from oasis
to oasis, holding meetings of the top-level Revolutionary
Commando Council, promulgating new laws, throwing out
the foreign devils, and pulling up the people by their camel
saddles.

"There are two journalists who saw other members of
the RCC," another diplomat commented. Then he paused.
"Or at least they think they did. One was taken out at
midnight and saw some young officer who wouldn't give
his name and didn't wear any insignia. The other thinks
he must have seen an RCC member because no one else
would dare speak as authoritatively as this man did."

Eventually I did find one young man to talk to, but
only one. Was he a member of the RCC? Allah only
knew! He was Lieutenant Ashur Amgiig, a twenty-six-year-
old flier who was more or less in charge of dealing with the
foreign press. "Dealing"—that meant occasionally speaking to one briefly in order to tell him he couldn't see
anybody in the government.

Lieutenant Amgiig was a laconic young man, dark-haired
and with the pock-marked complexion of so many Libyans.
As he leaned forward over his desk, wearing his nylon

flight jacket from the Americans, he reminded me of nothing so much as a "dead-end kid". Since so few things that I said seemed to interest him, I dug to the bottom of the ideological barrel at one point and suggested that his revolution might take as its motto the American generational motto: "Don't trust anybody over thirty."

His expression, so bored previously, brightened. He liked the saying, hadn't heard it before. "Those old people," he said then, shaking his head in much the way some fathers must be shaking theirs about boys his age. "They want to delay everything for tomorrow. We want to do it today."

But if the names and phone numbers of the captains were still top secret (making a government directory was *not* one of the things they were going to do today), the style and the substance of the Libyan revolution were beginning to be clear to everyone. It was a supernationalist regime, socialist, with a strongly anti-Israel foreign policy, and heady elements of the young and idealistic overthrowing the old and the corrupt. It was anti-foreign and was already taking the form of the one-party state à la Egypt. It was violently, passionately pro-Palestinian and they sent one million dollars to Fatah their first month in office.

To many observers, the revolutionary sounds in the deserts of Libya were strangely reminiscent of other times. "A lot of what is happening has an antique quality about it," one Arabist in Libya told me at the time. "It came out of Egypt in '54 and Damascus in '56 and Iraq in '58. The new revolutionary regime here, in its fervent talk about Arab unity, is harking back to a stage of Arab politics that everybody else lived through and has now discarded."

But though the Libyan revolution was very much in the Nasseristic pattern and though to these young officers Nasser was *the* hero, there were also differences here. The major one was their extreme Islamic moralism. In the beginning, for instance, when the officers began meeting, they met on holidays, pooled their money to buy cars to transport themselves to remote meeting places, and promised not to "gamble, drink or frequent night clubs or give up praying." Then they rethought their strategy, decided this would make them stand out too much, and purposely sent some of their group to night clubs so as not to attract attention. They must have had a wonderful time.

Now, public rallies opened with readings from the Koran and all over Tripoli the walls were covered with quotes from the Koran which dealt with social justice. Colonel Muammar Khadafi, the handsome young president, was making promises like: "We will reveal horrible secrets, including wine factories, dancing and Beatle performances" of the old "sanctimonious swindlers and fornicators." But as far as is known, this one real service which the revolution could have fulfilled for us international inquiring cameramen never was accomplished.

In aother speech, this one threatening the Western imperialists in Libya, the young colonel threatened (brevity was not one of his strong points) to "let the states involved, who own the bases in Libya, know that schools, institutions and universities will be turned into military barracks; houses, shops and offices will be made into ditches for fighting and resistance, that the Libyan soil will be shaken under the colonial bases and that we are either to die as martyrs defending our country or gain victory and that we appreciate both alternatives equally, but the owners of bases will lose because they are defending a false existence and are acting against the freedom of a people who fought with ardor."

When it actually came down to it, there was no need for all that ardor. The United States quietly vacated its $100-million Wheelus Base—the only base left in the area where it could train fighter pilots—a year later. And the British—who had kept Libya alive in its pre-oil dog days— were forced to leave, too.

The unusual religiosity of Libya's revolution was probably due to the fanatic Muslim fundamentalist sects on the oases. It was also due to the Byzantine court of old King Idriss.

Somehow, King Farouk's excesses were quite believable. Even his body was a bloated floating brothel and crap game all wrapped up in one flabby bundle of 280 pounds. But the stories one heard in Libya were shocking, because King Idriss was, basically, a good man, a religious man, an austere and honest man. But even here, strange sexual intimations—probably largely based on fact—asserted themselves. It was generally accepted that the king, who became a beloved national leader when under his leadership his Senussi sect resisted the Italians in the Second World War, had been castrated by the Italians. At any rate, he and his queen never had any children.

However, in an action typical of the Arab world, when he was a very young boy, King Idriss was assigned, as his "coffee boy," a young man named Omar Shelhi. Omar's duties were, of course, not exclusively reserved to serving coffee, and it soon became obvious that the king was inordinately fond of his servant. His fondness lasted through life. He brought the entire Shelhi family up to a level almost of royalty. Omar amassed a fortune of $125 million, and Omar's two sons, Omar and Abdelaziz, really became almost the sons of the king. It was his obsessive public coddling of the Shelhi family that nearly brought about his downfall, for the Shelhis waxed fat and feline in power.

There is, in fact, good reason to believe that the king had nodded his approval of what in Latin America is called an "autogolpe"—a coup against yourself—by the Shelhis, to bring the Shelhis to power. It was most probably for

this reason that the king, who at the time was vacationing
in Europe, gave so little response to the first news of the
officer coup against him; he thought it was the Shelhi coup,
his coup.

Indeed, these "strange Arab sexual practices" seemed to
flourish in Libya. One night in Tripoli, I accepted an invitation from an American oil official who had worked
there for several years to come over to his apartment to
have a drink. I accepted readily. Anywhere else, where
liquor was readily available, it didn't matter whether you
had a drink in the evening or not. But here, with prohibition in force and so much being made about it, people
were drinking with delirious compulsion whenever they got
a chance.

"Every Arab truck driver out there has an 'assistant,'"
the oilman said. "A very young boy. He's no assistant. And
you know, the damnedest thing happened at our camp out
there. We have Arab women working as maids in the oilmen's rooms—all covered up, of course. Well, one of our
men got one of these maids to uncover all the way. He
was astonished—he said she was really lovely. In fact, the
two of them got crazy about each other. She was just out
of her mind. What we found out was that an average
sexual act among these people takes about ten seconds.
The woman feels nothing. She had never had an orgasm
before, and she was nuts about this guy. She was just one
of four or more wives of some Arab and hardly ever even
saw him. But if he found out . . . Jesus! We finally got
them to break it up, but it wasn't easy."

In addition to these, shall we say "inherent" problems
of working in the Arab world, however, the foreign oilmen
were finding plenty of others. Once the revolution came,
problems abounded. This oilman shook his head and said,
"Just the other day one of our bosses caught a Libyan
messenger boy developing pictures of Colonel Khadafi in

the company's photo lab. He immediately told the boy to stop it because the company is supposed to have nothing to do with politics. The boy immediately reported him to the military and said he was an Israeli sympathizer. The boss was taken in and questioned for four hours and then released with an apology."

In another camp deep in the omnipresent desert, he further related, the Libyan workers had refused to accept five-inch mattresses to sleep on because they were an inch thinner than those of their American bosses.

"I'm leaving as soon as my contract expires the end of this year," he said flatly, as I was leaving. "If there is another war with Israel, American lives won't be worth a nickel around here."

But while the oilmen saw very clearly the "little picture" from their isolated oasis in the desert, what they did not see was the "big picture"—how the revolution of 1969 had happened and why.

There were two important elements to this. One was the primacy here, as in nearly every revolutionary situation, of the psychopolitical over the economic. Second was the coming of age of a new generation who wanted revolution not really, as they said, because their people were so miserable but *really*, as they would never admit, because their country's economic development had brought them to a point at which they were confident and knowledgeable enough to feel their country's and their people's humiliation.

"It was not a revolution of empty stomachs," one Western diplomat in Tripoli told me. "What they were rebelling against was the overall mold of Arab society. No young man in traditional society was even recognized as existing until the birth of his first son. They are trying to change the rules, to break out of the mold. They wanted status in the community in the Libyan context."

Before the early sixties, Libya was one of the poorest
countries in the world. Since World War II, it had totally
depended upon budgetary support from Great Britain—
support given in return for military bases. Then the country
struck oil. Literally. Out in those endless deserts, oil gushed
forth, making Libya, by 1970, the world's fifth largest pro-
ducer of oil (after the United States, the U.S.S.R., Vene-
zuela and Iran). American interests climbed in eleven years
to $1.2 billion and showed an annual return of 68 per cent
on investments. With the new money, young men were sent
abroad to study . . . only to come back to find there was no
place for them in the running of their country.

For almost all of them, the June war of 1967 with Israel
was the watershed. Not only were they humiliated as Arabs
by the Israeli victory, they felt doubly humiliated as Libyans because Libya took no leading part in the fight against
Israel. Tellingly, nearly every leader of the revolution had
some tie with the Palestinians—Prime Minister Mahmoud
Soliman al-Maghrabi, for instance, had been born in Palestine of Libyan parents. They gave the code name of "Palestine" to the revolution. As one young Libyan officer put
it: "We grew up in the shadow of the 1948 and 1956
defeats. The one in 1967 was like a national tragedy."

Immediately after the war, a group of young men calling
themselves the Popular Congress got together in Benghazi.
All educated in American institutions and all working then
for American oil companies, they organized the oilworkers
union and the portworkers union. It was these two unions
which then pressed the government—through strikes, and
refusal to unload American and British ships—to take a
stronger stand against Israel.

This agitation was followed by the naming, on October
1, 1967, of the first young non-establishment Prime Minister, Abdal Ahmid al-Bakkuush, twenty-seven years old and
a Ph.D. from the University of Wisconsin, who had taught

at Harvard and Berkeley. Bakkuush brought in other young men, but in ten months they were all out and the old establishment politicians from the upper classes were back in. It was that move, according to several of the best analysts of the situation, which led many Libyans to question the king's judgment. At that time, one American cable to Washington warned prophetically, "If nothing else, that ten months significantly lowered the threshold for extra-constitutional changes of government."

At the same time of this attempt on the part of young civilians to modernize through working within the political process, there was also growing—clandestinely—the coup of the young officers. They say today that they began meeting even in the 1950s, which would have made most of the conspirators the age of teenyboppers. They struck on September 1, catching all the political police in the country at their annual convention and overwhelming them, thus changing for once and for all the lineal political inheritance of their desert kingdom and tipping the balance toward radicalism in the larger Arab world.

The revolution, in effect, was the culmination of the dissatisfaction of an entire strata—civilian and military—of twenty-year-olds, all of them well-trained but dissatisfied at their lack of political representation and at political stances they considered humiliating and archaic.

"It was a horizontal cut, a generational one," one experienced Western diplomat here said. "In every family, one of the boys goes into the army. The officers who acted were simply the military branch of the civilians who tried to act before." And the first civilian cabinet of the revolutionary regime was made up entirely of the young civilians who instigated the demonstrations and union-organizing of 1967.

Khadafi immediately put the squeeze on the foreign oil companies, increasing oil-production taxes by $440 million

a year. Since he was only spending $480 million a year in
government expenditures of the $1.4 billion in revenues,
this left plenty over to leave $10 million "tips" when he
went to visit his other Arab leader friends.

Khadafi was soon more Arab than even Nasser himself.
He took over Tripoli's Cathedral of the Sacred Heart of
Jesus and converted it into the Gamal Abdel Nasser
Mosque. He was passionate about the projected "federation" of Egypt, Libya and the Sudan. Born in a goat-hair
tent to a family of desert nomads, he was acting a good
deal like a hell-fire-and-damnation preacher. It is said in
Cairo that at the conference in September 1970, to end the
civil war between the Jordanians and the Palestinian commandos, Khadafi stalked into the room, placed his pistol
on the table in front of him and told King Hussein, "The
best thing you could do would be to abdicate." Finally
Nasser himself suggested they were all so sick they should
call in a doctor. He turned to the young colonel and said
angrily, "The first one the doctors should examine is you."

Libya unquestioningly was turning away from British
and American influence, as so much of the Arab world was.
They were also using the Palestinian issue as cement in
place of the monarchy. They were submerging Libyan unity
in the larger problem of Arab unity and opposition to Israel.

It didn't matter that the British had supported Libya during the years when it had nothing—and got very little in
exchange. It didn't matter that British soldiers died freeing
Libya in World War II. Nor that, just outside Tobruk,
where the evil Beatle parties had been held, there was a
large Commonwealth War Cemetery. All that was over. It
was time for the British to leave, and time for us to leave,
and—most important—time for me to leave.

I got out of Libya with no problems other than a five-
hour delay at the airport. Nizar Jwehdah tried to reclaim
his scotch but was told by a dour young officer that

it had been taken to a warehouse "for safekeeping." He could go and get it if he wanted. The warehouse was fifty miles away, and his plane was leaving immediately.

Early evenings, when the strangely luminous African sky is broken only by the slow glidings of Kitchener's hawks over the Blue Nile, foreigners in Khartoum sit, as they have for years, on the outside terrace of the Grand Hotel. The white-robed and turbaned Sudanese waiters, far more dignified than most of the guests, serve gins while the merchants quietly spread out their cobra skins, cheetah-covered briefcases and ivory rhinos on the terrace floor.

"I remember after independence in 1956," a British diplomat was saying that night, cherishingly, for the Sudan, after all, was so recently his, "when a lot of Britishers here just disappeared into the Sudd." The Sudd—that immense Sargasso Sea of marsh and swamp in the south of the Sudan, big as England itself. "We called it 'the bog,'" he went on. "The British who worked down there we called 'the barons of the bog.'" He paused, took a sip of gin. "Just walked away into it. . . ."

Yes, I had read about the British in the Sudan. About how they had broken up into two groups: one fervently supporting the Arabs of the north, the other passionate protagonists of the black Nilotic tribes like the Dinka (who always stand, resting, with one foot on the other knee) of the south. Laurens Van Der Post, not a man easily taken in, says the Sudan under the British had the nearest thing to a Platonic government that the world has ever seen. The British did not settle here. Rather, shocked by the horrible excesses of the Arab slave traders of the north among the Negro tribes of the south, they sent some 1700 young men—doctors, veterinarians and soldiers—to "govern well and with honor." Because of this, he found the Sudanese

"free of the negations and crippling complexes and para-
lytic resentments one finds in other parts of the empire."
And I did, too. Even the Sudanese themselves talked about
the British almost always with reverence—"that was before
the government came," they would say of the chaotic,
brutal days before the British occupation came in 1898.

Just then, a neat little minibus pulled up on the road
alongside the Nile, and twelve unsmiling Russian technicians climbed out and marched sourly across the terrace.
Their part of the hotel was ringed with barbed wire—"to
protect them," the government said.

The Russians were the "new British" in the Sudan. There
were two hundred in the embassy, and new planeloads of
technicians were arriving every week. Yet here, as elsewhere, nobody liked them. "They eat three times as much
as other guests," the manager of the hotel told me, disdain
and disgust in his voice. "When the Russian soccer team
went to Egypt, their hotel there charged them 150 pounds
extra for all they ate."

The accents change, the influences change. One day it's
British, then American (the Sudan had been a U. S. Aid
"country of concentration" before 1967), then Russian
. . . in the Sudan and all over the Arab world. We Westerners were going out and the Russians were moving in,
not liked but needed.

But in the Sudan, having been so British, the process
had totally unique tones and nuances. The Sudanese had
not been called "the British of Africa" for nothing, for
these handsome, dark-skinned Moslems of the Nubian deserts were soft-spoken, rational and—my God!—even efficient.

On the way from Cairo to Khartoum, for instance, I had
met in the first-class compartment on Sudan Airways the
Minister of Information, Omar el Hadj Musa. Omar was a
tall, handsome black man with the engaging, slightly

skeptical smile and eyes of so many educated Sudanese. The next morning he sent his assistant to the Grand to pick me up and take me to his office.

Nowhere else in the Arab world did I see in government a performance like this one. Omar greeted me in his doorway, without formality or pretension. He was in his shirt sleeves. There was none of the false pride of so many other Arab officials, because the Sudanese have a saving admixture of Negro blood and culture or perhaps, too, because he was educated at Sandhurst.

"Who do you want to see?" he asked.

In any other Arab country this very question would have been a reason for convulsive laughter.

But here I ticked them off, starting (without much hope) with Major General Gaafar el Numeiry, who was president; the superradical foreign minister, Awadallah; the labor minister, Baashar, because he was also a psychiatrist. . . . To each request, he nodded efficiently and jotted down the name on a pad of paper. Then without a further word, he picked up one of five phones on his desk, dialed these people directly, made the appointments, and gave me the time and place.

"General Numeiry will certainly see you," he said, to my great astonishment, "but the time will be fixed later."

Then he looked at me and asked, "Do you have cards?"

I had just tried to have cards printed in Cairo, and like most things in Cairo, it couldn't be done. "I'm completely out," I explained, a little testily. "I've tried all over to have them printed, with no luck at all."

"But we can print them for you," he said unblinkingly.

"No, no . . ."

"But we have a wonderful little old machine. Just give me your data."

Precisely two hours later—I remember it because I had just had lunch—a messenger from his office arrived with

the cards. They were beautifully printed and in perfectly
fitted boxes. Was I still in the Arab world?

And of course, in the Sudan, you are only barely "still in
the Arab world."

What sets the Sudan apart is not only its many geo-
graphical curiosities and its two peoples, but its entire, dramatic history. The most unforgettable chapter in this history is, of course, the story of Colonel Charles "Chinese"
Gordon of the British Royal Engineers and the mad Mahdi,
formally known as Mohammed Ahmed Ibn el-Sayyid Abdullah, the warrior priest of Islam.

In many ways the two men were quite alike. Both were
mystics, both drew people to them with a certain wild
charisma, both were intent upon their missions, and both
were drawn by fate—God, they said—to spin out the substance of their lives in Khartoum.

Chinese Gordon, one of those magnificent nineteenth-
century British oriental adventurers like Richard Burton,
had already been on tours of duty to the Manchus in China
and in Equatorial Africa to stop the slave trade when he
became governor-general of the Sudan in the 1870s. He is
described as a man with eyes like "blue diamonds." Certainly his magic eyes, his melancholic withdrawals into
mystic contemplation for ten days at a time and his peculiar habits made him a favorite British hero of the times.
He said once of himself, "Talk of two natures in one! I
have a hundred, and none think alike and all want to rule
me." No one disagreed.

After his enlightened governor generalship of the Sudan,
he retired to England, only to be called back in the early
1880s to face the newly arisen Mahdi. A man possessed,
a man who saw himself as the prophet of Islam, the Mahdi
appeared, it was said, "like a sandstorm in the desert." He
would rid the country of the Egyptians and the British.

He did everything with a very sweet smile on his lips—whether it was sending a woman off to be tortured or examining Gordon's severed head. Alan Moorehead says "he was a smiler with a knife."

Soon after Gordon arrived, Khartoum was all but cut off. Silence fell over the desert as the Mahdi's dervishes prepared for the slaughter, while Gordon paced up and down on the roof of his palace on the Nile, scouring the silent deserts with their strange black veins that branch right up to the sloops of Khartoum. Before help could come, the Mahdi's dervishes demolished the city, killing everyone and taking Gordon's severed head to their fanatical leader.

But the Mahdi had only five months left of his life, most of which he spent reclining in his harem, his body anointed with sandalwood oil and his patched jibbeh exchanged for drawers and shirts of fine, scented material. Antimony was painted around his eyes by his favorite slave girl as he lay on pillows of gold brocade. But he died quickly, poisoned, it is said, by a woman he had outraged. And in 1898, General Herbert Kitchener, with a junior officer named Winston Churchill, and 20,000 men, took Khartoum. From that time on, the Sudan was British.

"In 1898, we just bashed our way in here," my British friend reminisced. "Queen Victoria and the white man's burden and all that. The last generation of the Sudan—they were really British walking-stick types. The young chaps today—no. And we don't really have any interests here any more." He paused. "And yet . . . I do think if we're careful, we might still have a role to play here."

When Britain gave the Sudan its independence in 1956, it left the country in an excellent economic condition, rich in cotton wealth and production. But thirteen years later, the country had gone steadily downhill. As much as the British had done here, they had not really prepared the

Sudanese for self-government; or perhaps it would be more fair to say they could not prepare them for what was coming in the Arab world.

The first governmental form was based solidly on Islamic traditions and forms, and before the May revolution of 1969, the old Islamic parties remained firmly in power. Most powerful by far was the Omar party of the Imam, a religio-political leader who was a direct descendant of the Mahdi. The Islamic parties wanted an Islamic constitution and no division of the political and the secular. Another Moslem force to be reckoned with strongly, particularly among the students, was the Moslem Brotherhood, largely discredited in the rest of the world but still powerful among students in the Sudan.

Soon after Sudan's independence, there was a first attempt by young army officers to get rid of these religious parties in the military coup of 1958, but the old forces staged a comeback. By 1969, everything had changed. The Islamic leadership was old and fractured, and when the young officers took over in that May, there was no resistance. One minister called it "an end to sectarianism." A Western diplomat in Khartoum, who speaks Arabic and is a noted Arabist, explained it in terms strikingly similar to what was happening to Libya.

"The old parties did not bring new blood in," he said. "They thought they could rule the country like a small village. Meanwhile, young men were being trained who were not taking part. Revolution was in the air. It is an old conflict. The traditional Moslems wanting a traditional society and those trained who want to apply their training but came back and were told to sit in the corner and wait."

Another diplomat commented, "The old politicians are out. This time they're gone forever and they won't come back." It was true. In April 1970, the Imam, El Hadi El-Mahdi, crusading anti-Communist, holiest of national leaders, leader of the Umma sect, was shot down by army forces when he gathered his swordsmen on Abba Island in the White Nile. It was on this island a century ago that the great Mahdi, his grandfather, announced that he was the God-summoned "one to bring freedom to Sudan"— freedom from the British and the Egyptians.

In the new Arab socialist state, Islam was most definitely still there, but as inspiration, not as leader. The modern secular state was clearly taking form. God was not dead, but he had a headache.

It was not surprising that Islam had come upon troubled times in the "New Arab" governments. Indeed, what was surprising was that it had held out in such a pure, unchanged form for so long. When Muhammed founded his faith in the sixth century, he was a rebel who turned the spiritual world upside down, a city man whose new beliefs transcended the limits of kinship and neighborhood and tribe and village by creating a sense of community among rival groups. More than any other great religion, Islam extended what one writer has called the "perimeters of tolerance," and even in its huge occupied areas the conquered peoples were permitted to maintain their own religions and languages. And why not, when Muhammed himself had based his new religion solidly on the Judaic and Christian religions?

But as time passed, the inherent barriers to change within Islam became more and more restrictive of the Moslem world. The Koran is considered the infallible word of God, and the Moslem world went through no Renaissance, as in Europe, in which everything was reinterpreted for a new time. Because it was unitary and infallible, the religion developed not a priesthood but a legal profession which specialized in the strict application of Koranic law to social problems. There was, in effect, no separation of Church and State.

In learning, Islamic education was a heavy burden blocking progress. In pious Moslem families, even today, children under ten are required to learn by heart the Koran's 6200 verses. Educators are agreed that such a gigantic outpouring of energy soon excludes the development of the reasoning faculties. Cairo is the center of Islam, but even at Cairo's famous Al Ahzar University, they are still confused over what needs to be done to adapt the religion to modern times.

As Islam spread to other areas in its first century of fantastic proselytization, elements of sensualism, sainthood and ecstasy came into it, and nowhere more than in the Sudan.

One night in Omdurban, the Mahdi's town, my guide, Ibrahim Mohammed Shagar, and I went to see a "zekr," one of the primary examples of ecstatic Islam. It was perhaps the single most arresting scene that I remember in the Arab world. We were on the outskirts of the city, in an area of dusty streets and low stucco buildings, and the faithful were celebrating the anniversary of their caliphs with marching, dancing, incense and hypnotic prayers.

In circles scattered here and there, in long lines, in half-open tents with Moslem holy men sitting on high chairs, the dervishes shuffled up and down in strange patchwork costumes, and the white-robed believers of Islam chanted and rolled their bodies back and forth to the beat of the drums. It was hypnotic: the rolling bodies, the rolling eyes, the tambourines and drums, the dust in the nostrils, the veiled women . . .

Ibrahim, a tall, good-looking young man with an ineffably sweet and gentle manner, stood with me, on the peripheries of the zekr. He was impeccably dressed in Western suit, white shirt and tie, and he stood properly, skeptically aloof.

"My father is a caliph in our town," he said, looking

with slight disapproval at the whole thing, "but I don't go
to things like this. I pray at home. The important thing is
to have a direct relationship with God, not to believe in
sects or caliphs. We young men only come here to watch
and meet girls."

He smiled. "When I was a boy, I used to have to beat
the drum for these ceremonies on Sunday night. I hated
all the noise, and besides I wanted to be home studying.
So I broke the drum."

I liked the idea of breaking the drum. It seemed to me
at the moment symbolic of the way in which young Sudanese were breaking all their religious and political traditions.

"How many times did you break the drum?" I asked
him.

"Five times." He smiled a big smile. "Finally they took it
away from me, and I didn't have to go any more."

It was true, the new regime was breaking a few drums,
too. It had allied itself with the pan-Arab, anti-Israel cause.
It was allying itself with the socialist world. They were
enforcing equality, and talked unceasingly about how
"every man in the government is here because of his ability." Calling themselves the "Free Officers," they took a
Koranic oath that each would have an equal voice in gov-
erning and that they would stay together, no matter what.

They were, of course, at times given as much to blinding
rhetoric and soaring hyperbole as their Libyan friends.
The official publication on the revolution claimed that the
Sudanese people were "perplexed and overwrought" (they
didn't *look* perplexed and overwrought, I thought), and that
they fixed their eyes on "the revolutionary vanguards of
the Armed Forces to rescue them from the bickerings of
multiparty politicians and chatterboxes." When I asked to
meet (or hear) a chatterbox, I was coolly rebuffed.

A Western diplomat analyzed: "They have a great vision
of the Sudan with crops springing up on all sides, natives

fat and happy. They think you can do it if you walk to work."

I had asked for an interview with General Numeiry, but I hardly expected to get it; it was clear that Arab leaders were not particularly forthcoming for the Western press. Besides, I knew from long experience that, in general, talking to leaders is about as fruitful as running as an Independent in Chicago. They simply never say anything.

Still, I was pleased when Pamela Painter and I were granted an interview, little knowing what a tremendous gaffe I was to make in it. That morning we went to the beautiful big shimmering white palace, built by the British. It was spacious and airy, with a gorgeous languid view of the Blue Nile. Just being there, you felt yourself fully ensconced once more in the sureties of the British empire. Except . . .

Ibrahim came in with a worried face at one point while we waited. "The President . . . can't see you," he said, as I thought to myself, "I told you so." Then he added that the minister of government would see us. Wonderful! Quoting a Sudanese minister of government in Chicago or Sioux City had about the impact of quoting an Amazon Indian in Ruanda.

Nothing more was said, and within a few minutes we were ushered into a very large and very elegant office-salon. At one end hung a spectacular embroidered hanging covered with Arabic sayings from the Koran. At the other end, a tall, well-built man with light-brown skin sat behind a desk. He had tribal scars—three long slashes on each cheek—and his eyes were slightly oriental with their heavy lids. He seemed vaguely familiar to me. . . . I had already written out questions, and immediately I was sorry I had done this, for the man proceeded formally to answer these . . . and in answers as innocuous as they were droning. I thought to myself, a minister of government and then all this vacuity!

"The May revolution takes scientific socialism as a philosophy and is innovating in the practice and application," he began, in answer to my question about the substance of the new revolution. "It is innovating those forms derived from the movement of the Sudanese revolution and motivated by its Islamic and Arab heritage as well as its African."

He made it crystal clear, in answer to a question, that there was no place for the United States in the new revolutionary regime. "Unfortunately, I have to say that the government of the United States works every day toward widening the gap between the United States and the Arab peoples," he went on. "There is no need to talk about reopening relations or aid unless American policy towards the Arabs changes."

It was all terribly, Britishly formal. And there was a strange juxtaposition of styles—a juxtaposition that made me feel slightly uneasy. On the one hand, there was the very formal form of the interview; the translator droningly translating the questions from English to Arabic and the "minister" answering in Arabic, which then was translated back to English. On the other hand, there was the twentieth-century revolutionary rhetoric of the answers that one felt should have been shouted and cried out and not formalized in this manner.

Were there Communists in the government? Was this true? Of course there were, but of course, he would deny it—until the summer of 1971, when they tried to overthrow him.

"I have repeatedly asserted this is not true," he said. "Cabinet members are not chosen on party affiliation but ability. There is no preference for any group in govern-

ment. Our contracts with the Eastern bloc are because they
support our cause. We base our politics on attitudes toward
the Palestinian revolution."

Again it seemed to me that either I knew this man or
had seen his picture somewhere. . . .

After what seemed an endlessly long period of all of this
dull and stilted hyperbole, there was a pause for additional
questions, and I asked whether he thought relations with
neighboring Ethiopia—which had been troublesome because the Sudan was harboring and often encouraging
Ethiopia's Eritrean rebels—were likely to improve. Pamela
seemed to sense I was about to say something horrendous,
and glanced with a slightly terrified expression toward me.
"We've heard," I went on, "that General Numeiry will meet
again with Haile Selassie."

With a quick, almost indiscernible action, she jabbed me
gently in the ribs and whispered, "That *is* General
Numeiry."

I know that, despite any amount of experience in the
field, you are always perfectly able to make horrible mistakes, particularly in countries which are new to you. Yet
it is always distressing when you do it. Of course. I looked
at him then, and it was perfectly clear that it *was*
General Numeiry. That was the explanation for my half-
recognition; I had seen him on his posters, but he looked
different in person and Ibrahim *had* said he was not available. . . .

If he noticed my acute discomfiture, he gallantly did not
show it, but went on answering questions. Yes, he had
come from a poor working-class family. He had studied at
Fort Leavenworth, that training ground for young revolutionaries from abroad.

And again—as it had with Muin and all the others—
the distinct feeling came out that, yes, you Americans are
splendid, quite superior, at technology, but you're hope-

lessly deficient at the spiritual and the social side of life. "I found Leavenworth highly advanced as a military institution," he said. "The instructors there were excellent officers. What I noted outside the camp there was a sort of ill-treatment of colored people—outside the barracks.

"I remember in one class the name of the NATO commander was known by only two cadets—myself and a Jordanian. There were fifty American cadets with us and the commander was an American. It shows the American people are living in a world of their own. I think this is most unfortunate."

Then he smiled and, in offering us coffee, asked pointedly: "Do you want your coffee black or white?"

He was, of course, fairly typical of the new generation in the Sudan and what it wanted to do. Here, too, the pattern was set: Nasserite younger officers; enforced equality; a socialist state; fanatic support for the Palestinians.

"The new generation is highly aspiring, with a lot of expectations," Dr. Taha Baashar, minister of labor and psychiatrist, had told me. "When the new generations find themselves unable to do what they expected, they become frustrated. Now they are in the stage of self-discovery. At the same time, tribal feelings are receding. They feel that the Sudan is a nation, especially when they see a government like this one with no parties. They see the people coming together."

This idea became a predominant one, too. To the Western mind it might seem peculiar, but in the Arab world the abolishing of parties was seen as a step forward. The competition of the old parties was looked upon as something divisive, something that kept people apart. What would bring them together—into states—was the unitary system of one inclusive party, one inclusive ideology, one inclusive government.

In great part, on the part of the young revolutionaries,

it was a reaction against what they considered to be the evils of tribalism. I was not surprised, on my next stop, to hear in Ethiopia that the radical students there looked upon socialism as the savior from tribalism. "They tell me," Aklilu Habte, the young president of Haile Selassie University, said to me, "that the only way out of tribalism is socialism." In similar ways, I knew, black tribes deeper in Africa, particularly on the west coast, looked upon Islam as the unifying force to take them out of tribalism.

Here, as nearly everywhere in the underdeveloped world, the surging need on the part of these new Arabs was to find some reason—and some form which they could offer their people—for escaping from the past.

CHAPTER VII

"Another Vietnam" in Eritrea
or . . .
Where?

▼▼▼

Vietnam was such an unending trauma for the American people that, even before it was halfway over, it became a tiresome—and often enough, misleading—commonplace, to speak of "other Vietnams" across the globe. The disease was no respecter of ideological positions. Che Guevara perished in Bolivia, his call for "one . . . two . . . three Vietnams in this hemisphere" echoing futilely from liberation-front office to liberation-front office. And at the other end of the spectrum, the State Department warned at regular intervals of "new Vietnams" in Laos, Burma, Guatemala and any number of places, as though they now were a marketable commodity like frozen fish or packaged kidneys at the Shop 'n' Save.

Still, even if a reporter kept these pitfalls in mind, it was good to find out—and to find out exclusively—that far from Vietnam we were involved directly in fighting some largely unknown but important guerrillas; that we

were doing some devilishly strange things in some devilishly strange parts of the world—like Eritrea.

Where?

I first found out about Eritrea one morning in Jordan.
I was standing at the cashier's desk in the Intercontinental
Hotel in Amman, thinking about all the money I'd spent
on unnecessary manhattans, while waiting for the Godot-
like commandos, when a little, almost prim, dark-skinned
man with glasses walked up to me and stood there blink-
ing. He was impeccably dressed, and his English—really
British—was just as impeccable. "I'm looking for John
Cooley," he said, referring to the respected *Christian
Science Monitor* correspondent. "They told me you
were an American journalist, and I thought you might
know . . ."

I explained to him that I didn't know, and then asked
him who *he* was. "I'm from the Eritrean Liberation Front,"
he said brightly, as an uncertain little bell rang in my
head. I had just read about an Ethiopian airliner being
hijacked to Aden by the Eritrean Liberation Front and,
having long been a collector of liberation fronts, I immediately sat the poor man down in the lobby and grilled
him.

His office was in Damascus, the closed city. I had heard
that many of the African liberation movements had moved
there from their old base in Cairo—they were closer to
direct Soviet advice and help there, and there were a lot
of swinging night clubs where the Socialist bloc swung in
that halfhearted way they swing. The talk was that many
of the Africans soon took up with Arab women and big
shiny cars. "Just find one," one knowledgeable friend had
told me, "and he'll lead you to all the others. They all
know each other."

I was interested in this movement, if only because it was
so crazily offbeat. It even occurred to me, since I very

seldom show very much sense in situations like this and am
easily aroused by romantic parts of the world, that, since
they were so little known, this would be an ideal movement to go to the mountains with. I had, after all, practically made a career of liberation fronts, that peculiarly
twentieth-century phenomenon of dissident young men and
women in underdeveloped and now-developed countries
(would even Russia have one eventually?) who, using
guerrilla tactics, were able to turn a government's strength
and bulk against it. I had been in the mountains of
Guatemala with the Fuerzas Armadas Rebeldes; I had
spent four full days with Fidel Castro in Cuba and hunted
down the tracks and story of Che Guevara, in Bolivia,
after he was killed; I had had the only full interview with
Regis Debray, the young French Marxist theoretician who
was with Che; I had covered the Viet Cong and the
Palestinian commandos; and I had carefully traced the
links between all of them, including most importantly the
links between Cuba and the American radicals.

But then came the obvious question: Is the story worth
the time and the stomach trouble? Clearly I had to find
out more about its importance.

After listening to Osman Saleh Sabbe tell me about how
Eritrea is the long, coastal Red Sea province of Ethiopia,
and how its 1.5 million people were almost half Moslem
and wanted to separate themselves from Christian Ethiopia
and join the Arab nationalist bloc, we finally got down to
business. Eritrea had been, I found, an Italian colony until
1941 when it became a United Nations Protectorate and
later entered into a federal relationship with Ethiopia. But
this relationship was abrogated by Emperor Haile Selassie
in 1962 and Eritrea became an ordinary province of
Ethiopia. It was in that year that the ELF began its opera-
tions, and since then it had held approximately one-quarter
of the area; it had continuously hijacked planes, thrown

bombs in the capital city of Asmara and even ambushed
Ethiopian troops.

The Eritrean province would be unimportant except for
the fact that it incorporates nearly all of the coastline of
Ethiopia. It is mostly a vast, often hilly desert, with only
sparse bush cover. The local tribes vary—from nomadic
Beni Amer who still wear Crusader costumes to one tribe
where a young man's manhood is observed by his present-
ing to his in-group the genitals of a man of a neighboring
tribe. (Western men usually stay out of this area.) Within
Eritrea, you can find every kind of countryside and
mood—from the picturesque, tree-lined Italianate capital
of Asmara to rugged mountain country or to the desert-
edged Red Sea coast.

Mr. Osman Saleh Sabbe finally gave me the name of
their contact in Khartoum, the capital of the Sudan, which
is also the seat of Eritrean Liberation, and soon I found
myself calling there at the Somali embassy, where Mr.
Ahmed Muhammed Hashim kept an office. I left my name,
and two days later he called for me at the Grand Hotel.
With him were two other casually dressed, well-educated,
dark-skinned young men.

They seemed to me to be very young, very eager and
very innocent, with little of the cynical hardness you find
in other movements of this sort. They were extremely
polite and a little unsure of themselves.

That day, as we sat in the huge, dark old room at the
Grand, the three young men started telling me more about
their movement. It had started in 1961. Since 1963, they
had been getting arms, training and money from Syria.
They had suffered many hardships. In 1964, they had between two hundred and three hundred men; now they had
four thousand and they could recruit more if they had
more weapons. They were changing their system because
they had had zone leaders and now found that tribal differ-

ences were creating little independent fiefs. They were solving this now by creating a general command inside Eritrea for the entire area. Between 1964 and 1967, the Ethiopian Army had driven thirty thousand refugees to the Sudan by bombing and burning villages.

Then, suddenly, the warm dark face of Hashim, our contact, took on a mischievous glow. He looked, at the same time, both apologetic and more than a little pleased with himself.

"Did you know," he asked, "that we kidnaped your American consul general in Asmara last fall?"

I looked at him in surprise.

"We kept him for seven hours. We wanted him to know about our movement. We thought he was poorly informed, and we wanted him to make the right reports."

Hashim went on to say that they had had some three hundred troops in the area that day in order to display their might to the consul, Murray Jackson, but that he was "convinced," so they did not show him all of them. In effect, the way they explained it, it was sort of a military briefing—not unlike the kind one gets from the American Army in Vietnam, but without the charts and pointers.

"We liked Jackson," another boy said. "He was perfectly willing to sign our statement, and he gave us some good advice." Advice? The world was, moment by moment, getting madder and madder. "He said if we'd strike in the city of Asmara every night instead of in the countryside, we'd be more effective."

So my newest liberation front had kidnaped an American consul general, in an extremely touchy and strategic and unknown area—and the story had never been reported. And what were we doing in Eritrea anyway? Where?

Before our conversation ended that day, I brought up

the most important point—we wanted them to take us into
the rebel-held territory in Eritrea.

To my surprise, there was no hesitance at all on their
parts. "We took some Swedish journalists," one said. Why
this was relevant I didn't know.

"We could go to Asmara," I interjected, "and meet some
of your people there."

They all shook their heads. "No," Hashim said, "that is
too dangerous. You would have to go from here to
Kassala [a town on the Sudanese side of the border] and
we would take you across the border from there. The
border is open there."

"How would we go?" I asked.

"By camel."

I was excited about the possibility of going into Eritrea
with the guerrillas, and if they had kidnaped an American
consul general, the story took on added importance.
Pamela was a little more ecstatic than I was about the
camel ride, despite her constant protestations that they
were "filthy, spitting creatures," perhaps because I was
having stomach trouble again. She had already spent a lot
of time in deserts, notably one six-month stay in the Sahara
where a rich Mauretanian sheikh wanted to buy her for
twenty white camels (a real fortune in the desert) and she
and her party barely escaped with . . . well, everything but
the camels.

But then came the overwhelming question of time. How
much time was the story worth?

"The most I can spend is ten days," I told Hashim flatly.
I knew that if you say three weeks, they will say, No, five;
if you say two weeks, they will say, No, three and a half.

Sure enough, Hashim shook his head, a worried frown
on his face, and said, "Three weeks would be the least. . . ."

Hashim came back the next afternoon, as always, un-
announced and at an unexpected hour. He looked dis-

couraged, down. "I'm sorry," he said helplessly. "We talked and talked . . . and it can't be done in less than a month."

A month!

"I tried to convince them," he went on, "but they say it's impossible. It takes ten days in and ten days out and you'd want to spend some time in the camps and villages."

There was only one decision, at least at the moment, to make. Two weeks yes; a month, no! Maybe later, not now.

It was on to Ethiopia. On to Murray Jackson.

The next morning at 5 A.M.—why, in the underdeveloped world, must planes always leave at 5 A.M.?—we left Khartoum for Addis Ababa, a place which still had a strange, mysteriously romantic ring to me. As we flew over that vast tableland, cut by chasmal veins and thundering waterfalls, I nursed some of my favorite historic remembrances about Ethiopia.

My favorite Ethiopian, without question, was the Emperor Theodore who, next to Rasputin, the Grand Mufti, and Attila the Hun, is my preferred historic character of all time. It seems that Theodore, born in 1818 to a small local chieftain, had started out as a reformer—he wanted to abolish slavery, reform taxation among the tribes and pay his soldiers instead of allowing them to plunder. In this frenzy of modernization, he looked toward England— but he looked with those mad rolling eyes that show up so disturbingly in all his portraits. Trouble started when Theodore wrote a letter to Queen Victoria inviting her to send some of her British subjects to visit him because "I long for the day when I shall see a disciplined European army."

Somehow the queen never answered, and Theodore, by then maddened even further by the failure of his attempts at reform, took prisoner about thirty British and other Europeans who were in his country. My favorite story

about Theodore—a man for all seasons—took place one
night when he went to visit his hostages in their dungeon.
"You know, I used to hear that I was called a madman
for my acts," he told the startled prisoners, "but I never believed it. Now, however, after my conduct towards you this
afternoon, I have come to the conclusion that I am really
so." A man before his time. No credibility gap here!

Theodore's untimely end came as the British troops finally entered the country in 1868. As he saw them ap-
proaching his fortress at Magdala, shortly before six thousand of his men died and he shot himself in the head, he
said serenely and happily: I knew they would come. I
wanted so for them to come."

The year before we visited Ethiopia had been Theodore's
centennial year, and he was now being deified as the emperor who had modernized the country. Young Ethiopian
girls were wearing their hair in the long braids on both
sides that came to be known as the Emperor Theodore
hairdo. But that was not the only odd thing about the
country.

It may well be—for the Western traveler—the strangest
place on earth. Ethiopians in the countryside, still today,
as they did in Theodore's time, eat raw meat cut right off
the carcass outside the door; the only change is that in
olden times they cut it off the live animal, pasted the skin
back on with a kind of putty and sent him on his way.

While I was there, the United States sent three more
men to the moon, but few of the Ethiopians believed it,
because everybody knows the earth is flat and the moon is
on fire; they said the men had gone to a high hill and
then come down again. It's that kind of country.

It may perhaps seem strange that Ethiopia, really more
part of Africa than of the Middle East, should be involved
in the Israeli-Arab conflict. But I soon understood the
downright peculiar reasons why this should be so. One

pretty young American Jewish girl I met in Addis, for instance, having decided to marry an Ethiopian student, first suspected that "something was rather strange" when she received her first letter from her future mother-in-law. The letter ended with "May the God of Israel bless you!"

Later, having settled in Ethiopia, she understood both the blessing and why there had been so little opposition to an Ethiopian son's (they are terribly ingrown people) marrying a foreigner, so long as she was Jewish. "They believe that they are the modern ancient Israelites," she said in some wonderment, "and that the Jews of modern Israel are sort of the modern ancient Ethiopians."

The great majority of the approximately sixteen million people of the Ethiopian plateau are Christians of the ancient Coptic Church, but they believe they have special and unique ties with Judaism. They believe that their own royal family, represented since 1930 by the Emperor Haile Selassie, the "Conquering Lion of Judah," is directly descended from the line of the Ethiopian Queen of Sheba, and the Jewish King Solomon. Ethiopian church art, which graphically depicts the queen of Sheba legend, candidly shows the two lovers in bed, pleasurably creating the new line of the Ethiopian throne.

At first I dismissed much of this. But the more I delved into the history books, the more it made a certain mad sense—as much sense as anything in this part of the world. The Ethiopians are dark-skinned, but they have Semitic rather than Negroid features. Many words in the Ethiopian language, Amharic, which is a Semitic language, are strikingly similar to ancient Hebrew words. Like the Jews, the Ethiopians believe in ritual cleanliness and practice circumcision on the eighth day—a practice shared by only these two people. In their ancient kingdom of Aksum, which flowered in 500 B.C., the Ethiopians had an Ark of the Covenant.

None of this is too surprising when it is remembered that in Solomon's time the Hebrew kingdom included the Sinai peninsula, which stretches to the mouth of the Red Sea, and that the Queen of Sheba declares in the Kebra Nagast, the Coptic Church's holy book, "From this moment, I will not worship the sun but the creator of the sun, the God of Israel." Says Father Petras, Coptic priest and professor in the seminary at Haile Selassie University: "Whether you say the Israel of 922 B.C. or today—it is the same Israel."

In political and military terms, it has also forged a real bond. There is a top secret twenty-five-man Israeli military mission in Ethiopia training the commando police who are fighting the Eritrean Moslem dissidents. Israel has given unusually large amounts of aid to Ethiopia. There is even an Israeli-backed kosher-beef plant in Asmara which produces one million tons of kosher beef a year, and Israel depends for much of its meat on that which is shipped up the Red Sea to Aqaba.

I soon ascertained, somewhat to my amazement, that Ethiopia was a crucial part of the whole Middle Eastern picture. For Israel, by wooing the African nations as she has been doing with great tact and success, could encircle the Arabs with her friends and leapfrog the hostile Arabs. Even in the Sudan, there were persistent (and most probably true) reports that Israel was sending arms through Uganda to the black southern Sudanese rebels to fight the Arab government in the north. But nowhere was the whole policy more important than in Ethiopia, with its long strategic coastline on the strategic Red Sea.

For the United States, Eritrea was equally important— for very special defense purposes.

Murray Jackson turned out to be a man of enormous charm. Rugged, square shouldered, with an easy boyish smile, savvy, quick, intelligent—it was impossible not to like him. He was also a type I would recognize a mile away. He was one of those Americans who are physically in such good shape, who are so extremely bright and do such specially sensitive jobs for different agencies of the United States Government that they become a recognizable type.

His last job had been as a political advisor to the military in Vietnam, where he had negotiated the deal with the South Vietnamese government to allow American planes to land on interior bases. Jackson knew a great deal about counterinsurgency and traveled all over Eritrea, even into the estimated quarter of it held by the ELF, on such curious business as "cultural missions." He was clearly no ordinary consul general. Asmara was a strange place for Murray E. Jackson of Eldorado, Illinois—unless you remembered that there were guerrillas here.

Jackson, smiling and charming, began the interview with a little historic diversion—by talking about the banditry always endemic in Eritrea. "Originally, there was this Shifta tribe of bandits," he began, in an academic spirit, "and three centuries ago an emperor dispersed them throughout the empire. The young men would go out and blacken their faces and become robbers for three months before the harvest. That's why the ELF has been able to attract young men so easily. But they don't stay with it, they become disillusioned, stay for a year and then come in for amnesty."

When I asked him how seriously he viewed the situation just then, he said, "There was an upsurge in April and June. They got into the waterworks and threw a satchel charge down the pumps. They also blew up a transformer out of town. Then early in July the commando police killed eight in an ambush." He went on to say that they totally identified with Fatah and Pan-Arabism, though they are

not Arabs ethnically, but he insisted that they were alienat-
ing both the Christians and the Moslems in the population.

"What about the refugees, Mr. Jackson?" I asked. I
wanted to see what he would say about the thirty thousand
Eritrean refugees in the Sudan.

"Most of these refugees are Beni Amer tribesmen," he
said, leaning forward, warming to his subject. "They are a
nomadic people. Their only allegiance is to green grass and
cows. They pledge allegiance to their tribal chiefs. Why"—
he chuckled—"they still wear quilted dresses and chain
mail from the time when the Crusaders came down this
far. Production of chain mail stopped years ago in other
parts of the world. They still train their horses in maneuvers
of the knight and spear. They have Renaissance jousting."

"But the number of guerrillas," I asked, "how do you
estimate them?"

"Maybe eight hundred to one thousand ELF. In sympathy, most Moslems listen to Cairo radio. Most speak
Arabic or Tigré, which is close to Arabic. The villagers
are close to the soil, they're apolitical. The agitators come
to the villages with arms; we know cases where they've
taken men out in the ditch and shot them. The villagers
are also at the mercy of the army, which does the same
thing. The villager is buffeted. His natural inclination is
toward Islam."

It did not surprise me when Jackson advanced the idea
that the only answer to the insurgency problem in Eritrea
was economic development. American officials in this area,
as in so many, believed in economic development as a
cure for political and social and psychic needs, just like the
alchemists used to believe they could make gold from base
metals.

"There are compelling reasons to believe that if we give
these people reason for a better life—political stability—
this will be solved," he was saying. "The government

started a project for the Beni Amer. . . . Two million dollars advanced from the development bank . . . six hundred tribal leaders in Keren to talk to the governor general of the province . . . They are buying shares in the company. . . . The owners will have a third interest, the government a third, private sources a third . . . profits to be split . . .

"You also have to have a military side," he went on, suddenly switching to the other side of the coin that hadn't worked in Vietnam, and Latin America and surely wouldn't work here. "You also have to have a commitment on the government's side. People don't fight wars in Africa for ideological reasons but for personal gain. . . ."

I thought the historic background had now been sufficiently explored, and so I asked him frankly about the kidnaping. "I hear you were kidnaped," I said.

Since he had been forewarned by the embassy in Addis that I knew about the incident, he was prepared. "I was out visiting the western lowlands when suddenly five or six men with rifles appeared on the side of the road," he began. "They were nervous. They told us to drive off the road. Then their leader came out. I was flying the American flag. They told us the usual stuff—that they wanted Eritrea to be separate, that Ethiopia was colonizing it. They were pretty well indoctrinated. They made a fetish of speaking Arabic. . . ."

I began to press him with specific questions for answers which I needed to write my article. But it wasn't until I asked him the name of the British man who was with him that he suddenly drew back. His face, so pleasant up to then, suddenly took on a distinctly irritated look. "Now wait a minute," he said, his voice peremptory and stern. "I don't think this is cricket at all. I agreed to talk with you, but I don't want anything written about this. Why, my life's

at stake here. I have to stay here, I have to travel around
this place. . . ."

I don't know if I looked at Murray Jackson with the
coldness I suddenly felt toward him, but I do know I didn't
say anything for a few seconds. He was a key person,
though there were others, in involving the United States
directly in an ugly little war which its people knew very
nearly nothing about. He was spending American money
to do this, and he didn't want American citizens to know
about it.

I had no personal feelings about these guerrillas at all.
All guerrillas seem a little insane to me, and many argu-
ments could fairly be made against them. After all, most
of the "Moslems" in the area whom they said they spoke for
were actually also tribespeople and at least half animist.
Perhaps up to half were Christian, and Haile Selassie's desire to keep his country together, in the face of all comers,
was an admirable and quite necessary feat.

But I did object to his arrant assumption that the "other
side" had no ideals—the kind of assumption that lay at
the base, for instance, of all our wrong assumptions in
Vietnam. Most of all, I objected to the disdainful, angry
attitude such officials assumed when you found out for
American readers something they wanted to keep to themselves. I'd faced this in Santo Domingo, and I'd faced it in
Vietnam, and I was frankly sick of it.

"I'll be very careful," I told Murray Jackson, in a tight
voice.

The rest of the Eritrean story? Put very simply, it is this.
The United States has an unusually large military mission
of one hundred men in Ethiopia. We provided about $150
million in military aid in the 1960s—the highest amount of
any country in Africa. Our military mission worked directly
with the large Israeli military mission of twenty-five men,
and they directly trained the 3300 Ethiopian commando

police who directly assault the guerrillas. What's more, our pilots, ostensibly on mapping missions over Eritrea, were actually looking for guerrillas. When they found them, they called in the commando police.

Later that day, when I was talking to another high American official who knew the whole situation, he said, "What troubled me was that after Jackson was let go that day, the commando police came in and blew up all the houses in the neighboring town as punishment for allowing the guerrillas to be around. I don't like that—it puts us too closely in league with everything the government is doing."

Nor did I like their so-obvious attempts to mislead, which were then belied by their constant contradictions. Jackson said first there were no more than six men; later he showed me a picture he had taken with twelve men on it. He said they were without ideology, that "wars in Africa are fought not for ideology"; then he said the young men who captured him were "well indoctrinated." He said the refugees were just Beni Amer tribesmen who moved back and forth across the border. Luckily I had stopped at the UNRWA office in Khartoum, which oversees these refugees. The official there told me clearly that these were "not nomads but real refugees" driven out by the "crossfire and the burning of villages by Ethiopian troops." In fact, they were so non-nomadic that UNRWA was settling them at a village called Umm Saqataa and the Swedish Red Cross had donated money for a permanent hospital there.

After I left Ethiopia, and wrote several articles, the Eritrean story continued to blossom, and indeed I would suppose it would continue to do so. But my stories were the first and definitive ones. One of the shy, soft-speaking boys, who had sat with me in the room in Khartoum, had been killed when he attempted to hijack an Ethiopian airliner. I saw his picture in the papers. Late in 1970, another 10,000 refugees were forced over the border after the Ethiopian Air Force bombed the northern Eritrean town of Keren. This, it was said, was in retribution for the guerrilla ambush slaying on November 21, of Major General Teshome Erghetu, commander of the Ethiopian Second Army.

Early in 1971, Senator Stuart Symington's Foreign Relations Subcommittee looked into the matter of "secret agreements" with Ethiopia and for the first time the State Department admitted that U.S. bombs and ammunition had been used against the Eritreans. But basically the Symington findings—which were angrily revealed to the public— were simply *my* findings. I had told them first. It is things like this that make one proud to be a journalist.

Meanwhile, Eritrea, a spot which probably not one person in 10,000 would have recognized in 1965, was almost daily in the news. The guerrillas were getting more and more daring—one day they wrecked a train only eighty miles from Asmara by removing the tracks and plunging it into a ravine after removing the passengers. Libya, with its golden goose, sent them $7 million. To replace the greatly threatened Kagnew Station, the $60-million communications station in Eritrea which is run by the U. S. Signal Corps and the U. S. Navy, the United States was planning a substitute on Britain's Diego Garcia Island in the middle of the Indian Ocean. And Admiral John S. McCain, commander of U. S. Pacific forces, said, "What Malta is to the Mediterranean, Diego Garcia is to the Indian Ocean."

In short, this little war—like so many "little wars" in the world today—refused to die but instead kept getting bigger.

Perhaps we *need* a presence in Ethiopia. I do not deny national defense necessities, and I believe in the use of power—but the intelligent use of power. Perhaps it is in our best interests to support, without any other alternative, a seventy-eight-year-old emperor who has made no provision for his succession. Perhaps we need Kagnew Station so much that anything goes. Perhaps we need Ethiopia, the only country in West Africa where we now have landing rights, port rights and overflight rights, so much that no other considerations come into play. It is, after all, a world where our strategic choices in the world are shrinking daily.

But wasn't it precisely this sort of policy—a policy that thoughtlessly supports whomever is in power and is atavistically against any new revolution—that led to the fact we have so few choices left? Wouldn't it be better to have formulated a more intelligent, long-range policy for the whole area, so we would not need these stopgap measures? Wouldn't it be better to just stay out of touchy areas like counterinsurgency in a powder keg such as the Middle East and concentrate on more traditional diplomatic and military influences?

And is it really intelligent to tell such obvious falsifications to a reporter—downright lies which are so easy to check out? Once again, I was angry. As I sat down to write several stories, which got a great deal of attention, I thought, with a coldness I never used to feel toward American diplomats, "They must think the rest of us Americans are very stupid."

CHAPTER VIII

Trying to Get a Visa to Saudi Arabia
or
Would You Like a Subscription to the
Ladies' Home Journal, Mr. Prince?

vvvvvvvvvvvvvvvvvvvvvvvvvvvvvvvvvvvvvvvvvvvv

I never bought an Edsel or Lyndon Johnson's story on the Bay of Tonkin. To me, the Brooklyn Bridge was clearly a fixed feature and everyone knew that Judge Harold Carswell didn't like Negroes.

Yet we all have our moments of mad swings of fancy, and I am not immune. When I went to the Middle East, for instance, I suffered a moment of illusion in which I truly believed it was possible for me to get a visa into Saudi Arabia.

The thing was I really *wanted* to get into Saudi Arabia, for it seemed to me to be one of the last really "out" and odd places left in the world. There you had a "country"— a desert kingdom, really—with eight million nomadic people spread thinly over 870,000 square miles—one-fourth the area of the United States. In 1958, it had only 200 miles of roads.

There you had the nerve center (except that everybody was largely asleep) of the entire Arab world. It was the

Arabia that the real "Arabs" came from, establishing in the seventh century a great empire extending from the Atlantic to the borders of China. Their individualism, said Glubb Pasha, the British officer who formed the Arab Legion in Jordan, "often leads to jealous rivalries, to an extreme sensitivity on what they consider to be personal honor and to a certain lack of communal loyalty and public spirit." In short, they gave the modern world such niceties as the vendetta, the blood feud, the alphabet, child slavery and Islamic purity.

They also gave the world the Arabian kings, and in particular the empire of King Saud, who, before he died in 1969, was known for giving away $20,000 in tips during an ocean voyage to New York, keeping a harem of forty to fifty wives and concubines, and fathering 150 children. As George Weller, our Middle East correspondent, who also manages to be a superb journalist, man and raconteur, once put it: "Old King Saud moved in a state of sexual fatigue, game but weary, while doing his royal duty. He had more than thirty palaces, dined with gold knives and forks, had his own zoo, and was the last of the big, big Arabian spenders."

George, who had known Saud in his many travels around the Middle East, described meeting him thusly: "Saud held your hand warmly while his large myopic eyes searched yours through their heavy lenses, seeking hopefully for a sign of disinterested friendship."

How wonderful it would have been to have offered that "disinterested friendship" and to hope that it would become "interested!" But by the time I got to the Middle East, unfortunately or not, the time of the Sauds was past. He was already dead; he died in gold-encrusted exile in Greece after losing his empire to his unflamboyant, buttoned-down, monogamous brother, Faisal, in 1964.

Faisal was sober, Faisal had only one wife, Faisal was

going to break the image of Saudi Arabia as a place where you did nothing all day but drive air-conditioned Cadillacs over fields of Persian carpets all the while shooting pheasants through the open top.

Camelot couldn't last forever, I suppose.

I first applied for a visa one morning in Amman. I took a taxi over to the Saudi embassy, where a good-looking young man looked at me rather intensely when I said I would like to get a visa.

"You *would*," he said.

I thought that was what I had said. "Yes," I repeated, "I would."

His face remained intent. "Well, we will send a cable to Jeddah," he said. "They will have to reply. It is no use to check here. Where will you be in several weeks?"

I said I thought I would be in Libya.

"Fine." He made it all sound so simple. "We will send it to Libya."

A few days later, forgetting it was the beginning of the Moslem feast of Ramadan, I again went to the embassy, this time to check on my "visa." The embassy was closed tight, but eventually I aroused a guard who fortuitously spoke some English.

"Closed," he said firmly.

"When open?" I asked.

"Open new moon," he said, pointing to the sky.

I did go to Libya soon after this and I checked at an appropriate time with the Arabian embassy there. They were all very pleasant and polite, if a little startled at my sudden appearance. Yet . . . when we checked for permission, there was none. I left, but more determined than ever not to give up.

My next move was to wire my office to contact the Saudi embassy in Washington and to get *them* to do something.

This, most often, works, because pressures from a Washington bureau chief usually convinces the hesitant country of one's sincerity and, what's more, one's legitimacy.

Sure enough, within a few days, I got a cable back from my office saying the Saudi embassy was assuring them a visa for me and that I could pick it up at the embassy in Ethiopia, since that was where I was headed next.

Meantime, as I told various people about this little drama, I began to get tremendously amused smirks in return. Sitting one night on the terrace of the Grand Hotel in Khartoum, I was talking to a young British diplomat who earlier had been assigned to Jeddah. When I told him I had it in mind to go there, he looked at me with the same bemused and intent expression that I had first encountered in Amman. Then out came a quick bark of a laugh.

"I remember the years I was there," he said, shaking his head. "There were four British girls whom one of the princes had given visas to on the condition that they go there to sell magazines." Another belch of a laugh. "Hah! The second day they all came running to the embassy, saying that wasn't what he had in mind at all." He paused. "We managed to get three of them out," he said, "but the fourth one disappeared completely. We never did find out what happened to her."

Then we thought of other stories. Pamela remembered that a friend of hers had been with the Dutch embassy in Paris some years ago when a handsome young Dutch bride was kidnaped. She had caught the eye of one of the princes and was found six months later in Saudi Arabia. Another, a woman geologist, who had a good job with an oil company, was able to enter the country only as a "nursemaid" for an American family. And we laughed over the old story of the German cabaret dancer "kidnaped" to an Arabian harem. When a German newspaperwoman finally

penetrated the forbidding country and told the captive she
would help her to escape, the girl told her to mind her
own business, she was quite happy there, thank you!

Since Saudi Arabia had already struck me as rather a
peculiar little land, I began to delve into it. Who could
not love King Saud, for instance, who had forty sons, and
$40 million to spend for his court out of the oil income—
which climbed in the 1960s from $500 million to $1 billion.

Saud was even democratic . . . in his own harem, where
he took off his glasses before visiting, so all the women
appeared equal to him. But the strict Islamic laws against
displaying femininity were severely applied. The religious
police allowed no faces of women to be seen, and even
mannequins were decapitated and dress-pattern illustra-
tions were headless. When his rebel daughter, Princess
Hassa, once asked the king whether he wanted his harem
to read and write, the king replied, "No, we keep slaves
for that kind of work."

But while Saud was traveling the world searching for
God-knows-what, his brother, the hawklike Faisal, was
stealing out into the desert, hunting with falcons, enjoying
erotic Bedouin poetry, and teaching *his* sons the old simple
way of life; thus consolidating his following among the
tribes. Eventually, when Saud's pilots, sons and half-
brothers began to defect to the Nasserite camp, the Ulma
of Moslem notables replaced him with Faisal.

The fun part was gone, the dreary parts remained. Faisal
took over like a Cromwell, determined in his sober way
both to reform the country and to ease it, at a historic
caravan-pace, into the fifteenth century. He confronted the
Islamic authorities by starting the first girls' schools, and
he sent Saudis to the United States for education. Harems
became largely a thing of the past, and "magazine sales-

girls" were frowned upon. Still, women stayed at home
while men even did the shopping.

For Faisal—who has a strangely ascetic and holy face
which one of my friends who knows him says is "misleading"—knew the wolves were at the door. In the summer of 1969, a group of younger officers, mostly pilots, attempted a coup à la Nasser but were apprehended only at
the last moment. It is said in inner circles that the mal-
contents were thrown out of an American transport plane
over the desert.

Faisal thinks he is surrounded by enemies, and he is.
The Palestinians (there are some 100,000 of them in key
positions in the country and they "tithe" 20 per cent of
their salaries to the commandos) didn't subvert him only
because he bankrolled the commandos to the tune of millions of dollars a year. He also supported Egypt since the
closing of Suez. He could afford to take a stronger position
than most Arabs on Zionism, and he did—Israel was far
away, and the Egyptians were fighting the war.

"Our enemies are firstly Communism, then Zionism,
and finally imperialism," he said in a speech in 1970.
"Communism is Zionism's first son. The Jews invented
Communism. Communism fights the Arabs, for they created Israel. Who benefited from the creation of Israel? The
Russians, who succeeded in penetrating our region. Who
lost out? The Arabs and the West." It must make a great
deal of sense, if you are sitting out on a sand dune.

Nor is it surprising that there are forces that want a
change. The country is one of few in the world which has
neither parliament, constitution, civil laws, property records
or a real census. Every Friday after prayers in the big
cities, they amputate the right hands of thieves (the oil
company doctors are now allowed to provide cauterization,
however) and flog adulterers. It is not unusual for a man

who has practiced adultery to receive six hundred lashes, but now he gets them in installments—sixty lashes a week, for ten weeks. Alcohol is forbidden. On a lesser moral level, during the week the "religious police," who get their salaries from the mosques, keep order, watching that shops close at the proper time and that women are properly dressed—which means totally—and totally means covered with an opaque black cloth. (Religious purity is a wonderful thing—it has kept me on the peripheries of many kingdoms.)

The Ulma—a body composed of sixty-nine imams whose status supposedly is based upon their wisdom and their mastery of the Koran—is all-powerful. These men blame everything on "progress," and quite properly blocked the construction of a telephone network because it would "lend itself too readily as a medium for adultery." Certainly, no one is really going to disagree with *that*.

But there *are* important changes going on. A bureaucracy is growing, and a system of laws and codes and a civil service and schools and even resettlement schemes. Of a total government income of $1.5 billion, $656 million is now appropriated for national development. Saudi Arabia will not stay the same.

But for those who find Saudi Arabia "intriguing" there are other spots in the Arabian peninsula which are even more "fascinating." At the bottom of the world's biggest sandbox, in the southwestern corner, lie South Yemen and North Yemen, the two "progressives." By the 1970s, both were governed by regimes highly in sympathy with and modeled after the Palestinians.

In North Yemen, a country of between six and seven million persons, the old imamate fell in 1962. Having survived a bitter war in which 300,000 Egyptian troops fought against a return of the imam and 30,000 died, this "Yemen Arab Republic" developed a relatively moderate government. The other government—that of the Peoples Republic of South Yemen, with its capital in Aden—became even more radical, being modeled after the ideas of the Popular Front for the Liberation of Palestine.

The war in the North was extremely bitter, and it is now well known that the Egyptians did indeed use poison gas there—a pilot who had flown there once regaled me with tales of skulls hanging from trees. But there is also unquestionably an absurd side to the entire thing.

The Yemenis know when the Saudis are likely to attack, for instance, by the availability, on the border, of British sovereigns with a picture of George V on them. These coins have been the medium of exchange since the arrival of the British. When the price goes down on the local market, in Aden or Yemen, it means the Saudis are infiltrating by bribing the border tribes. When the banks receive a lot of them, they signal the government which strengthens the border. They are also made of a higher percentage of gold than the original, since the Saudis insisted *their* coins should not be inferior.

Even southward, and across the Red Sea, much the same political transformation is going on. Somalia changed in 1969 to a more or less socialist country, when young militarists took over in a Revolutionary Council thus turning that key nation, which juts out into the Red Sea and the Indian Ocean, into a Russian-leaning nation. The reason given at the time was to expunge "musug-musug" from the body politic—this was a newly invented Somali word for everything from mismanagement and corruption to injustice and ordinary mistakes.

As you go eastward, things get, if possible, even wilder. First you encounter the Dhofar independence movement, a Maoist-oriented guerrilla movement instructed by Chinese advisers and dedicated to freeing the eighth-century enclaves of Muscat and Oman. Muscat is a blazing white

city whose port is guarded by Fort Mirani, the ancient
Portuguese fortress. Until recently the gates were closed
at night and anyone who went out of his house had to carry
a kerosene lantern (no flashlights, please) because the Sultan opined that people carrying lanterns were less likely to
sin than people walking in the dark. Again a reasonable
assumption—like the Saudi ban on telephones.

Until his son miraculously overthrew him in 1970, the
Sultan had turned Muscat into one big prison; he had
locked up his only son and reached what was certainly the
heights of xenophobia, by locking *himself* up in his palace
for five years. He painted the windows of the palace blue,
so no one could see inside, and then he frolicked with his
150 concubines and 500 slaves. Nobody could travel, not
even around the sultanate, and he forbade cars, drinking,
smoking, playing the oriental oud or the drums and listening to the radio. The Sultan was totally dependent upon
the British soldiers who kept him in power.

Then on July 23, 1970, the Sultan's twenty-eight-year-
old son, Qabus, who had been educated in Europe and
then locked up upon his return, overthrew his father's regime. "I would have liked to have a normal relationship
with my father," he was quoted afterward as saying, "but
he was a man ruled by fear."

The overthrow must have been something to see. A dissident sheikh in league with Qabus arrived at the palace
with ten soldiers during the intense heat of the afternoon
and took over. In the melee, the old Sultan, as he cocked
his gun, shot himself in the foot. He refused to be moved
until Lt. Col. Edward Turnhill, the Briton who had com-
manded one of the Sultan's regiments, promised to stay
with him. Colonel Turnhill held the Sultan's hand and the
Sultan wouldn't let go until his wounds were dressed.

As I traveled slowly down the west coast of the Red Sea
—an area that in contrast seemed as radical as a hippie

commune—I kept looking thirstily over at all these outrageous princedoms, kingdoms, sultanates and liberation
movements on the east coast. But everything would be all
right—I still had the promise of the visa that was to arrive
in Ethiopia.

Pamela and I were together again in Ethiopia and both
headed (in our minds, at least) for the forbidden Arabian
peninsula. One morning we got our signals crossed and we
both arrived at the Saudi embassy within an hour of each
other. I arrived jubilantly, for I had just received *another*
cable from my office assuring me still again that the visa
was already waiting hungrily for me in Addis Ababa.

When I swept confidently and happily into the cubical
modern house which is the Saudi embassy in Addis, I immediately ran into the worldly, wise-looking Greek woman
who seemed to run things there. I thought it a little strange,
but her face immediately broke into a broad grin.

"You are Miss Painter's friend," she announced.

"Why, yes . . ."

"She was just here. I told her, too . . ." At this point,
she broke out into uncontrollable giddy laughter. "It is
very difficult . . . very difficult."

"Forgive me," I said, a little irritably, "but *what* is so
difficult?"

"The visa." She started to laugh again. "They won't even
give *me* a visa and I am their representative."

"But *your* embassy in Washington told *my* bureau that
the visa was waiting."

She shook her head gravely. "No. Nothing has arrived,"
she said.

"But why . . . why?" I persisted, still somehow believing that rational judgments could be applied. "I am a
journalist. I merely want to write about the country. It
could be helpful for them."

"A journalist!" Her eyes opened wide. "All the worse,

my dear," she went on. "And you are not only a journalist, you are a woman besides. And single. All the three things they do not like." Her tone suddenly grew confidential. "My dear," she said, "forget it! You will not get a visa."

"But . . ."

"They do not want journalists, they do not want tourists."

"But why?"

She grinned broadly. "They say . . . that there is nothing to see there."

Showing her the telegram only elicited more tumultuous laughter, until her eyes were wet. Finally, I began to understand. The embassy in Washington was only being courteous to our bureau. But in fact, visas were only issued through Jeddah, through the Foreign Ministry, and the number had to be telegraphed to the embassy abroad. None of this . . . had been done.

And soon I discovered some other things.

When Pamela and I met later that day back at the Addis Ababa Hilton, a gorgeous new hotel on a knoll overlooking the city, we sat in the coffee shop and compared our common experiences.

"And she told me," Pamela was saying, "that even if a married woman gets a visa, her husband has to sign for her and she can never be out of his sight. And do you know what else?"

I waited expectantly.

"She said that occasionally women *did* get into Saudi Arabia. She said that recently she had had a group of Ethiopian girls coming through . . . and that they were going to be selling European magazines. They got visas to do this. They were all young and pretty, she said, about age sixteen. She said it was surprising that Western magazines should be so popular in a country like Saudi Arabia."

A pregnant pause.

"She then said it was a shame we didn't fall into acceptable categories . . . something like selling magazines or . . ."

"Or . . . ?" I paused breathlessly.

"Being acrobats or aerialists in the circus," she finished up. "They were the last women to get in."

CHAPTER IX

Love and Sex in the Arab World
or
Under the Sheikhs

▼▼▼

I don't know whether Arabs are lousy lovers or not, though I have my suspicions. I do know that I, a single and usually lone Western woman in their midst, was treated better by men in the Arab countries than in practically any other area I have worked in.

The expectation of "problems" was there when I arrived, for what we in the West think about Arab men is in many ways uncomplimentary. Before I left, one of my friends, the Washington *Post*'s devilish columnist, Nicholas von Hoffman, regaled me, tongue-in-cheek, with the story of the Western girl held captive for several months by Arabs in a tent.

"All they did was make love to her, beat her and feed her hashish," he said. I shook my head and answered, in the spirit of the story, "That's no good—I don't like hashish."

Even after I arrived, that second night in Cairo, I remembered the beautiful journalist Maha saying to me in her feline way, "You Western women like Arab men. You think they are brutes."

One day in Israel, I asked the Israeli Arabist, Yehoshophat Harkabi, what conclusions he had come to about Arab sexuality and marriage, something that I had had great difficulty discussing with even highly educated Arabs. "We find with Arabs," he explained, "that there is a distinct yearning for the Jewish women and at the same time a fear of impotence with them."

I nodded. "I have had the same feeling about Arabs," I said.

He smiled. "From your own experience?"

Now *I* smiled. "From observation."

"Tell me," he went on. It was obvious he was interested in this. "How *were* you treated by the commandos? Did you have any . . . trouble with them?"

It was difficult for him, like many others, to accept the fact that I had been treated not only well but even with gallantry—or perhaps they were just too fanaticized to care about women. I explained what I found to be the predominant theme in the Arab male's treatment of me—an overwhelming desire, or so it seemed to me, to prove they were cultured, that they were "not savages, not barbarians."

"That's astonishing," he repeated several times. And when I told him that my days with the commandos almost inevitably ended up either in an elegant private home or an elegant French restaurant, he was even more astounded.

Much of what Westerners have come to think of the Arabs is plainly vulgar, particularly in these last years during which the entire Arab world has taken on such an aura of unreality. The West's unselective derision and contempt for their whole way of life has led to gross exaggerations and falsities and nowhere more than in the sexual field, where the word "strange" has come automatically to be put before "Arab sexual practices." But this doesn't mean, I hasten to add, that there are not *plenty of strange Arab sexual practices.*

I remember a long talk at a party one night in Cairo with an attractive Western wife, who must go unnamed because her husband had an important job there. Her conversation kept coming back to Hassan, the Egyptian riding master with whom she went riding several days a week. When she spoke of him—it was unmistakable—her voice took on a buoyant tone and her eyes shone. It was Hassan did this . . . Hassan did that . . . Hassan said this of me.

Then she spoke, with bitterness and shock, of the traditions in the village where Hassan lived with his several wives. "Do you know what the weddings are like?" she demanded. "I have seen the girls going in the carriages to their weddings . . . crying their eyes out. They told me there that the bride is then taken into a room with her mother, his mother and the bridegroom and stripped and then made to kneel down, where she is deflowered manually by either her mother or the man. Then the sheet with the blood is thrown out to the guests. You can imagine a young girl who has not even seen a man before and suddenly——"

"Marriage is difficult at best," I agreed.

But, in truth, the more I heard of these "traditional practices" the more horrified I became.

In the Sudan, for instance, I was given at the Information Ministry a most interesting pamphlet, "The Development of the Sudanese Women's Movement" by Zeinab El Fateh El Badawi. In the booklet, she wrote, "When the women's movement started in 1947, we felt at that time that the Sudan was the most disagreeable of all the countries in which to be born a woman. Women in the mass were isolated in the harem, absorbed in their engrossing household duties, with no education, and with superstition as a dominating power in their lives. . . .

"Girls, backward and uneducated, had to endure the in-human operation of Pharaonic circumcision, their right nostrils were pierced to hold heavy wedding rings, their lips were tattooed, and they had to go through the agony of the eventful forty days of the marriage. The dominant status of the men was maintained largely on the basis of the humiliation suffered by the women."

I asked to see Zeinab El Fateh El Badawi, in Khartoum, and she was kind enough to come over to the old Grand Hotel one evening and sit with me on the outdoor patio overlooking the Blue Nile. She was a beautiful, dark-skinned woman with five children and apparently a rare modern husband for this part of the world, for he per-mitted her to work in the university. She was one of the first results of Miss Clark's girls' high school.

"Miss Clark started the high school for girls in 1941," she reminisced. Miss Clark had been one of those British-ers who came to the Sudan to "do good" and did. "She said she would do it if only three girls came. First there was the problem of girls dropping out when they were forced to marry. So Miss Clark made a new rule—once they started, they had to finish."

To some, this may all seem like colonialist imposition. But women like Zeinab *know* what the customs were, and are, really like. She talked about the women who never re-ferred to their husbands by name and never appeared out-side the home unveiled. To get attention from her husband a woman would refuse to talk, sometimes for months or a year. He, in turn, would give her gold bracelets to make her talk. (In the West, I thought to myself, they give their wives gold bracelets to keep them quiet!)

But asked about the "unspeakable things" like Phar-aonic circumcision or clitorectomy—which in real terms means that young girls between the ages of five and nine had their clitoris chopped off by a midwife to "keep them

chaste" and at nine were given in marriage if they hadn't
bled to death—she grew flustered. No, it was more of a
withdrawal . . . from something she could write about but
not talk about with Westerners. She did say, "Yes, it still
goes on, and many nine-year-olds die from it." But the
"eventful forty days of marriage"? She simply refused to
talk about it, and soon excused herself.

Everywhere in the Arab world women were simply a
gray, undifferentiated background for the real actors—
men. In this world, it was the men who kept looking at
themselves in the mirror and posing. It was the men who
danced, except for belly-dancers, whose hypnotic contor-
tions were actually a form of masturbation for the pleasure
of the men watching. It was the men who were the temperamental creatures, the creatures of feeling, while the Arab
women were the drudges and plodders. It was the men who
held hands with each other and sniffed daisies as they
walked to battle; they who were considered the chalices of
artistic feelings and tastes.

Because of the unreal and harsh protection of women,
the only spectrum of feelings here was expressed between
men and not between a man and a woman. Much of this
was homosexual, but much was not. It is simply natural:
when you hide women away under those black shrouds,
they cannot develop any of the myriad elaborated relationships with men or even with other women. They are stilted,
frozen beings, draped and covered over like the furniture
in a dead house.

What something like clitorectomy really means, for the
girls who live through the primitive operation, is that as a
woman she can never feel sexual desire, never really enjoy
sex and love. I could only wonder whether women thus
mutilated physically could possibly come out not mutilated
emotionally. How could they know or feel love—for their
husbands or even their children? It was no wonder that so

much of Arab society was so sick and that relations between the sexes were so degraded!

But what is it in Arab history that caused these peculiar patterns in love and sex to develop? How did the Arab woman become so oppressed while her Jewish "cousin" was free and respected from earliest Jewish times? Why should these archaic practices continue here, long after the impact of the West?

One of the reasons for the differences among Jewish women was that among the early Jewish tribes, unlike in Christianity and in Islam, the puritan idea of sex as a sin never bloomed. Sexual desire was considered normal but to be exercised within the marriage institution. Cohabitation was supposed to be joyous and at one's own wish. Women could marry or not marry—in fact, they probably had more freedom within society not to marry in those days than American women have today. But then the Jewish people were always far ahead of the world around them in matters of morality, ethics and individual responsibility, although even today very Orthodox Jews thank God in their morning prayers that they are not women.

In the Moslem world, on the other hand, women never had any of this type of freedom. The Koran says, as though it were written only for men, "Women are your tillage." The word for marriage is that used for the sexual act, as though that was all that marriage was. The Koran also says clearly: "Men have authority over women because God has made the one superior to the other and because they spend their wealth to maintain them. So good women are obedient, guarding their unseen (parts) because God has guarded them."

Even when women did not like this, what could they do against such forces of tradition? One Arabic proverb, reflecting a man's right to throw his wife out and divorce her at whim, reads bitterly: "A woman never knows whether she is going to eat the meal she is cooking."

It should be noted, however, that the dark and ingrown world that the Arab woman found placed around her grew much worse after the Mongol hordes destroyed and perverted the advanced Arab civilization in the thirteenth century—the same time that the persecution of the Jews, who formerly were prized in Arab society, began.

Before this, women rode to battle with men and were not necessarily veiled or in "purdah." A niece of the Prophet Muhammed's wife, for instance, refused the veil saying saucily, "Since God has stamped me with beauty, it is my wish that the public should view that beauty and thereby recognize His grace unto them." This was common in that era.

It was after the savage Mongols swept across the Middle East, barbarizing everything and everyone, that women became those veiled ghouls, covered in black like carrion crows and unable to move outside the home unveiled. They were in "purdah" as a soul would go to purgatory. Their husbands could divorce them by the simple act of saying "I divorce you" three times, and the woman's only respite was that under Moslem law she was able to keep her own property. The man could also legally take up to four wives, but he was—legally at least—saddled with the impossible injuncture to love and treat each one equally.

In Islam, the woman's sexual morality became so obsessively important because it, in effect, was what guaranteed the prestige of the males in the family. If she flaunted this, she was destroying the morality of the family—and the overwhelming shame that perhaps only Arabs experience so morbidly in their shame-oriented culture could then be expunged only by the destruction of the woman.

As the perceptive Lebanese woman sociologist, Dr. Sania Hamady, says in her studies of the Arab temperament, "The woman is the property of the nearest male kinsmen. Woman's sexual behavior is her total honor, and most of a man's honor."

"To a great extent, sex is always related to shame in our country," Haifaa Chanawani, a leading Egyptian woman sociologist told me one evening at a garden party in Cairo. "The virginity of a girl has a tremendous value of its own." She pointed out a magazine which specialized in advice to readers. "All the letters they get are linked to shame about going with a girl who is not a virgin. All through our history, families were afraid girls would bring shame on the family."

Not even the recent emancipation movement in Egypt has led, yet, to any real amount of *sexual* freedom for women. "A girl would be ruined," Amina El-Said, the greatest Egyptian fighter for women's emancipation, told me flatly. "It is not accepted. Maybe in ten years—who knows?"

And so in the conservative Arab countries today and even in parts of Egypt, despite the government's attempts to change this, peasant and lower-class girls are ritually killed by the males in their families for sexual straying.

Psychiatrists and sociologists say that all women in societies like this suffer from these barbaric customs, but unquestionably the educated girls suffer most. They are not about to be killed for "straying," but they live always with a writhing tension within them.

"I go abroad, and I do what I please," a talented young woman writer told me one afternoon over tea in her parents' beautiful, antique-filled apartment in Cairo. "But when I come home, I can't even go to Upper Egypt alone. It is very hypocritical. It is not what we do but what people will think. I think there are few happy families here. It is very difficult, because I come back to the ones I love most, and I can't speak to them directly about these things—I have to go around them. Sometimes—" she paused and swallowed, her emotions very close to the surface, "I think it will drive me mad."

But even she was surprised at the Yugoslav diplomat who had told her at a party, "Hah! Your men would not marry a girl who was not a virgin—and we would not care to marry girls who were."

It would be incorrect and unfair, however, to ignore the healthy parts of Arab personal life, the responsible parts. For most Moslem men are highly responsible to their families, and they have their own structure of thought about family life which to them has both dignity and integrity. This is probably best told in the words of Lady Duff-Gordon, the sensitive and perceptive Englishwoman who, dying of tuberculosis, spent the last years of her life in Egypt at the end of the last century and wrote the famous *Letters from Egypt*.

She consistently makes the point that, to the surprise and even chagrin of the British, Arab men considered the British males' treatment of women abominable and judged that "the English are unkind to women." She quotes an old Turk of Cairo who was being chaffed by an Englishman about Mussulman license in sex. The venerable Muslim replied, "Pray how many women have you, who are quite young, seen (the Eastern phrase for the biblical "known") in your whole life?" When the Englishman could not count, the Turk rejoined, "Well, young man, I am old and I was married at twelve, and I have seen in all my life seven women; four are dead, and three are happy and comfortable in my house. Where are all yours?"

As in all restrictive cultures, there are ways of getting around the cultural roadblocks. Since Arabs live by the injuncture that appearances are far, far more important than reality, they are given relative freedom when outside their own culture. As they say in one of their many expressive proverbs, "In the country where you are not known, pull up your clothes and satisfy your need."

In the same spirit, a man may overlook something if it is not generally known. Dr. Hamady tells the story of a husband who caught his wife in bed with another man. After drawing his gun, he told the man he would let him go if he swore always to keep secret his relationship with his wife. Afterward, he divorced his wife, and there was no problem—the only thing that concerned him was his reputation.

In real life, many strange accommodations occur. In cases where a man's first wife would not accept a second wife, "secret marriages," in which a couple signs a marriage agreement with two witnesses present, are undertaken. They are respected by law, and children born of such unions can inherit family wealth.

Then too, as Egyptian society sees more and more people being uprooted by changes in the countryside, by the war and by industrialization, these old mores do begin to change. One sociologist did a study on marriages that resulted from ads placed in newspapers. He found that the women involved were largely beyond the accepted marriage age of twenty-three. They tended to be divorcees or widows who could offer, in place of youth and virginity, money, furniture and the willingness to marry a poor man.

The men tended to live in remote areas (oil refineries, for instance), to be of simple village origin, to be willing to set aside the dowry which approached some $700. In effect, he concluded, they were "marginals"—people who did not belong to the traditional society any more and so did things in new ways. And Egypt has more . . . and more . . . and more . . . marginals. Like every society, when marginalization becomes predominant, the old strictures of traditional society, including the sexual, break down.

But there is something else that is breaking down traditional Arab family life even more, and that is the economic problems: the need for money. In Egypt, for instance, it is neither idealism about emancipation nor revolutionary ideas that are gradually freeing the Egyptian woman. It is money, which not only talks but also shakes the world.

As much as in his Arab heart he hates it, the young Arab man has been forced by low salaries, since the revolution and the high cost of living, to accept what would have turned him into a roaring Mongol before—the working wife. "Before, when a man wanted to marry, he asked about the girl's father and how much money he made," Hassan Abdul Kaddous, Egypt's foremost novelist about the young, told me one day when we were chatting. He smiled slightly. "Now he asks where she works and how much she gets. I believe myself that economics makes the real difference between a man and a woman. If she's dependent upon a man, it's different."

He recalled the schizophrenia he himself had felt as a boy about the position of women and the schizophrenia all educated Arabs feel—but in his case, it was particularly dramatic. His father had been a famous actor and his daring mother had been the notorious Madame Rosalusas, cosmopolitan and editor for whom the famous Egyptian magazine of the same name was named. "I was brought up in my grandfather's house," he said, "and he was a sheikh. There was such a big difference between the society my parents lived in and the society I was raised in. My aunt had no right to meet any man. If the girls of our house looked from the window, I was given a stick to beat them. My mother lived among men, so I was very astonished. Once when I went to see my mother, I saw her sitting among men. I was horrified—is my mother mistaken or are they mistaken? This is what made me a revolutionary. I knew it was impossible that my father and mother were wrong. It couldn't be. Society had to be wrong."

What many observers in the Arab world call the "remarkable transformation of the Egyptian woman" began only in 1962. Before that, there was a feminist movement, but it had accomplished little. Then, President Nasser not only decreed full equality between men and women in the constitution promulgated that year, he also nationalized properties and industries. Many clever but now impoverished women of the upper and middle classes seized the opportunity with a passion and alacrity that can only suggest to the skeptical that they may well have been waiting (genteelly), behind those closed doors for the opportunity to escape.

"It was remarkable . . . remarkable. . . ." a prominent young woman journalist commented. "They just spontaneously went out en masse and got jobs. Some had only their good taste to offer—they became interior decorators. Nothing, but nothing, would have made men accept it but this."

Along with this movement, there came, almost immediately parallel, the astonishing spontaneous movement of older women going back to school. Cairo University, which not too many years earlier had no women at all, by 1969 had some two thousand *married* women. One went back to school with her two grown daughters and graduated with them.

But despite these dramatic changes, even educated Egyptian women remained somehow shy and gentle, unlike many other Third World women who, once released from tradition, became harsh little public tigers. "Even though she is no longer in purdah, she keeps a purdah of her own will over her heart and attitudes," was the way Amina El-Said, explained it. "Our job is to tear that away

and to get away from the shyness and timidity in the face
of public opinion. The Arab woman is still new, raw. She
is a wonderful being, but with real contradictions."

Amina El-Said is probably the single most dynamic
woman in Egypt, and perhaps in the entire Middle East.
It was she who pioneered women's studying at Cairo University twenty-eight years ago; she who used to play tennis
while the furious traditionalists threw eggs and tomatoes
at her. Now the editor of the influential Arab woman's
magazine, *Hawa,* she is still a dynamo—an unforgetting,
unforgiving dynamo.

But it should be noted here that it is actually the peasant
or fellahin women—so restricted and often despised by
their society—who in many ways hold the key to the development of Egypt and the Arab world. For it is their
unbridled fecundity—enforced by custom, ritual and fear
of peremptory divorce for lack of child-bearing—that is
destroying all hopes of development. Birth control has been
spread in Egypt as in practically no other country in the
underdeveloped world, and there, it is up against no strong
religious barriers. But it *is* up against the barriers raised
by the enslavement of women, for women fear that if they
do not bear many children their husbands will take another wife or divorce them. And it is up against ignorance
(one village man told the birth control nurse he liked the
21-cycle birth control pills better than the 20-cycle ones
because the first divided evenly between his three wives).

In other words, emancipation for women in the Arab
world is not just an idealistic dream—today it is a necessity if these countries are not to sink back into decadency
and hopelessness. Men so seldom see that by imprisoning
women they are imprisoning themselves.

It should be pointed out, too, that there are not only
the various types of Egyptian women in the Arab world.
They are important because Egypt is the epicenter and

stylesetter. But there are also the super-conservative Arabian women and the relatively uncovered Berber women. And there is still another group of Arab women—the fanaticized young girls of the Palestinian Arab world, the daring Leila Khaleds, creatures of Western education now turned against the West and willing to hijack planes, risk their lives and those of how many innocent others . . . for their "cause."

Leila, the Palestinian commando girl who became the Joan of Arc of the movement, represented a new, restless generation of Arab women. They were bursting the bonds. Yet, I wondered. They could do this so long as there was a "war" to be fought. After that was over, would women keep this freedom or be forced back under the veil as they had been in Algeria? There, after fighting valiantly in the resistance, they were only rewarded by the "revolutionary" Arab Algerians with being put back in their place.

The imperatives of tradition are strong. I would color them black.

In July of 1971, I was in Leningrad when the embassy in Moscow put through an urgent phone call to me: they had a message from Cairo which needed answering immediately. Mrs. Gehan Sadat, wife of the new Egyptian President, had agreed to a long, in-depth interview with me—her first with a regular Western correspondent—and when could I return to Egypt?

I was delighted. Here, indeed, was a new type of Arab woman, and, more important, a new type of Arab first lady. I knew that in the ten months since her husband was catapulted into the presidency of Egypt and into the leadership of the Arab world, shaking the diplomatic world by his proposals for ending the war, Mrs. Sadat had been gently shaking worlds, too.

She was trying to shake the veiled seclusion of the rural women of Arab lands.

Discreetly, but forcefully, she was taking a political role. With her husband's blessing and encouragement, she ran for and was elected to the Arab Socialist Union, the official party. She started a feminist organization within the party that was to co-ordinate all women's activities in the country. She had, by the simple, astonishing example of her appearance in public (Mrs. Nasser and other Arab first ladies had almost never appeared in public) become the prototype of a new type of Arab first lady. I knew, too, from her pictures that she was a stunning beauty and a woman who dressed with an unusually tasteful elegance.

The night I met Gehan Sadat at their beach house near Alexandria it was easy to see why, at first, her beauty closed people's eyes to her other qualities. At thirty-seven, she was a mature beauty, with fair skin, then suntanned and freckled from days in the sea, gray-green eyes, coal-black hair and a dazzling smile. Wearing a long, flowered dress, she looked more like a heroine from a romantic novel, as she moved gently back and forth in the swing in the villa's vast gardens.

But when she spoke it was clear that there was also a great deal of substance to the woman. "I am against the exploitation of women," she said in a deep, gentle voice, as a cool evening breeze blew in off the Mediterranean, "but I believe in being efficient, in working legally. I believe in everything simple and gradual—that way you reach what you want."

Mrs. Sadat's way to emancipation for Arab women was to show the men that they could do things—to prove it, not simply to say it. "Certainly there are barriers in the way of women," she went on. "Sometimes they are traditions. But you know, I feel that if a woman wants to prove she is efficient, she can. The way to prove you are efficient is to be it. If I want to *say* something, I *do* it."

Whenever she spoke of her husband or their four children, she radiated happiness. It was obvious that, after twenty-two years of marriage, she was still terribly in love with Anwar Sadat, and she liked to reminisce about their early life together.

Had she ever, in those days, dreamed that she might be the wife of the President of Egypt? She laughed. "I remember once before the 1952 revolution," she began. "We had been married one month. My husband wasn't working. He was out of prison (he had been imprisoned for fighting against the British colonial rule) but not yet in the army. It was a hard time.

"To try to forget, we went to a casino just to spend time. We were waiting to see if the army would accept him again. It was the beginning of our life, and I was very tense. Then a fortuneteller came and asked to see my palm. I never believed in that, but to bring my husband out of his mood, I told the man to look.

" 'You will have four children,' he said, 'mostly girls.' (This turned out to be true.) Then he said, 'Do you know, madame, you will be the first lady of Egypt?'

"There we were, with no salary and no job, not knowing how to face our family and friends. It was something unbelievable. He asked my husband to have his palm read, but he said no. 'After all,' he said, 'I am her husband. If she is first lady, I must be the President.' We laughed the entire night about this."

In the next few years, Sadat became a major conspirator of Nasser's "Free Officers," and Gehan encouraged him in this. Her love for politics and her passion for revolution matched his—they grew out of her patriotism, she said.

It was the fact that he was a revolutionary, indeed, that attracted her to him. Sadat and Gehan, daughter of an

Egyptian physician and a British mother, had met when she was only fifteen. It was the day after he came out of prison for conspiring against King Farouk. "We met at my cousin's home," she recalled. "He was something new for me to see. I like this sort of man. The fact that he was a revolutionary was one of the main reasons I married him. I felt he was an exceptional man—very honest, very faithful to friends and family, a man of very good values. Believe me, I did not ever change my impression of him, though we have been married for twenty-two years."

It grew darker over the broad open gardens that surrounded their spacious modern villa, decorated tastefully inside with formal, European-style furniture. The evening wind blew in from the sea. An impression of her was emerging—she struck me as gentle but strong, discreet but determined, capable of great passions but at the same time balanced, sensible and good-humored. Then she went on about their life together, bringing into existence an Anwar Sadat that no one else knew.

When they married, her father had exacted a promise from the young revolutionary that he would not involve himself further in politics, endangering the security of his daughter. Sadat agreed, but later he found the promise impossible to keep and he felt guilty and disturbed about it. A few months before the revolution, he told his wife how he was torn by it.

"I told him," she said, "that 'the promise was given for my sake. But I married you because you are a brave man. If I felt that you left politics for my sake, I would be unhappy. I am proud of you.' I pushed him and told him not to worry, that the promise was for me."

A few months later, the night of the revolution in which Farouk was overthrown and the age of British colonialism in Egypt ended, Sadat suddenly returned from his post in Sinai. "He asked me what I would especially like to do that

night and I said I wanted to go to the cinema. It was a
cowboy film." She laughed. "He still likes cowboy films.
Later he told me he wanted to do something nice for me,
so I would have a good memory in case he was killed."

When they came back home that night, he received a
card from Nasser saying, "The project will start today."

"I read it," she recalled, "but I didn't know what it
meant. He started to put on his military uniform. He said a
friend was ill and that at midnight it would be easier to find
a doctor if he had his uniform on.

"As he left, I said, 'If you are in prison, this time I won't
visit you.' I don't know why I said it—I sensed something.
He stopped and said, 'Why do you say that?' I said, 'I
didn't mean it.' 'Are you serious?' he asked. 'No, no,' I
said, 'I'm joking.'

"Early the next afternoon, he phoned me and said,
'Please listen to the radio.' I was ready to quarrel. It was
the first time he had ever spent the night away. He said,
'Just listen to the radio.' I felt at this moment something
serious. I said, 'God bless you.'"

She switched on the radio to hear her husband announce
the success of the revolution. "I forgot about visiting the
prison and everything, when I heard him," she continued.
"Of course I was proud. I was flying. I'm very attached to
my country."

In the next years, as Sadat became speaker of the congress and then the Egyptian vice-president, while Mrs. Nasser and the other wives of high officials stayed totally in
the background, it was Gehan Sadat who quietly but ef-
fectively established a woman's presence. She was the first
woman to go the the front lines at Suez after the 1967 war
to visit the troops and to work in the hospitals. She personally fed and comforted the worst napalm victims,
sometimes while bombs were falling.

"I went to the front lines to let them know we were with

them," she said simply. "Morale rose when they knew
that the vice-president's wife was there. Some of the officers
asked, 'How could he send you?' I simply said, 'He sent
me, and I want to be with you.' I don't want to say I'm
brave, but I'm not afraid of bombs at all."

She started a highly successful "business" among the
poor women in her husband's village, Tala. "Once when
I went to the village," she related, "I found this very poor
lady, crying. 'My husband is playing cards,' she said. 'I
have five children, and he doesn't give us any money.' I
gave her money, but I knew this was not any permanent
solution."

What she did was to find twenty-five sewing machines
lying unused in a village basement, to rehabilitate an old
police station and to help the women establish a "welfare
society" which sewed undergarments and lingerie to be
sold in Cairo. They were soon so successful that the first
woman came to her, saying, "My husband respects me
now, for I earn money."

Perhaps the thing that pleased her most, however, was
that, after she was elected to the conference of the Arab
Socialist Union and after she had taken her place there
several times, an old fellah from Upper Egypt, who was
also a member, told her: "After seeing you here, I respect
my own wife more. I tell her, 'The President's own wife is
there with us. She is just like the rest of us.'"

At home, Mrs. Sadat's ideas about child-rearing follow
closely her generally harmonious outlook toward life. "I
am like a friend as well as a mother," she said. "They tell
me all their problems. I do not try to force my ideas upon
them, but indirectly I try to give them confidence and a
sense of justice and responsibility. I am exactly like one of
their friends, but I also believe that respect is very es-
sential.

"They are very proud of their father as President, but I

always impress upon them that this is not a permanent way of life. Gamal, our fourteen-year-old son, wanted an expensive shirt once, for which his allowance was not enough. After his father became President, he thought he could have the shirt. I told him, 'The presidency means your father has more responsibility, it does not mean you have more allowance.'"

In closing, I asked her how she would feel if the war were to start again? How she would feel if her own son, Gamal, had to fight when he came of age?

She sat for a moment, thinking. "Every mother hates war," she said, finally. "War is a terrible thing. My husband is doing his best—his utmost—to find a peaceful solution. But if we fail, sometimes values are more precious than life. All our people are against war.

"At the same time, you do not want your children to live in refugee camps. If the war occurs again, Gamal will serve the same as any other boy. There are no exceptions."

There was no question about it—Gehan Sadat had come to represent to many, many Egyptians a new kind of woman. To the women, she had come to represent a revitalization of the women's movement that bloomed so winningly after the revolution and then gradually withered. Why? Simple apathy. Simple lethargy.

Perhaps Gehan Sadat's discreet and gradual but determined way was the only way. . . . But would it be enough?

By now it was dark—dark over the shores of the Mediterranean where the Romans and where Napoleon once ruled, dark over the Nile where the Pharaohs built their temples to death, and dark over the deserts where the Bedouin roved. All of them part of the complex world that is Egypt.

Gehan Sadat's way of trying to change the place and role of women in that society was complex, and yet at the

same time simple. I left feeling that perhaps no woman in
that country was more complex—and more simple—than
she.

But what is it that draws us *Western women* into this
maze of Middle Eastern sensuality and injustice and fascination? It has drawn us since the last century and doubtless will draw us forever—away from our own more just
and tepid societies.

For us, ironically, there is a peculiar freedom—a feeling of being removed from the usual *Anglo-Saxon* divisions of male and female, young and old, educated and uneducated, and where they all belong. In a place like the
Middle East, a Western woman is as in a pressureless
chamber, floating free in a society, belonging neither to
the men of it nor to the women of it.

She is a single satellite, neither of it nor from it, able
to savor the possibilities of every position in society, yet
forced to take none, delving here and then withdrawing,
feeling both superior to the men and submissive to them
but never having to take the final consequences of either
position, identifying with the women and pitying them and
despising them for their acceptance of the way things are
just as on different levels we have despised ourselves for
acceptance of the world as it is.

And—yes—I suppose that is what draws me, too.

CHAPTER X

Across the River Jordan—The Moral Trauma in Israel

It was all too simplified, too monolithic, the Arab side! Once I left Egypt, with its cynical humor, its kindly cowardice and its saving sense of historic proportion, I began to feel as if I were in a sound tunnel—the same voices and the same wild cries echoed starkly about me as they catapulted off the walls to come back and back and back at me. The same maddening propaganda, day and night, morning and noon, over and over! It was as if I were facing a hard blank wall, with no veins and no cracks and no smudges.

And so when I went to Israel, it was at least in part an escape from intellectual vacuity and this stifling totalitarian thought. It was an attempt to regain my sanity about what was real and what was not real in the world.

And if I am to be honest, I must admit that my first reaction upon arriving in Israel was a somewhat schizophrenic one. I have talked to other correspondents who made this cycle from the Arab countries to Israel, and many of them went through the same fragmented experience.

Since childhood I had always had a very romantic and highly idealized idea of Israel. Yet my first months in the Middle East had all been spent entirely in the Arab countries. I would be less than honest if I did not admit that, after week after week and month after month of this bombardment of propaganda against Israel, I began to be troubled. I wondered: "Is it possible that there *is* something to all these stories about Israel? That what I had thought all my life was completely or in part wrong?"

Still, I arrived in Israel with a sense of relief, with the feeling that here I could certainly find what for lack of a more realistic outlook we journalists still call truth. Yet, for the first couple of days, if again I am to be very honest, I must admit that I found myself looking with extreme suspicion upon everything and everybody. The Arab propaganda had got even to me. It suddenly became clearer—clearer to me in visceral terms, which after all are what ultimately matter—how even educated and rational Arabs can be so totally, fanatically, unthinkingly caught up in the perfervid emotions of the campaign against Israel.

When I finally reached Tel Aviv, checking into the Tel Aviv Hilton, at first my sense of unreality reached new heights. All this activity, all this energy! ("Such an energy, this country," my Israeli friend Boaz Evron was to comment. "Sometimes I forget myself. I can see why it scares the Arabs—it scares me!") Everything so modern and . . . all those American tourists! (Who would not be amused by the two American Jews with the omnipresent United Jewish Appeal walking out of the expensive Hilton gift shop and one saying to the other in a voice of surprise: "These fellows are good businessmen!") Suddenly it was "Shalom" instead of "Salaam," and the beautiful sea was stretching out from your toes and the Israelis were already

out running and exercising on the beach when I got up
at 6 A.M. to write.

What had happened? Where had I left behind the sloe-
eyed, scratching Arabs sitting around their tea tables, hurt
or sulking or crazy, as the case might be?

I soon discovered, however, that this initial picture of
exuberance, as true as it is, was only part of the picture of
Israel today. Beneath it, Israel was living out a deep moral
trauma. Where was the picture of Israel from outside, the
superstate, the hijacker of radar stations, the runner of
blockades, the surest of the sure and bravest of the brave?
These pictures, which I, too, had held, were in many ways
as false as had been my prejourney ideas of the Arabs.

For Israel was a deeply troubled country, and that made
me admire her far more than I would have admired the
superstate. (There is doubtless a flaw in me that superstates and even aspiring superstates bring out the worst in
me, leaving me with an irresistible impulse to kick them.)
The always latent feeling of persecution and the sense of
imminent abandonment that has both strengthened, en-
riched and torn the Jewish soul was what was really overwhelming the Jewish people in Israel and not, as many
outsiders saw it, an overbearing superiority complex.

What Israelis call their "Massada complex" had reas-
serted itself. There were signs around the country reading
"Massada Shall Not Fall Again." Massada: the fortress
whose dusty golden ruins stand atop a remotely barren
mountaintop southwest of the Dead Sea. It was here that
the Jewish Zealots made their last stand against the Romans
during three long years. Finally the Jews in the fortress, on
the brink of being vanquished, picked ten to kill the rest;
then they drew lots for one to kill the nine, and then this
one killed himself. This siege complex again was all too
prevalent, and this uncertainty about things—this eternal

questioning and fear of extinction—showed itself in many ways.

When a survey was taken of Israelis asking which people would be the most happy in the future, the majority answered that it would be the Americans and only 11 per cent answered that it would be the Israelis. Many Israelis were questioning the ultimate compatibility of the "hard line" against the Arabs and the preservation of Jewish humanistic values. Or, as one put it: "Can Israel maintain the martial posture of Sparta and the civic virtues of Athens?" And the young Israeli boys who faced three years in active duty in the army and then reserve duty until age fifty-five talked drearily about "the desert view" or "Bedouinism"—Israeli terms for the drying up of the mind and soul that came from too much desert military duty.

Outside, it looked as if Israel were the winner; but inside, it did not feel that way. People were scared and, more, they were often traumatized. Everything—every reference, every question, every anger and yearning—revolved around the Arabs. This was natural; they were a tiny Jewish vessel being tossed on a turbulent Arab sea.

One American diplomat characterized the new mood and the dilemma in these words: "We have a simultaneous hardening and softening. There is a hardening on a governmental level and underneath an intensification of worry. Casualties are mounting. There are incidents with the Israeli Arabs. There is a feeling of hopelessness, that it will never end."

Or, as one Israeli diplomat told me, "It looks like we're losing just a few men on Suez, but the fact is we can't even bear the loss of that small number. We're too small a country. Every loss is like the loss of a family member. That's why we've got to strike harder and harder."

The first day I paid my respects to the government information office, I found myself talking to a charming

older man from South Africa named Petan. "Yes, we've
heard about *you*," he said at once when I entered his office.
I didn't exactly understand then the reason for this initial
(but only initial) hostility; later I discovered, rather to my
astonishment that I, a long time admirer and sympathizer
with Israel, was considered an enemy—simply, in general,
because I had reported from the Arab side and because,
in particular, I had raised the question of whether Israel
was mistreating or torturing prisoners in the occupied territories. I was astonished. Even the Soviet Union does not
react like that any more—only the most dismal of the underdeveloped countries do. I was simply doing my job, and
it was unthinkable to me that advanced, educated Israelis
would take this defensive attitude—unless they felt very,
very threatened.

Then he sighed and said, immediately, "There's no
question that we're losing the propaganda battle." I thought
of Israel over the years, about how doggedly it had wooed
the world propaganda-wise, and I was startled. "We see it
with the New Left kids who come in here every day—and
with the papers of Western Europe. The Arab countries
have been able to show themselves as the underdogs, and
that underdog image is hard to beat."

He got up and stared for a moment at the map of the
Middle East in which Israel, even with its territories tripled
by its victories in 1967, still remained a tiny enclave in a
huge Arab land mass. "Just look at that map," he said.
"Yet it has become the fashion, so to speak, to represent
Israel as a brutal militaristic power intent only on crushing
its sadly inefficient neighbors who are unable to compete
with Israeli technology. We're the strong aggressor—we're
the establishment to these kids. There's not much romance
here. Everything is too modern, too Westernized. There's
not much romance in selling gladiolas from a kibbutz. It's
not like Arabs on horseback."

Petan grew even more despondent as he talked. "There's not much we can do," he continued. "Take our kibbutzim on the borders. They dig in. The children sleep in shelters. But they stay. The other side was the green part of Jordan —now there's nothing there, because the people didn't stay. We get blamed when they show a picture of a father with a dead child in his arms.

"I"—he paused and shook his head slowly and sadly— "was going to send a photographer to get a picture of a girl soldier who had been killed. Everybody was shocked. 'She has parents,' they said. 'You can't do that.' We have too much concern for life to do this." Then he voiced an oft-repeated expression and one which I came to feel had a good deal of validity: "Whatever the Arabs do, the outside world says, 'That's the way they are.' Nobody expects as much of them. They say 10 Israelis killed, we say none. BBC looks and calculates it must be five. We can't win."

The next day in Tel Aviv I was having lunch with a highly successful young Israeli businessman, named David Cohen, and with Peter Jennings of ABC, an earlier friend of mine. We went to what the Israelis call an "oriental" restaurant, a crowded, busy, noisy small upstairs restaurant in which you are served by busy, Oriental Jews whose service would not be recommended by Duncan Hines but whose food was superb. There was nothing personal, I soon found out, in their non-verbal attitudes toward customers; it took an hour and a half for everybody to get his food, regardless of race, religious creed or national origin.

"That's the general who created the guerrilla units that took Sinai," David said at one point, pointing to an unprepossessing open-shirted man sitting two tables away from us. "He's one of the most famous men in Israel and look he's complaining. . . . He can't get served either."

As we talked, it turned out that David, like more Israelis

than one would think, was more than a little anti-American.

"Go ahead—tell her. You Israelis are not as friendly to us as we think, are you?" Peter baited him.

"No, we don't trust you," David answered. "We know that Johnson was simply going to let us go down the drain when the Straits of Tiran were attacked." I wanted to say how similar that sounded to some of Isam Sartawi's denunciations of Johnson that night in Amman. . . .

Then David suddenly became very serious. "If you want to write about something, you should write about the moral questioning," he said. "Everybody's living through it. The government can't give you help, it's a personal problem. There's something about the Jews—they can't kill. It's not natural. The Jews care more than any other people in the world for human life. . . ."

David, it turned out, had been a member of the Irgun, the most brutal Jewish terrorist group during the Palestine war of 1948, which led to the division of Palestine and the creation of Israel. "But we never killed civilians, even then," he said. "I remember one night five of us came out of a theater and there was a howling Arab mob. One of us had a grenade, but if he threw it in the crowd a lot of innocent people would get killed. He didn't throw it. I got away, but he was literally torn apart, ear by ear and . . ." He paused.

"But, David," I protested, simply because I knew that this wasn't *all* the record. "There *were* massacres on your side, too. Like Deir Yassin."

His expression changed. Deir Yassin, the Arab village where more than three hundred villagers were taken out during the war and shot by terrorists of the Irgun, is a haunting memory for any thinking Israeli. "Ah yes," he said slowly. "Yes. . . ."

What was to strike me forcibly was the fact that Israel

was no longer the Cinderella of the Western world, for the simple reason that Cinderella could never be an occupying general. They were living in a state where 40 per cent of the GNP was going for defense and where the average of twenty deaths a month they were sustaining at that time was equal to 1500 American deaths a month. The war had actually saved Israel—before the 1967 war, emigration was so high there had been a sign at Lod airport, reading "Will the last one out please turn off the light?" But it had also saddled Israel—and the world—with the new image of the Jews as victors.

There was a strong disappointment here in the gradual realization that the rest of the world did not like the Israeli so much as victor as it liked him as struggler.

The world was uncomfortable with these unpersecuted Jews, and the Israelis were bitterly cynical about the fact the world didn't like them so much now that they were so successful.

Too, as with Americans, there was a certain lack of form among the Israelis. They had destroyed and built everything so fast there was no time to create new forms. And the brazen, open person, so attractive in pioneer days, becomes less attractive as a boss or a sergeant. He has none of the style and manners and civilized forms that, for instance, the British have and which brought them through the worst of times with their style and their dignity intact.

The changes in the Jewish state should have been expected, of course. No country ever stays in that early, romantic, superidealized, hypercharged state in which Israel was born. That generation passes—always—and a new generation comes which is more practical, more businesslike, more pragmatic and less soulful; a generation that despises even the dreams of its parents. It struck me that Israel had simply matured, and very few people seemed to want to realize this. This unwillingness and inability to live

within the strictures of this new state was distorting the
entire Israeli existence outside it and making people uncomfortable within it.

The country itself remained as vibrant and lovely as ever.
Tel Aviv buzzed with activity and with a nice, totally
unique Jewish-Middle Eastern-Berlin-cosmopolitan-Ameri-
can flavor. Its outdoor cafés on the broad avenues were
filled with the usual lively people and the youngsters were
more handsome and more breezy than ever. The road to
Jerusalem was still one of the most glorious drives in the
world, ending as it does with the breath-taking entry into
the old city while the desert views all around it tore at the
soul and soothed it at the same time.

If you drove north from Tel Aviv, you traveled along
the brilliantly blue Mediterranean that slapped at your side,
ringing with old voices. Caesar was here. . . . The Crusaders were here. . . . Paul walked here. . . . One day,
in a driving rain, I stopped by myself to see the golden
ruins of Caesarea, the old Crusader city on the sea. It was
a wild and windy day, and the rain seemed driven down
like pieces of glass. The rain swirled about me with such
life and power that it seemed to me all the historic energy
of the centuries was, in that moment, there.

Such a little country to have so much! From a high
apartment building in Tel Aviv you could see the outskirts
of Jerusalem. You could drive the whole length of the
country in a couple of hours. Such a little country to be
the reason for more than 100 million people to be locked
in total combat over it! Such a successful country and . . .
such a troubled country!

Some Israelis saw the problems clearly. A friend of mine
at the Foreign Ministry, who is a very discerning man, discussed the Israeli complex about the whole world being

against it. "The publicity is not against Israel," he said,
"but there are just more reporters here now. Before, many
would not report anything bad about Israel because of anti-
Semitism. Now Israel is open to objective reporting for the
first time. It is part of the new role of the state." Yet . . .
there was no question about it . . . they were finding it
very hard to be treated in this objective way.

Another man who saw very clearly what was going on
and analyzed it was Dr. Amnon Rubinstein, the young,
vibrant, incisive dean of the Law School at Tel Aviv University and a particularly popular newspaper columnist.
"Israelis today are very pragmatic," he told me as we sat
one evening in his office and chatted. "They are very strong
in terms of the visions and idealism of the earlier days.
They've gone through everything . . . revolution . . .
change . . . There is no end to anything. I think this produces a feeling of realism, yet also one with paradoxes.
There is more idealism and personal courage here than in
any society I know. But the idealism today takes different
forms. Today people are not satisfied working without re-
wards. The old kibbutz spirit is dead. The younger generation is far more sophisticated and pacifist. There is a black
humor. A few days after the war, they gave a revue in Tel
Aviv called *You and I and the Next War* and another
one *Catsup,* which made fun of Israel as a 'brave little
country.'"

It was not like that, of course, in the "early days." Immediately after the creation of the State of Israel in 1948,
nearly the whole world applauded roaringly. Support of
Israel in the United States was so complete that it was
nearly impossible to find any realistic mention or analysis
of the brutal conflicts between Arabs and Jews between
1917 and 1948 which laid the troubled basis for the new
state. In the first decade of its existence, Americans con-

tributed more than $1 billion in gifts, largely through the
United Jewish Appeal, and bought another $500 million
in bonds. Another $250 million in private American in-
vestment went into Israel plus another $800 million in U.S.
aid. Unlike any arrangement with any other country, the
United States permitted tax-deductible donations to Israel,
and very nearly all American sentiments were with Israel.

(These close human, political and economic relationships
between the United States and Israel led to both practical
and ethical questions in the field of foreign affairs. Was it
right for American foreign policy to be so inexorably tied
to one small country—a country whose friendship immediately cost us the friendship of every other country in a
vast and strategic area? Was it right for one national group
in the United States to influence American policy on the
Middle East to the extent it does, when policy ideally
should be made for and by the interests of the majority of
Americans? Did this not lead to the danger of increasing
anti-Semitism at home? These were sticky, touchy questions—questions that still have not been answered.)

But mainly the Israelis did it themselves, and the saga
of their first twenty years of building up their state is
one of the great historic sagas of all time. For them, it
was Israel or destruction. The passion of a return to Zion
had informed Jewish religion and Jewish passions for centuries. "Next year in Jerusalem" they greeted each other
in their Diaspora all over the world, but by World War
II, they considered it not a dream but the only reality
possible. Unless they had their own homeland and their
own nation, like other nationalities, the Hitler-hurled Jewish
refugees reasoned, they would be persecuted to the end
of time. If, indeed, they lasted that long. And so they
became even more filled with the sense of a biblical inevitability of a return.

But how did all of this start? What was it in Jewish history that led to this "mad dream" of a return to this tiny scrap of the world's land?

Jewish history is so rich, so complex and so open to many and even contradictory interpretations that one could not hope to do it justice in less than a major book. So let me mention just a few salient facts here—facts which are, however, necessary if one is to understand even a little bit of the magnificence of Jewish history and a little bit of the Middle East conflict today.

The key to Jewish genius lies in the fact that the Jews, a Semitic race who gathered in the shadows of ancient times in the area now Israel, were the first people to believe in one God. This sounds like a simple enough idea, but it isn't. Believing in one abstract, ethical god, at a time when the world about you had lascivious male gods, languorous female gods, angry gods of war, fecund gods of harvest . . . and marvelous tales of their banquets together . . . meant some very special things. It meant there were no pagan resurrection rites, no mythological wars between the gods. It placed an overweening web of spirituality around the Jew's life, curbed licentiousness and created the inner discipline which still today is a hallmark of most Jewish people. It gave birth to an intense intellectualism—a direct consequence of making God abstract.

Throughout their early history, the Jews, like most of the peoples around them, were constantly conquering and being conquered. For a time they were exiled in Egypt, until they were led back to Israel by Moses. Still another time, they were exiled in Babylon, until a small group returned to Israel. It was not until the Romans, tired of the endless Jewish resistance to their rule, exiled them from Jerusalem after the destruction of the second temple in A.D. 70 that they were completely scattered in their fateful Diaspora—a Diaspora that probably kept Jewish culture always young and seeking because it never found a homeland and thus peace and death.

What had been Israel became the home of the other Semitic tribes and the Romans. As the Jews were dispersed throughout Europe and the Middle East, they performed brilliantly in every culture. As the excellent Jewish historian Max Dimont puts it: "When a civilization was philosophic, like that of the Greeks, the Jews became philosophers. When it was composed predominantly of poets and mathematicians, like that of the Arabs, the Jews became poets and mathematicians. When it was scientific and abstract, like that of the modern Europeans, the Jews became scientists and theoreticians. When it was pragmatic and suburban, like the American, the Jews became pragmatic and suburban. The Jews were part of, yet distinct from, the civilization in which they lived." What they did along the way was to lay the ethical basis of the entire Western world.

Everywhere, too, the Jews, with their demanding religion and their special place in society, acted as a weather vane of the sickness or health of a society. In the blossoming Moslem world of A.D. 700 to the 1300s, the Jews were treasured citizens. During those times in European history when nations were thriving, the Jews were prized. Always . . . always . . . it was when a civilization was troubled or traumatized or endangered or in decline that the Jews, along with other minorities, were persecuted. And in Europe it was when a new, unsure middle class arose after the Middle Ages—a new middle class which wanted the commercial positions that only the Jews had been permitted to hold—that in many countries Jews were at least temporarily expelled.

It was not until the last century, Dimont points out, that a spasmodic anti-Jewishness turned into virulent anti-Semitism. This, he says, was an entirely new historic pattern. It meant not just disliking individual Jews but disliking

the race and plotting for its destruction. As the world so
tragically knows, this horrible trend led to the extinction
of between five and six million Jews at the hands of
Nazi Germany—a number that was, however, exceeded by
the number of Christians killed by the Nazis.

When anti-Semitism began to arise, in Europe, Jewish
leaders turned to Zionism—to a return to Israel—as a last
desperate hope. And from 1882 on, many Jews worked to
make this dream a reality. In what is known in Hebrew
as the "first aliyah," 25,000 Jews "ascended" to Israel between 1882 to 1904 to "build the land and to be rebuilt
by it." The "second aliyah" brought 40,000 more Jews
to Israel between 1904 and 1913; this group was highly
influenced by the developing socialist ideologies of the day
and believed strongly that a Jewish Renaissance in Palestine
required the development of a Jewish working class and
peasantry. Most of these Jews were East European. In the
"third aliyah," between 1919 and 1922, 35,000 Jews emi-
grated, primarily from Russia. But even by the end of
the third aliyah, only 11 per cent of Palestine was Jewish—
and very little concern was shown for the native Arabs.

The next twenty-five years in Palestine were as tormented
as any twenty-five years anywhere and at any time in history. It is possible to prove anything about these years.
Jews say they bought most of the land from the Arabs
and wanted the remaining Arabs to stay. Arabs say the
Jews deliberately drove them out through terror and through
plans to extend the state even deeper into Arab territory.
Jews say the Arabs could have had their own Palestinian
state if, after the 1948 war, which was started by the
Arabs, the surrounding Arab states had not seized those
territories. The Arabs say that the Jews never wanted any
Arabs around at all—if they had, they argue, why didn't
they allow any Arab refugees to return to Israel after
1948 or compensate them for their land? The Israelis said

they would compensate them, but only after the obstreperous Arab states recognized the State of Israel.

Where is the truth? It is a little bit here and a little
bit there. And many times, it is nowhere. For the important
element in the Middle East conflict is not that the Jews
did *this* at a certain time or the Arabs did *that* at another.
The important thing is how different are the two peoples.
The Jews, while often traumatized underneath, are rational
people on an action level. They live in a largely democratic,
finely functioning state in which very nearly every citizen
takes an active role. The Jews are the ultimate activists,
while the Arabs are the ultimate sulkers—the men who
would rather lose than have anyone hear them say a "dis-
honorable" thing.

Perhaps only one thing further needs to be pointed out
at this time—this is a warning not to compare things in
the Middle East today too literally to other times. Today
is not Nazi Germany again. As strange and irrational as
it may seem, the Arabs genuinely fear the Israelis. Dimont,
an eminently fair Jewish scholar, warns that "rightly or
wrongly, the Arabs think they have good cause to fear
the Jews, because in their eyes the Jews have dispossessed
them from what they consider their land. The Arabs are
playing the political game the way it always has been
played, mobilizing fears to unify dissident factions. It is
anti-Jewish, yes, but certainly not anti-Semitic."

The first years of the Jewish state—despite the always-
present threat of the Arabs—must have been ecstatic. "It
was as close to an idyllic society as any I have ever
seen," one Israeli friend told me. And most felt that way.
This enormous confidence and understandable pride in
what they had accomplished in so short a time lasted
through the 1956 war over Suez and came to a peak right
after the enormous victories of the 1967 war. This victory
made, initially, generous conquerors out of the Israelis,

many of whom then were ready to give back all the Arab
territories they occupied during the flash-flood war in exchange for peace, but it made even more sullen and furious
enemies out of the Arabs, driven by this further humiliation
into an even more pathological position.

As William Polk has put it: "Taunted by the notion
that they were merely, in the words of the Balfour Declaration, the 'existing non-Jewish communities in Palestine,' infuriated by their own incapability to act, their
inability to coalesce into an effective national unit in the
face of the European or the Zionist challenge, ever trying
to prove that theirs was not the 'empty land' depicted in
early Zionist literature, the Arabs retreated from reality into
a world of myth, posture and pretense." And while the
Arabs, in their failure having grown more and more fanaticized, became surer that they must purge themselves of
the "stain" of Israel on the map of the Middle East, the
Israelis began questioning—moral questioning.

This moral questioning, of course, revolved not only
around the war but largely around the questions of the
occupied territories, those 50,000 square miles of Arab
land and those one million Arabs which Israel took under
occupation after the 1967 war.

What do you do, the Israeli started asking with troubled
eyes, when you are caught in our dilemma? We have
this war we never wanted, you see—we were about to be
attacked. Now we have 1,300,000 Arabs, most of them
hostile and smoldering, in territories we feel we have to
occupy for our own protection.

Some Israelis were saying, "Give them back, we are not
occupiers of other people's lands." Most said, "No, give
them back and these people will rise to destroy you as
they have promised for twenty years." "But if you keep
them," still others argued, "don't you realize that with only

2.5 million Jews, you soon won't have a Jewish state—
which is the reason for all this suffering and killing?"

And there were the other nibbling, nagging, niggling
questions. How do you, as Jews, who have suffered more
than probably any other single people in the world, justify
the suffering you now are inflicting on others, even if they
instigated it? Are you really treating them, as the Clovises
and as many Europeans and even young American Jews
contend, not like human beings but as "obstacles"? How
can your fathers and mothers be sure their children will
not be as indifferent to the Arabs' suffering as your persecutors were to yours? Have you created a new race—
Israelis and not Jews? And what is an Israeli Jew—what
is the justification for the state itself—when most Israelis
no longer practice Judaism?

While the Israelis suffered over these questions, there
was also occurring an unquestionable hardening of Israeli
attitudes—toward the Arabs and toward peace as well. In
the spring of 1971, a Louis Harris poll showed the growing hawkishness of the Israelis; with 53 per cent of them
thinking that "Arabs are lazier than Israelis," 74 per cent
finding them "less intelligent than Israelis" and 67 per cent
"inferior to Israelis." Was this a "racist" attitude?

The same poll also showed an increasingly hawkish attitude toward the occupied territories. Eighteen per cent
wanted to retain all the occupied territories and 3 per cent
wanted to expand them. Only 4 per cent would return
all the lands, and substantial majorities wanted to keep
the key areas of East Jerusalem, Sharm el Sheikh, the
Golan Heights and part of the Sinai desert. By a 58 to
34 per cent margin, Israelis found it difficult to feel sympathy for the Palestinian refugees because they believed so
many of them wanted to see Israel destroyed, and only 2
per cent wanted them to be allowed to return to Israel. The
predominant view (57 per cent) was that the refugees

should be settled in Arab countries with Israel paying
them compensation. Were they not being as indifferent to
others' sufferings as others had been to theirs?

In some of his writings, Amnon Rubinstein, one of
Israel's most perceptive sons and analysts, has pointed out
that this suspicion and distrust of everything outside—this
innate hawkishness—is deeply imbedded in the Israeli soul.
It exists not only in the older generation of Jews, he says,
but coexists in the sabra with his well-known openness.
This is because of the Jews' historic distrust, first of the
Gentile or *goyim,* then of the Arabs, then of protection
by international bodies. A distrust that is often based on
fact but often is not and only reinforces itself. He further
points out that, in Hebrew, the word *goy* means both
"Gentile" and "nation." In Israel, Jews were to become
a nation like all other nations, and thus escape these centuries-old fears of the always-persecuted wandering Jew.
But though the nation has been smashingly successful, the
fear—succored by the new reality of a sea of surrounding
Arabs—did not die.

Key to all of these debates—a dark catalyst here as in
the Arab world—were the Palestinian commandos. To the
Israelis, they were "terrorists" and nothing more; captured,
the commandos in Israel were treated as civil and not
political prisoners, and the Israelis called them not *fedayeen*
(those who sacrifice) but *meshablim* (the dark forces).
They had good reason, often enough, to despise them, for
while many of the commandos showed extraordinary courage in crossing the Jordan River border, others showed
extraordinary cowardice—their kind of attack was to throw
a bomb into a school bus.

Still, very few Israelis, I found, were any more willing
to try to understand the real motivations and sufferings of

the commandos and the Palestinians than the commandos were willing to understand theirs. But some were.

I was sitting in the office of our stringer, Jay Bushinksy, and another journalist in the big Beit Ma'ariv building the second day I was in Tel Aviv, and we were talking about the wonderful panoply of "characters" in Israel. "You should see them," Jay was saying. "One is more fascinating than the other."

"She should see Begin," the other journalist said. "He was commander of the Irgun and now he's . . ."

"Or the doctor," Jay went on. "What a marvelous character. Whenever he would see the Israeli police mistreating an Arab in any way, he'd go up to the policeman and insist that he be arrested too."

"Or Yalin-Mor," the other young man said. "He was commander of the Stern Gang, and now he's a prominent dove."

I perked up. "Could we get in touch with him?" I asked Jay. The former chief terrorist, now a dove! It was too good to be true. The next evening I saw Nathan Yalin-Mor.

He lived then in a roomy modern apartment on the outskirts of Tel Aviv, and I immediately liked the man. He had one of the most engaging faces I have ever seen —indeed, I could not take my eyes off it. It was a round face with a large handle-bar mustache, and it was both very sensitive and rather comical. He looked like a Jewish character actor of the old school, from Poland or Hungary. It turned out he had been born in Poland, so that settled that.

Yalin-Mor was worried. "Nothing can endanger our national existence," he ruminated that evening. "But in the course of time our country could be turned into a state not very pleasant to live in. It could become a garrison state. The repressions of the Arabs could also come to apply to Israeli citizens, and everyone who talks against repressions could be considered a traitor.

"Sure we'd win another round. But is that the aim of our lives . . . to have wars without end? We have the Army Reserve now until age fifty-five. It would be like France at the time of Napoleon, where every consecutive victory meant taking older and older soldiers."

Yalin-Mor was one of a group of Israeli peaceniks who thought his government was all wrong in its treatment of the Arab commandos, and it came to me after talking with him for a while that he understood the motivations of the "terrorists" on the other side because he had understood his own.

"To me, it is no surprise that many Israeli Arabs are joining in Arab terrorist acts," he told me that night. He smiled. "I do not use 'terrorist' in a pejorative sense," he added. "I myself was called a terrorist, and I knew I was fighting for the highest ideals of life. Collective punishment . . . only pushes the Arab population into the hands of the Arab resistance. I remember how interested we were for the British to put collective punishment on the Jews. It would only build barriers between the British and the Jewish population. People who know something about national liberation movements should know this. Mao wrote that the terrorists are the fish in the water of the people. Well, collective punishment makes the water more abundant.

"Harsh punishments work only for the benefit of the organization, for the people with no courage then fall by the wayside. The movement starts to attract only the most idealistic element. There are terrorists of several types, some who want to be executed because they believe that helps their nation's fight and they believe they gain eternity. It is silly talk to think they will be frightened by executions. The Israeli government works for Fatah by giving the impression it is going to annex the Arab populations in these areas. It gives credit to their political theories and makes them look like a national liberation movement."

He showed me one article he had published which was astonishing for its forthrightness. "Palestine has given birth to two nations," he wrote, "the Hebrew and the Palestinian Arab nation. Both nations have just claims to the same motherland, like two children who claim the love of the same mother. We are not entitled to deny the just right also of the Palestinian people to this country. They, too, are attached to it not by the virtue of some caprice but of the fact that they have been living here for thirteen centuries; by virtue of the fact that for generations they buried their dead in this land, developed a national-popular culture in it.

"It is regrettable that one may hear Israeli leaders in the highest offices, including the Prime Minister, the Foreign Minister and the Minister of Information, denying knowledge of the existence of the Palestinian nation. They have forgotten, or they prefer not to remember, that only twenty-one years ago statesmen and also leading intellectuals negated the existence of the Jewish nation. A nation exists from the day that a certain society attains independent national consciousness, and that needs no confirmation from outside."

I read this with great interest, while he smiled a gentle, somewhat sad smile. "When that was published in Australia," he interjected, "there was a Jewish typesetter and he put an extra line of his own in." His eyes sparkled. "It was, 'This is bloody rubbish!' "

Occasionally, when Yalin-Mor talked about things less serious, he got an impish look on his face. "I could be critical of many things the Arab terrorists do," he said, "as a man of the same . . . metier. But I don't think I'll give them any advice."

The only time when he lost, momentarily, his charming
manner was when I referred to the "Stern Gang." He almost winced. "Ah yes, the Stern Gang," he said, almost
sadly. "The British called us that. We called ourselves
the Stern group. Just as now *we* call *them* 'terrorists.'"

Later, after I left Yalin-Mor, I thought about him . . .
and about everything. Such a charming, gentle man. Yet
I remembered that the Stern Gang had been one of the
most brutal of all terrorist gangs of all time. He had been
in on the murder of the Swedish mediator, Count Folke
Bernadotte, whom the Jews thought was giving too much
land to the Arabs. It occurred to me to remember that
Yalin-Mor had been sipping a lemon squash in a café
that night in 1948 when the announcer broke into the
music from the loudspeaker and said, "Count Folke
Bernadotte was assassinated in Jerusalem today." He had
put down his lemon squash and calmly listened to the
details—details he had helped plan. "I suppose they'll be
looking for me," he said to his companions. "Let's go."

It was no accident that those responsible for Count
Bernadotte's death were never punished—the new State
of Israel rewarded the Stern Gang for their assassination
with no prosecutions.

The debate on the "terrorists" went on and on in Israel.

"It is very serious," my friend Boaz Evron, the well-
known commentator for the newspaper *Yediuth Aharonot,*
told me one day. "You have two peoples with absolute
demands. What the Arabs are thinking about is really
genocide. On the other hand, we could destroy them. What
I fear is that if Israel gets into a paroxysm of anger,
it will destroy everything between Turkey and Aswan."

"What will the Arabs turn us into?" I wrote in one
story about Israel. "That is the question, unspoken and,
more and more often, spoken."

The government seemed convinced that its position was

correct. The Arabs, they argued, would eventually give up under the pressure of enough "punishment." They only understood a strong hand from Israel and only respected a strong hand. The application of more and more Israeli air power to Suez and even to the interior of Egypt would eventually bring the Arabs around. It would be gradual, for hadn't the war gone on already for thirty years? But, eventually, they would be forced to sue for peace or see all their own internal development fall by the wayside of the war. The important thing for Israel was to keep the cease-fire lines. Moreover, Israel could not give up one piece of the occupied territories until a permanent peace treaty —with concomitant recognition of Israel—was signed.

Even those "doves" who were in strongest opposition to this Golda Meir-Moshe Dayan government policy had few answers. Their "answers" tended to be more in the area of the kind of attitude Israel should take than in specific suggestions. Of these doves, who only managed to get a meager five thousand votes in the 1969 elections, the leader and the finest spokesman was Yehoshua Arieli, a big, kindly man who is professor of history at Hebrew University.

The day I saw him in his office, he looked discouraged . . . perhaps saddened is a better word. He talked of the Middle East being caught up in an "anonymous process. Nobody makes it. It makes itself. It is the logic of the situation, not of man. I don't see how anything could change."

To Dr. Arieli, the first step for Israel was to realize that she and not the Arabs must take the initiatives—the policy of strong-arm offense was counterproductive—and then to make the qualitative change in attitude that would enable a new step to be taken. "I always said we should differentiate between our side and the other," he told me in his measured, thoughtful way. "The possibility that the

other side will make a gesture of peace is nil. The regimes
are dictatorial, unstable. Hatred against Israel has been indoctrinated into the masses for twenty-five years. It is a
typical situation of international tension in which both
fear every change of the status quo and the situation in-
creases the insecurity about what the other side should
do. If we take a unilateral step, we don't know how the
other side will react."

But the next step? That, as we used to say when we
were children, was the killer. And here it was quite literally
that. My friend from the Foreign Ministry said one day
in Tel Aviv, as we sat lunching in the Gondola, "Tell
us . . . Tell us what to do? What should we do?" And
I had to admit I thought that some of the things Israel
was doing were clearly counterproductive, but even if these
things were corrected there was not the slightest assurance
that that would cause the Arabs to talk, or even bring
peace any closer in the slightest. Later I was to change my
mind about this.

In the Israeli universities, there were admirable depart-
ments of Oriental studies, where some of the finest scholars
studied and restudied the Arab world. There were ten
scholars at Tel Aviv University alone. But on a popular
level, little of this understanding of the Arab world seemed
to creep through. "You know Arabs," a cabdriver told me
bitterly. "If you give them an inch, they take everything."
Another said they were "the type of people who only
understand force." Professor Rubinstein probably put it
most deftly:

"There is a general contempt for the Arabs," he said.
"The people generally despise them. But they don't hate
them. And they despise them not because they lost the war

but because, for instance, of the way they treat prisoners. They wanted to make friends with the Arabs after the 1967 war. There was even a snob appeal as to who had Arab friends. Now all that is past. A year ago, we could still talk to the Arabs. Not now. Every day the roots of the conflict grow deeper."

It was clear the Israelis thought of the Arabs as some exotic, untrustworthy "tribe." But how much difference was there, really, between a Western European looking down on the Orthodox Jews, with their strange archaic ways and curls, and the modern technically oriented Israeli looking down on the Arabs, with their strange, archaic ways?

On the other hand, the parents feared their children would learn to hate the Arabs, and did everything they could to expunge any signs of hatred—an attitude refreshingly different from the hatred inculcated in Arab children by *their* parents. Still, over and over, I noticed a strangeness about this self-conscious determination not to hate the Arabs, who after all were daily bombing, kidnaping and killing Israelis. To a great extent, the Israelis came to treat them almost as if they did not exist. It occurred to me as I wandered around Tel Aviv that perhaps they could not bear to allow themselves the luxury of reacting spontaneously; they were afraid they might find in themselves the same hatreds that throughout history they had found in their own persecutors.

Sociologists and historians say that the young in Israel were far more apt to accept the Arab as inferior and worthless than the old. And the older people were more and more concerned over the increasing isolation of their country and their young people in the world. For while these older Jews were, in the best sense of the word and not the pejorative sense, "cosmopolites," that is men with a truly sophisticated and yearning knowledge of the world, of other peoples, of the sciences and the humanities and languages, the young people were not.

One aspect of this was the curious disinterest on the part of the young in language. Hebrew, obviously, was a very limited language, spoken by only a minuscule number of people in the world. For this reason, eight years of English study are compulsory in the Israeli schools. But it is astonishing how few young Israelis were speaking anything resembling workable English.

The first weekend I was in Israel, I rented a car and drove up and down the country, picking up hitchhiking soldiers as I went along. Usually I had a carful of five or six, and I must have given lifts to at least between 120 and 150 in all. They were almost uniformly pleasant, grateful, cheerful and good-natured. But to my surprise, and eventually to my irritation, only one of all these young people spoke any English at all, and his was not very good. This deficiency, which was also pointed out to me by several Israeli English teachers, disappointed and disturbed me. I had learned five languages, mostly by myself, and I am, after all, a citizen of a country with the world's most international language.

I found, too, a curious and hesitant ambivalence among the older Jews about the young. "When I was a child here," a fortyish official in the Foreign Office told me one day at lunch, "this was the most idyllic country you could imagine. Today it is changed. Perhaps all countries go through that pattern. And yet the youth today . . . they are able technocrats."

A sixtyish kibbutznik who arrived in the midst of Israel's most idealistic period thirty-five years ago, Mrs. Chava Shing, whom I met one day up at Kirjat Tivon in the beautiful Nazareth hills, put it this way. "I don't know. . . . Somehow it didn't turn out the way we thought it would. It's good, and the younger generation is good. They fight hard and work hard and we have no troubles with drugs and those things. But"—she paused, unsure herself as to how to classify her sense of unease—"we didn't expect it to be like other countries. We expected more idealism, less class consciousness, less materialism."

With Israelis of the older generation, who were the giants of the creation of the Jewish state, there is today a slight yearning for paradise lost, for the years of the great victories—and the great sacrifices—and perhaps, too, the years of absolute moral certainties. As for their children, they never knew quite so viscerally that it was paradise because, unlike their parents, they had never known hell.

But the difference is not only generational in Israel, it is national and international. There are distinct differences between the Jews of Israel today, who comprise 16 per cent of world Jewry, and the Jews of the rest of the world.

The discrepancies—often more than that—between the ideas of young American Jews and the Israelis comes out constantly. On the radio one day for instance, young American Jews were discussing war and peace with Israelis and there was a marked difference in attitudes. The Americans felt Israel was so hung up on security that it precluded any progress toward peace. "We understand why you are preoccupied with war. You feel your survival is at stake," one American said, "but we can't see how you'll ever achieve peace unless you look at the Arab view of things. We know there are no pat solutions, but we don't think the path you're following is likely to bring peace."

An Israeli youth answered, typically, "It's all well and good to talk about understanding the Arabs, but we know that if we don't survive, we won't worry about Israel-Arab relations twenty years from now." Another said, "When

they blow up bridges and bus stops, then countermeasures
don't bother us at all."

The Israeli youth are so less ideological than their parents.
They spurn ideology. They are even bored with Zionism,
and one of the reasons is a feeling of uneasiness about
the state at this moment. They feel that the leadership
—almost all of which comes from the generation of the
second aliyah and is thus highly ideological and passionately Zionist—is so out of step with the young. "The state
is created now, why do we need Zionism?" asked one
young sabra.

This new man, this sabra, is a little embarrassed by
the bravado which attended the early years of the state.
The "Exodus" syndrome, which is so popular with American Jews, frankly horrifies him. "They don't think you
should get praised for doing something that is your duty,"
one government spokesman told me.

All of this has created a new Israeli with few of the
complexes, emotional scars and traumas of his parents. But
it has also created a new Israeli with little of their fascination, with none of that splendid metaphysical mystery that
has always characterized the Jews and with little of that
gut and intellectual humanitarianism that set the Jew
apart . . . and finally, tragically, aside. It is simple—he
finds the constant nagging reminders of his grandfathers'
sufferings tiresome, and he is not much interested in the
Arabs' sufferings either.

It is even possible to ask today: Is this new Israeli really
a Jew? This is not a mischievous question. For the simple
fact is that in this "Jewish state," fewer and fewer of the
population practice Judaism. Among the young, almost
none do. There is no question that the secularization of
the Israeli state is proceeding steadily. The Supreme Court
ruled in 1970, in the Shalitt case, that people can have
Jewish nationality without practicing the Jewish religion,

thus changing the entire basis of original Zionism and, in effect, opening the country to non-Jews.

What, then, is it to be a "Jew"? Boaz Evron, columnist and philosopher, puts it this way: "I'm an atheist, but when I read the Bible, it's not a religious book, it's a national book. When you know Hebrew, the Bible is the feel of the country, the shape of its national consciousness. Zionism has changed. It is now a tool in the hands of the government to mobilize world Jewry. Now we follow our own interests, and when we hear of the troubles of Jews elsewhere, we're not sure we have an affinity.

"What is Jewish here today is not exactly religious. What counts is that there is a nation here. I feel it. My friends feel it."

To older and Orthodox Jews, this outlook is anathema, and contradictions between Jewish religiosity-Jewish nationality and spirituality-materialism seemed for many to come to a head last year with the fire started in the Al Aksa Mosque in Jerusalem by a fanatic Australian Christian, Denis Rohan.

What Rohan, who was adjudged mentally insane, did was bring attention to the Jews' centuries-old promise to rebuild the temple of Solomon which stood until its destruction by the Romans in A.D. 70 on the site of Al Aksa. The rebuilding of the temple was one of the spiritual purposes of the return to Israel.

However, until 1967 the site and the mosque were in Jordanian hands. The reality of the question never emerged and the promise was never challenged. Since then, rabbis point out, there has been utter silence on the question of rebuilding—not only because of the inappropriateness of destroying other religions' holy places but because it is clearly of no importance to modern Israelis.

"Israel today is schizoid," said the rabbi of a large synagogue in Jerusalem. "The State of Israel was founded on the idea not only of a return to a piece of land, but of a spiritual return. The great moral driving force that brought Jews to the shores of Palestine in 1948 was the literal belief that we were chosen by God to give back to the world a body of faith. Now we have the comforts of materialism. Actual physical rebuilding of the temple is not necessary—it is only symbolic of putting emphasis on the spiritual as well as the material side of life."

This type of comment is typical of a vague amorphous disappointment many older Israelis feel with their state today. A disappointment, ironically, that comes of the very success of the new state . . . and of the enormity of the creation of a totally new Jewish man, the Israeli. For what troubles the older Israelis, underneath, when you really get down to it, is the fear that this new man, so efficient in work, so courageous in war, so brilliant in conceptualizing, does not have the basis of suffering that made of his fathers unusually humanitarian men and made of the Jews such an extraordinary people.

Ironically, it was only in their return to the promised land after nearly two thousand years, only in their return to the mount where the temple was to be rebuilt, that the Jews for the first time in their history created a secular generation for whom the old Jewish customs, so guarded and cherished all those years in exile, no longer matter so passionately.

It was not only "What will the Arabs do to us?" but "What have we done to ourselves?"

There are doubtless those who will think that many journalists today are being "easier" on the Arabs, who have quite enough foibles and brutalities to keep regiments of critics busy from Ramadan to Ramadan, than on the Israelis. In part, perhaps this is true—I have mentioned before that all of us have the tendency to expect less of the Arabs than we do of the Israelis . . . or of ourselves.

But I think that this, too, is fair, and I do not really think that it is condescending. It is not making value judgments on the Arab way of life to say that because of a different cultural formation it simply does not have the psychic or mechanical tools, *at this moment in history,* to grapple evenly with the West in a military or commercial confrontation. It is a society torn and fragmented, feeding on its own entrails, furious with the world and with history for passing it by. To say this is not to be contemptuous of Arab society but to understand and even to sympathize with it at one particularly difficult moment of its history.

Israel, on the other hand, in much the same manner as the United States, is able to go through these traumas because basically it has faith in itself. It is a country able to question and to change as a result of the new answers it finds lodged deep in its collective psyche—this is a strength and not a weakness.

The weakness comes from the other end of the spectrum—from the inability to question anything, as though the slightest questioning will open the gates to a dark and churning abyss. Russia was like this for so many years; the Arab world is much like this today; and there are forces in Israel like this, too.

And this is the major difference between the Arab countries and Israel. The monolithism of fanaticism in much of the Arab world is like a blank white wall, with no cracks, no way over and no way around—the sun shining on it stuns the eyes and wearies the soul. Israel is like a huge and variegated but, in the end, harmonious stained glass window. Each part is different, individualized, not only a different color but a different shape.

And yet there is a great irony here.

The many parts of Israel all fit together. They work
as one. While the unflawed single surface of the Arab
world is like the white robe the Arab covers himself with
—it only serves to shroud the atomization, the loneliness,
the desperation, the inner turbulence and the contradictions
inside him.

CHAPTER XI

The Occupied Territories

Gaza was Yanta all over again, Yanta or a Vietnamese village just after the Viet Cong had come into town. There are places in the world where you can walk in and know at a glance that you have reached the outer limits of hatred and desperation and human degradation, and Gaza was one of those awful and dangerous places.

From nearby Tel Aviv, correspondents took turns driving the hour and a half to Gaza, and when they drove they raced through at top speed. It was not only that bombs were being thrown every day, but that the desperate Palestinian refugees, who had lived in tightly closed refugee camps since 1948, and the Arab commandos who now infected the camps like diphtheria were bad bomb throwers. There's nothing worse than a sloppy bomb thrower. He can aim for the military jeep two hundred yards ahead of you and get you.

Jay had been wanting to go down to Gaza, because the incessant terrorism was continuing unabated despite

everything the Israelis did or did not do, and I wanted
to go, too. So one Tuesday morning we set out with an
Israeli correspondent whom we will call Joseph. Joseph
drove to Gaza every day to cover it for his newspaper,
yet even he was nervous as we drove into the outskirts.

"It's along here that it's bad," he said, glancing at the
little knots of Arab men lounging by the small, low shops
between the citrus groves on both sides of the road. "There's
no work, and they stand around, day after day."

I had expected to see more of a change as we left
Israel, passing by several famous kibbutzim and I was
surprised that the landscape did not really change that
much; that there was not a precise line where Israeli agri-
culture and know-how ended and Arab lethargy and slop-
piness and fatalism began. For, contrary to Israeli propaganda, the Arabs can "make the desert bloom," too.

As we drove along, Joseph pointed out new citrus crop
improvement methods which the Israelis were teaching the
Arabs. Soon we passed blockhouses, now half-destroyed,
which only the week before had been abandoned by UN
personnel because of the rampant terrorism—as soon as
they left, the Arab refugees had swarmed down on them
like destructive locusts, carrying off even halves of walls.

It was when we came into the town that the mood of
Gaza—as forbidding as any mood I've seen anywhere—
struck you in the face, like a blow. Gaza is a white, Arab
town, with stark streets, and buildings that are two and
three stories high. There are few observable trees or gardens. On Omar El Mukhtar Street, the wide, main boule-
vard that ran down to the sea, the shops were stiffly,
ominously closed—the curfew for streets that misbehave.
Here and there a shop had been bricked shut as punishment to the owner for watching a bomb being thrown
without attempting to stop it. A brutal white heat hung
over everything in this city where once, if we are to be

trusting of legend, the blind Samson destroyed the Philis-
tines by pulling down the temple of the god Dagon. Had
much improved since then?

This was an "occupied city," and so I was surprised
at the public scarcity of Israeli soldiers. Only occasionally
you could see a young, tense-looking Israeli sitting on a
curb, nervous, keeping guard over the pregnant emptiness.

"See those shops," Joseph said, pointing to several
bricked-up shops in the center of the main street. "That's
where a bomb was thrown last week. It barely missed an
Israeli jeep, but it hit and wounded several Arabs. When
the soldiers came by to question the shopkeepers, they
just stood in the doorways and said they had seen nothing. They must have seen something, even if they didn't
know the man, which they probably did; so their shops
were closed up."

It was not surprising, of course, this bitterness in Gaza.
For twenty years, 350,000 Gaza Arabs, most of them refugees from Palestine, had lived under Egyptian military
administration, with very little done for them. The Egyptians had publicly tortured and hanged any Arabs who
co-operated with Israel. The 200,000 refugees lived cooped
up in stifling refugee camps far, far worse than those in
Jordan; they lived under a constant dusk-to-dawn curfew,
and in the prison of the camps at night, the reasonable
bitterness they initially felt turned them into desperate,
dehumanized creatures. In many respects, people raised like
this, from childhood, cannot be entirely human.

Even economically, Gaza was condemned to be a never-
never land, a peripheral result of the world's illegitimate
needs. The few wealthy, feudal land-owning families in
Gaza, who descended from the time of the Turks, grew
citrus fruit and sold it abroad. With the foreign exchange
they got, they loaded up ships with refrigerators and ap-
pliances—all the things that the well-to-do and new rich

Egyptians wanted but could not get directly in Egypt because of Nasser's rigid import restrictions—and took them to sell in the "free port" of Gaza. From there they were taken to Cairo. It worked because Gaza was not really part of Egypt, so the import quotas didn't apply. Yet it was enough of a part of Egypt so you could bring the goods in—but not the people—without the restrictions. In short, Gaza was the economic whorehouse of the U.A.R.

When we found Colonel Schmuel Tiran, the Israeli military spokesman in Gaza, it was clear that he was frustrated and bitter and unhappy, too. A small, wiry man with an excitable nature, Colonel Tiran was angry. He did not really want to listen to our questions—he wanted, understandably, to pour out his own problems. "This was a swamp before we came in," he said, immediately. "Twenty years a pressure cooker and all pointed toward Israel."

When I asked him about the "commandos" (the word I had arbitrarily decided to use simply for descriptive purposes), he exploded. "Do me a favor," he said, his voice rising to a highly emotional pitch, "and call it terrorism. Don't call it an underground. I was in an underground. An underground fights the occupying power . . . as we did it. We had people in the camps in Europe. I wanted to bring my mother in and the British would not allow it. Radio stations hindered us, and to destroy one, I and several others went fifty meters, crawling on our bellies with explosives on our backs. Then we went back outside the wires and announced that the building was going to explode in ten minutes, and that the British inside should leave the building for their own sakes.

"They wouldn't leave, so two boys crept back again, and pulled the primer out of the explosives. It was only when nobody was left inside that we exploded it."

I thought to myself of the difference between Colonel Tiran and Yalin-Mor, but I said nothing. He continued,

"It is a dirty business throwing hand grenades so they themselves are never hurt. It's always the civilian population. The leaders never do anything by themselves, they approach somebody, usually between the ages of fifteen and twenty, and put a grenade and five pounds (about $1.50) in his hands. Afterwards, when we catch him, he'll tell you, 'I would have done it without the five pounds because they'd call me a traitor or they'd kill me tomorrow.'"

Colonel Tiran said the terrorists were men and boys who had left Gaza earlier, then infiltrated back from Jordan or the sea. "I can assure you that after two and a half years there are very few," he said. "We know every one. They never do anything themselves, they just approach somebody else. When we ask the boys who throw the grenades, why they do not throw them *at* the trucks, they say things like, 'Do you think I'm crazy? They'd shoot back at me.'" He snorted. "This is the ideology back of it."

It was not, perhaps, surprising that he had some grisly horror stories from Gaza. "One girl was completely destroyed," he said. "Several boys came to a house one night, identifying themselves as terrorists, and demanded the girl come with them. They told her, 'We haven't had a woman in six months.' I saw her afterwards. . . ." He paused. "Two days later, two men took another girl. After raping her, they bound her ankles and hung her in a well. Another girl was witness to this and they warned her not to tell the story. The girl in the well drowned. These same men later called an Egyptian UNRWA nurse into an orange grove and told her to give them all her money, if she didn't want the same thing to happen to her. People are deadly afraid of this. One said to me, 'We'll always be more afraid of them than of you, because you don't kill or rape.'"

Colonel Tiran, like most Israeli military officers, is no typical military man. Israel is such a small country with such complex human beings, with such variegated talents, that nearly every individual carries the talents and training and layers of human experience of three or four average people elsewhere in the world. After a while, we began to talk about social patterns in Gaza, and the colonel turned out to be something of a sociologist as well as everything else.

"You add to everything the basic problems of the Arabs, which is that it's a shame to work, that work is for women . . ." he went on, as we drank coffee made by his bobbysoxed girl soldier-secretary. "Neither the military nor the economic problems will be solved, because the Arab family has within it the seeds of its own destruction. The man has to buy his wife, he has to work for the eight hundred pounds (approximately $160) to pay for her. Then he treats her like a prostitute. If he has a girl baby, he in effect 'sells her' to the high school so she can eventually get a better dowry. He sends her to be educated to get more money; but if she is educated she doesn't want to be sold. Then there is another situation. The boy goes to Egypt for college. He comes home and finds that his father has taken a young wife, that his mother is now number 2, washing the floors. He is in a quandary. He's not willing to give up his own future right to have a number-2 wife, because it is promised in the Koran. Yet he loves his mother. One day the two young ones are alone in the house, and . . ." He shook his head in a knowing way, back and forth, that spoke quite clearly for what happens.

"We have introduced birth control here, you know," he added. "At first the men took it away from their wives. Now the men are coming for it. They're living in 1969 now, and we brought 1969 here."

When I asked Colonel Tiran about the numbers of houses

destroyed, he blew up. "We have not destroyed any houses," he fairly shouted.

"But . . ." I began to say.

"Eight houses destroyed because a Jewish merchant was killed and none of the neighbors happened to see the killer, who walked right in and out among them."

"Only eight?" I began to say.

"Only eight," he shouted.

Jay and I looked at each other. We both knew this was not true, but there was no use pursuing it.

After leaving Colonel Tiran, we drove around the town. It was noon or after, yet none of us wanted to eat. "Do you mind waiting until we get back to Tel Aviv?" Jay asked. I said "No," with a vehemence that surprised even me. It was a strange feeling—I didn't *want* to *eat* in Gaza, and neither did anybody else. By now there was a little more activity on the streets. Some farmers had set up stalls of fruits and vegetables, and a few people were shopping, for this was the hour open for buying. Yet it was mostly a silent, quick coming and going; few people were talking or stopping. Now we drove slowly around town—somehow in the hot, bright, high midday sun, Gaza seemed a little less ominous—down to the blazing blue sea, where the small warehouse and pier that were the "free port" stood empty, and the attractive, modern houses once occupied by the United Nations (remember when there was a UN emergency force in Gaza?) stood empty and abandoned.

As we passed one low commercial building, Joseph said suddenly, "There's Fayez Abu Rahmeh. He's a very interesting fellow. A lawyer who tries most of the cases of terrorists." He looked questioningly at Jay and me. "Get him," Jay said immediately. "We'd like to talk to him."

Fayez was a rather typically good-looking Arab—medium-sized, well-built, dark, with a well-trimmed mustache.

He had both a sad and determined look about him, and the two of them were blended with a pleasant, outgoing manner. It turned out he was a friend of Muin's—Muin was from Gaza, too—but of course, they had not seen each other for years. The four of us retired to a pleasant hotel, one of the few still open, which was ironically called Nasser House because Egyptian officers used to stay there. It faced the street from behind a beautiful flower garden, and it was run by a formidably built elderly Englishwoman who greeted us correctly at the door, before ushering us into a cool, old-fashioned European parlor and serving us coffee.

In every way, Fayez was an Arab as Colonel Tiran was Israeli. In fact, the comparison of the two—coming so fast on the other's heels—was almost disarming, it was so typical of the generalized differences. For while the colonel was precise, while he dealt in facts, of today, while he spoke with the rat-a-tat intensity of a submachine gun, Fayez roved, he spoke in terms of historic justices, and abstractions. His voice low and sweet, and cajoling, like an ancient Arab storyteller's.

He sat down on the couch, with its pink-flowered covers, sipped some coffee, then spoke. "The people are frustrated." His voice sounded as though he was delivering a sermon. "They want to be resettled. They don't see any end to it all. Everybody is moving in a vicious circle— the Tuesday and Saturday meetings are as endless as the Tuesdays and Saturdays of the weeks. One looks to it and thinks it should be a very simple case. The Palestinians ought to have self-determination. They ought not be occupied by anybody. They have been robbed of self-determination from the dawn of history. The powers from North and South created the bridge of Palestine. Everybody suffered from the armies. In the time of the British Mandate,

we were considered in the Class A of the countries of
the League of Nations. . . ."

I asked him whether Israeli programs of economic aid
—in which I had been told the Israelis were teaching the
Gaza Arabs farming and marketing—were of any help.
"The Israelis are teaching us so many things," he answered,
his voice filled with irony and bitterness. "Sound barriers,
dynamite, hand grenades. And these teachings are mutual."
I put that down. It was a good quote.

Then he went on, "Occupation was bad for everybody,
for the occupiers as well as the occupied."

"But you had an Egyptian occupation before," Joseph
interjected.

"It wasn't really an occupation," Fayez said. Oh come
now, I said to myself. "They entered as helping Palestine
Arabs. Before that, I went to high school in Jerusalem
because there was no high school here. In Gaza today,
there are four full high schools for boys and girls. One-
third of the population of the Strip are students. Science
and education are the only means to get out of this dilemma."

"The schools . . . were built by UNRWA," Joseph interjected again.

It was interesting watching them. The two men were
obviously friends. Neither one represented the full possibilities for fanaticism on his side, and each respected the
other. Yet they sat there and contradicted each other. Each
one challenged the other with his new claim to truth.

"How are prisoners treated and how many houses have
been destroyed?" I asked Fayez.

"There are probably a thousand prisoners in Gaza now,"
he said, "and they are held in rooms that hold fifty prisoners.
They get two tiles. Then we come to article 53 of the
Geneva conventions—the destruction of houses under col-

lective punishment. On October 31, eight houses were destroyed here, and two hundred tiny shops in the local market, as well as a building of three floors with fourteen rooms owned by the deputy head of the high school."

I glanced at Joseph and asked him if this were true. He would know. He had been covering Gaza every day and he was an Israeli and a journalist. (I will trust a journalist any day above *anybody* else.) "Yes," he said. "That's right." So Colonel Tiran had lied about this. It was not surprising, because the destruction of houses is something the Israelis simply will not be honest about. Besides, he probably would not classify the two hundred "tiny shops" as "houses," they were so gerry-built. Still, to the Arab people they were "houses," the only houses they had. Again, the vast difference between Israeli perceptions (formed by their own higher standard of life) and Arab perceptions (formed by *their* lower level of life) stood out clearly, and with it were truth and rationality.

"I am against bombing, blowing up, shooting any civilian, Israeli or Palestinian," Fayez went on. "If they want to coexist, then the infliction of pain on the civilian population operates against this. . . ."

"What about the terrorists?" I said. "Are they organized . . . ideological?" I was thinking of what Colonel Tiran had said.

"They all belong to the commando organizations," Fayez said.

And I asked him about Arab allegations of torture.

"The problem is the Red Cross never sees the prisoner during interrogation," he answered. "The shortest period before anyone has seen a prisoner is eighteen days, and the defense attorney does not see him for from eighteen days to two months. All my cases tell me they are tortured. They have testified this in court. Personally, I believe it but how can we know? The Red Cross says it does not

want to believe Israeli torture, they even want to believe it
is not done on orders but perhaps by individuals. What I
wonder is . . . why use the courts at all if you're not
going to follow their practices? If you use the court at
all, all the other steps should be in conformity."

For a few minutes Fayez and Joseph talked. Joseph,
in covering Gaza, like the good newsman he was, had
gone to one of the Arab high schools and talked to the
young people. At first, he said, they had been friendly
and had openly discussed their problems, even asking him
about scholarships abroad. "Then when I started to leave,
they stoned my car," he told Fayez.

The Arab shook his head, as if to say, "And . . . ?"
He turned to me. "The Israelis want more contacts. It is
we who withdraw from them because they are the victors."
He snorted, genteelly. "The Israelis say, 'Shalom, why
don't you come and negotiate?' The Arab says 'Hi, why
don't you get out?' "

When we finally took leave of the elderly British propri-
etress, she stood in the door in the hot sunlight and intoned,
like a bearer of bad tidings from an ancient Greek drama,
"Day after day the roots of the tragedy grow deeper.
Before this, when anybody talked about peace, they called
him a Communist. Now even a boy of fifteen years understands what you are talking about. It is worse now than
twenty years ago. There is more hate now."

Once in the car we drove fast, very fast, back toward
Israel. "If only the Arabs would recognize that we won.
If only they would acknowledge this," Jay said.

Joseph was quiet. Then he said softly and slowly. "They
think we're the victors. . . ."

I thought, but only to myself, "Yes, there is the problem.
The Jews lost for so long they cannot bear being denied
this victory by the Arabs . . . just as the Arabs, whom
history has chosen as the counterpoint to the Jews, cannot

bear the defeat. How they defeat each other, and how they defeat themselves!"

For the first month after the six-day war, something very peculiar happened in the occupied territories. The walls—both physical and psychological—came down between the two peoples for the first time in twenty years. Israelis flocked to the markets of Gaza and the West Bank to buy, and one day in Jerusalem—they called it the Day of Euphoria—when the long-closed gates between the two peoples, suddenly were opened, Jews and Arabs fell into each other's arms. Israeli Jew was invited home by Palestinian to dinner; and Arab, by Jew. In the Knesset, the doves were largely in power; they were momentarily ready to give back the territories for any assurance of peace. That was the first month.

The Arabs could not bear this new "humiliation." Most of the one million Arabs in these territories already had fled from the Jews during partition. It was probably too much to expect them to embrace their conquerors, especially when they were the same people who had originally driven them from their homeland.

Still, things were relatively quiet in the occupied territories from June until August, when the Arab governments met in Khartoum and made their famous vow of no negotiations and no relations with Israel. For the first time at an Arab League meeting, as well, the Palestinian guerrillas came as a full member. The stage was set for the beginning of all-out terrorism and guerrilla warfare against Israel, and the possibilities were rich as never before. For while previously, with only 300,000 Israeli Arabs inside the country since 1948, it was difficult for an Arab to be a guerrilla within Israel, now the Palestinians had 50,000

square miles of former Arab lands under Israeli occupation
and one million Arabs. The fish had suddenly found an
abundant and hospitable pond to swim in.

There was Gaza—horrible Gaza with its cowed and
snarling people. There was the desert vastness of Sinai,
abutting Egypt on the Suez. There was the strategic high
tableland of the Golan Heights, formerly a Syrian arsenal
of army posts. And, most important, there was the large,
fertile, developed West Bank, formerly of Jordan, where
many of the most educated and advanced Palestinians had
lived uneasily under Jordanian rule since 1948 and now
lived angrily and even more uneasily under Israeli rule.

These territories were the gnawing hunger of the Arabs
and the throbbing in the brain of the Israelis. To the
Arabs, the fact that Israel continued to hold them and
showed so little disposition to give them back proved beyond a doubt what they had always, in the dark of night,
really believed about the Jews. It proved they were hungry
expansionists, that the Israeli saying, "From the Nile to
the Euphrates," was a real and living testament to the
day when the "Zionist imperialists" would seek to claim
the entire Arab world. The Arabs also point to the often
undiplomatic words of General Moshe Dayan, who has
readily declared of new Jewish settlement in the occupied
territories: "The land belongs to the people who live on
it—terriorties will be ours if Jews settle them." And to
the harsh words of hawks like Major General Ezer Weiz-
man, who has said, "If you don't keep giving the Arabs
a bloody nose from time to time, the Arab balloon will
blow up. We are going to live like this, hacking at each
other, for some time to come. Do I have to preach to
my children that I have the right to the land of Israel
only where there are no Arabs? Or do I preach to them
that I have a right to this land because it is mine by right?"

To the Israelis, on the other hand, the occupied territories were a burden but also a protection. They were determined not to be left undefended and alone again.

My first evening in Jerusalem I stood in my room, with tears in my eyes, looking out at the sun going down over the old city. I thought then that Jerusalem was perhaps the most beautiful place I had ever seen, and I must have sensed something because I thought to myself, "Why did it have to become such a symbol of hate?"

I had come there to try to assess the Israeli occupation. I knew that it was a crucial element in this whole awful jigsaw puzzle of the Middle East. Moreover, the *character* of the occupation was supremely important. I shuddered inwardly even as I went about trying to assess it, for whatever you might find and say that is even slightly anti-Israeli would bring out the vipers of anti-Semitism in many people waiting in their dark caves for something—anything —to hold against the Jews. Yet it existed—it was absolutely impossible to ignore it.

It was everywhere, hanging over everyone, Jews and non-Jews alike. One day in Jerusalem, for instance, Jay called me from Tel Aviv. He was coming that night to Jerusalem to see a West German television movie on the occupation and did I want to go? "Of course," I said, though in a way I feared it.

The showing was a semiofficial one, and we piled in along with many Israeli officials. A tall, blond, Teutonic announcer emceed the show, which went into Israeli prisons where Arabs were held, to farms where the Israelis were teaching the Arabs farming methods, and into the tormented towns of the West Bank. For a moment, I felt almost faint. Here we were, I had to remind myself, sitting in *Jerusalem*, in *Israel*, watching a *German* criticism of

Jews as *occupiers*. I walked out, not talking to anyone.
It ripped at my insides.

In the next couple of days, I systematically began to
gather facts about the occupation. It was a strange one,
and in many ways a very liberal one. I found that millions
of dollars worth of agricultural goods from the occupied
areas were being traded every year with the Arab countries,
some of it going as far as Saudi Arabia and the Persian
Gulf. Israel had initiated new vocational-training programs
for occupied Arabs and had aided them with advanced
agricultural methods. Ninety-five per cent of the mayors
in Arab towns were the same as they were before, and
the Arabs were free to listen to Radio Cairo, which constantly spewed out vicious anti-Israel propaganda because,
as the military spokesman in Jerusalem told me, "We don't
want to act like the Russians and pull down the curtain."

Yes, it was a strange occupation. An American diplomat
in Jerusalem, after being somewhat critical of the occupation, shook his head in some confusion. "But it's damned
curious," he said. "On the one hand, the Arabs are very
bitter. But just the other day I was talking to the wife
of an Arab mayor who had recently been deported to
Jordan. She was going to join him. She knows the Israeli
officials well, and she said, 'They're nice people with a
job to do.'"

Throughout the Israeli occupation there were two strains.
One was the unmistakable thrust among the Israelis of
wanting to help modernize the Arabs, of wanting to be a
revolutionizing force among them. The other was the punitive attitude, a pedantic impulse to punish the Arabs
harshly for every misdemeanor so perhaps they would
grow up to be "better boys" (which they certainly had no
intention of doing).

On the first and more positive side, the Israeli Histradrut,
the famous old socialist labor federation, was organizing

Arab workmen in and around Jerusalem. It was strange
to see young Arabs sitting under pictures of the old European Zionist-Socialists. The Israelis had established a good
network of vocational schools in the occupied areas and
were teaching thousands of Arabs skills they had never
before known. In addition, about fifty thousand Arabs
from these areas were working with Israel, almost always
at salaries far higher than those they had received before.

The Israelis wanted to break the old political structure
of the West Bank, where a handful of educated upper-
class Arabs held feudal sway over the masses. In Jerusalem,
for instance, for the first time, voting was put on a free
basis for Arabs after the six-day war. Before, under
Jordan, you needed position, male sex and money to vote,
and only a small percentage did so. Once the Israelis made
the change, to their enormous surprise, some ten thousand
Arabs showed up at the pools in Jerusalem to vote in the
November 1969 elections. But as so often tragically happens in the Middle East, something intervened to throw
all the effort at harmonious change into chaos.

Denis Rohan set fire to Al Aksa Mosque in Jerusalem,
and all the Arab candidates withdrew in a typically Arab
protest—symbolic, futile and self-defeating—against the
Israelis, whom they accused of the arson. Otherwise,
ironically, they may well have elected an Arab mayor of
all Jerusalem—both Arab and Jewish.

And did these efforts to "help" and "reform" their Arab
subjects work?

The Israelis, of all peoples, should have known that
economic development does not ease national humiliation
—particularly when it came with their obvious disdain
for the Arabs. It is too slow, and it is operative on a
totally different personal and national level from humiliation. You don't wipe out centuries of hate with Impalas

and washing machines. It is like rock and water—one
cannot stand in for the other.

Or as one Arab labor organizer in Jerusalem told Rubinstein, "There is one thing I can't forgive you for—it's not
easy to hate you. I want to be like you . . . and I want
you out."

But besides these creative efforts, there were the punitive
ones, which turned the Arabs into a fuming, furious raging
mass and made them unequivocally reject all the friendly
gestures.

First there was the supersensitive question of Jerusalem
—the city holy to Jew, Arab and Christian alike—and the
city that had been given in 1948 by the UN to the Arabs
but occupied by the Israelis in 1967.

The Israelis were making it very clear they had no
intention of giving up Jerusalem, for under Jordanian
administration, until 1967, the Jordanians had denied the
Jews access to some of their holy places, in particular the
Wailing Wall. Now, the Israelis were being fair about
access for all religions to their holy places, but they were
also sealing their hold on the city through the typical
Israeli maneuver of "creating facts" so that when and if
peace negotiations ever did come, Jerusalem would already
be marked as an Israeli city.

On the former Jordanian side of the city, for instance,
two new Jewish apartment complexes were being built
that would house forty-five hundred families; there were
plans for three more developments to be built to house
another nineteen thousand Israeli families. To do this,
some four thousand acres of land, 80 per cent of it Arab-
owned, were expropriated. Though offered compensation,
the Arab owners refused, as always, because this would
mean accepting Israeli actions.

The energy put forth in cleaning up, restoring, trans-

forming and Judaizing Jerusalem was extraordinary, and
the man directing it was the superenergetic, not very likable Teddy Kollek, the famous mayor of Jerusalem. I
went to see him one morning in his office, and he said
briskly, "Our city plan for the year 2010 may seem pre-
sumptuous, but it's more to see that we don't fall down on
the traffic patterns and on safeguarding certain green areas.
We're doing things like determining the width of the roads.
It's not a detailed plan."

Kollek was red-faced, puffy-jawed, sarcastic and acerbic.
One wondered if somehow he always had a stomach ache.
When I asked him for a list of the "international com-
mittee" the Israelis had put together to try to give gloss to
their illegal annexation of Jerusalem, he said, sneeringly,
"You wouldn't know any of them."

It happened that, after I finally did get the list of artists,
architects, scientists and other notables, not only did I
"know" them, I had interviewed and had dinner with
many.

When I said, cheerfully, and with no more evil intent
than making small talk, "Well, you have some problems
here," he snapped:

"And you don't have problems in Chicago?"

And when I got up to leave, saying, "It doesn't sound
to me as if you'll easily give up Jerusalem," he shouted:

"Not easily or any other way!"

It was easy to understand how Israelis like him got under
the skin of the Arabs . . . and everybody else.

Another Israeli action—a highly questionable tactic
which deliberately provoked the fury of the Arabs—was
the destruction of houses. In effect, if a bomb were thrown
a shot fired, the house from which it issued was destroyed.
In many cases, all houses on the block were also destroyed
as a warning to the populace that silence is not enough,
that they must report all terrorist or anti-Israel activities,

even if the perpetrators were their sons or brothers. In addition, the well-developed women's social service groups on the West Bank were ordered not to help families thus evicted. This "collective punishment," as Moshe Dayan termed it, sent shivers up the spines of many who remembered similar things done in World War II and wondered how Jews could use these tactics against other peoples.

There are cases where whole villages were simply destroyed immediately after the 1967 war, such as the three villages of Latrun, housing some six thousand persons, and the area of Kiabel Beit Eskalya near Hebron, where Arab villagers were replaced by Jewish settlers for no given reason other than that both these areas resisted in 1948 and lay on desirable land.

The Israelis thought they were acting with a total understanding of "Arab psychology." They told the Arabs that the "house is guilty" for housing the terrorist and so it must be destroyed. In other cases, using the same "Arab psychology," they had put whole villages on day-after-day curfews (toilets, outside the houses, were unavailable for use during this time) and made village men crouch in the sun all day in the village squares, just as the women in Amman had told me.

It was not only the discomfort involved in exercises like these, but also the shame that was so devastating. "Arabs do not necessarily fear pain or death," said one American-Arabist diplomat, "but they do fear shame. This is shame, and it is something they run from. They leave." Many also felt that the methods, besides being against the Geneva conventions which Israel had signed, were ineffective. "It is not only that the destruction of houses is bad and against the conventions," said one Red Cross official, "but that it is so counterproductive."

And always there was the question of maltreatment of prisoners, even of torture. Since I had got involved in investigating this in Jordan, I felt obliged to stick to it. Moreover, I was angry at the Israeli government's reaction. I simply could not believe that *any* government was so perfect that someone in it couldn't be doing anything wrong, especially in an emotionally supercharged atmosphere like that of Israel's.

First I went to the military government spokesman in Jerusalem, an unsmiling young officer named Michael Shashar. Mostly we spoke about the military government in the occupied areas, and when I mentioned the stories of mistreatment of prisoners, he had ready answers. "The stories about torture are part of the whole Arab context of wishful thinking," he said. "Psychologically speaking, it is part of a bigger context. A prison in an Arab country is a really horrible place. They get indoctrinated that the same thing will happen here. They expect their opponents to act like them, but it doesn't occur."

Shashar, did say, however, "But of course, security measures are never a pleasant thing. . . ."

Jay Bushinsky had also been working on the story, and he was told by Colonel Yosef Calev of the Israeli Adjutant General's Office that there is absolutely "no physical breaking" of prisoners. But, he said, "Sometimes there may be a slap. There are no brutal methods, but it sometimes depends upon the behavior of the person being interrogated. The interrogator may get mad and slap the prisoner."

The case that had disturbed Israeli journalists was the case of an East Jerusalem restaurant operator, Kassem Bau Akr Tamimi, who had been arrested on suspicion of collaboration with the commandos. He was held for a time, until in the middle of one night his body was brought to his wife to be buried immediately. Nearly everyone close to the case suspected that Tamimi had died in prison of maltreatment. Marks on his body seemed to confirm this. But the Israeli police announced that the marks

on his body were from a fall down the stairs which resulted
in fatal liver complications.

What irritated local journalists most was the fact that
police officials, such as District Chief Shaul Rosalio, even
refused to discuss the case. This type of official arrogance
was common. And there were other similar cases.

According to military court procedures, which here as
everywhere were totally arbitrary, lawyers could not see
clients often until as much as three months after their
imprisonment. "It is always the same answer," Felicia
Langer, an Israeli Communist lawyer who had defended
many Arab prisoners, told Jay Bushinsky. "They don't
want you disturbing the investigation. If there were beat-
ings, by the time three months have passed, the marks
have disppeared. Though I have seen some with marks
still on them, it is hard to prove."

What was most disturbing to many, was the fact that
the Israelis had doggedly refused to okay the one proof
that could be offered definitively in their behalf—allowing
the Red Cross to visit the interrogation centers. When I
went to see the Red Cross representative in Tel Aviv, he
spoke forthrightly. "During interrogation they try to break
the man, so to speak," Jacques Moreillon said. "Israeli
military rules do not permit physical pressures, but if you
are using psychological pressure, you do not want the prisoner's morale boosted. Can they take the risk that because
a man has seen a Red Cross delegate, he won't tell them
there's a bomb behind the house? Still, we are trying to
establish a practice to allow us to check those interrogators
who do not respect standing instructions. It is a very
subjective matter to judge. We feel we have to check not
only the state, but the individual. There are certain things
unbelievable to the mind, here as in America; certain
things which act as a cushion to the mind. We want to
establish a system here by which this can be decided.

"There are a substantial number of similar traits in Israel and in America. They are the only two spontaneously humanitarian states I know. But we want to put safeguards and railings on before it is too late. . . ."

There I was, deeply involved in a story that I had not even wanted to do but that I was tricked into by my free time in Amman. It raised questions that, frankly, I was not eager to get into. But there *they* were, some thirty-five hundred Arab prisoners, about a thousand of whom were held under administrative arrest, that is to say they are held indefinitely, without charges. They deserved some attention, too.

There was no question that most Arab governments, in particular Iraq and Syria, have often brutally mistreated and tortured Jewish prisoners, as well as others and their own, in the past. There was no question that Israelis were far more humanitarian than the Arabs. Was it fair to "pick on them"?

All these things crossed my mind. But there were too many contradictions. The Israelis said on one hand that the Arabs broke down immediately and told everything they knew—then they said that they needed uninterrupted three-month interrogation periods in order to get them to talk. The Israelis said there was no one imprisoned for his beliefs, but the Red Cross had a list of two dozen "conscience arrests" and, of course, there were the thousand under administrative arrest, where there were no trials and no charges brought to bear.

What perhaps worried me most was that the subject was simply undiscussed in Israel—undiscussed and un-written about in the press. No country can afford this type of "world of illusion."

So I wrote an extremely cautious article, an article which presented the question but offered no answer. That was all I could do. It was my personal judgment that there must have been torture and at least serious mistreatment in some individual cases. Almost surely, the government did not bless this, but it was done by individual interrogators. In other cases, Arabs exaggerated and imagined. Still, the government denied it . . . too surely, too vehemently.

In all conscience the silence had to be broached.

Among the Arabs of the old order whom I met in the occupied territories, perhaps the most elegant was Anwar Nusseibeh, a manicured gentleman who had been a minister in Jordan and had various business interests. The always perfectly dressed Nusseibeh was permitted to travel back and forth between Amman and Jerusalem, as did many Arab businessmen, even under the occupation. He received me cordially in his elegant old home near the American-colony hotel in Jerusalem and we sipped Arabic coffee and ate much-too-sweet Arabic confections as we talked.

"The mood?" he said. "It is more hopeless as time goes by. No. I don't think it is more resigned, but it is more bitter, more frustrated. When we were keeping things more or less on an even keel, there was hope that a settlement could be reached. It kept people going." He paused. "Now, as hopes recede . . ."

A strain went through my conversation with Nusseibeh that came and went like a flickering candle as in all my conversations in the Middle East. It was the theme of what was happening to Jerusalem, of how the Israelis were changing it. "I think they are trying to change the whole character of Jerusalem," he said, "to give it a totally Jewish character. I think the purpose is to impose a Jewish character on Jerusalem and squeeze the Arab population out. They certainly do not want these Arabs. They want a Palestine empty of Arabs. But it is wrong to move people because they belong to a certain race or religion. Eventually we will have to live as neighbors."

Nusseibeh lifted his tiny coffee cup to his lips and sipped the sweet, dark liquid. "It's fantastic, this psychosis of isolation of the Jews. This time they have created their own ghetto. They have done it to themselves. Nobody told them to live by themselves." He paused, and repeated again, "They've done it to themselves."

I found the Arabs living under Israeli occupation unquestionably more open-minded and, though this is strange, even more moderate than the Arabs elsewhere. In some ways, they were more bitter, but they were as bitter about the Arab governments, which I heard criticized nowhere else—and even the untouchable commandos—as they were about the Israelis. One of the most fascinating of these men is Mahmoud Abu Zuluf, the editor and publisher of *Al Quds,* the largest West Bank Arabic newspaper and one, indeed, which was financially supported by the Israeli government. That never stopped him from criticizing Israel, but he was, above all, a rational man.

I, unfortunately, did not get to see Abu Zuluf personally, despite the fact we had a series of appointments, which had to be cancelled for one reason or another, but I know in general his attitudes, which are important because they show the dichotomous attitudes many Arabs live with. "The situation for the occupied Arabs is getting worse," he told a *New Yorker* correspondent, "and much of the blame is due to the Arabs themselves. The Al Fatah movement is a failure—a waste of good men, time and energy. The little hurts they give the Israelis are nothing to the hurts the Israelis give them back. And the governments of Jordan, Egypt, and Syria seem to become more impossible every day, with no sign of democratic regimes on the horizon. They refuse to state the facts and let the people think

for themselves. As long as military officers rule these countries, there will be no popular revolution, no democracy,
and I fear that there will be at least three more decades
of military rule. It is very depressing. Sometimes I wish
I were a young officer in an Arab army, so I could organ-
ize a coup myself and establish democracy. But that is a
dream, and dreams are the Arabs' curse."

Under the Israelis, he said, life was not bad. There was
freedom of the press and speech. "On the personal level,"
he said, "I can honestly say I haven't been stopped and
searched any oftener than most Israelis have, and I haven't
yet run into prejudice or hate. I go swimming with my
family at the Israeli beaches, and people there give me
no offense. But I do not speak Hebrew, and I do not feel
Israeli. I am an Arab who believes in Pan-Arabism—
the Arab nation. I lost my inherited property in Jaffa,
and I cannot get it back unless I become an Israeli citizen.
I will not do this. I cannot in good conscience join the
enemies of the Arab nation."

I left early one morning to drive north through the occupied areas of the West Bank—through Ramallah, historic Nablus, and to Nazareth—to try to see a little more
of this curious occupation. My first stop was in Ramallah,
a pleasant, spreading town of low but attractive houses,
tree-lined streets and a prosperous-looking business district.
It was, of course, different from Israel; there was none of
the tremendous, energetic rush of the people as in Israel,
none of the nervous tension in the air. Yet this was still
a prosperous and pleasant area; in the Middle West, these
towns would be considered thriving market towns in a
prosperous farming area. Certainly they were not, as I
was expecting, run-down Arab backwaters, as Israeli propaganda would have it.

My first stop, at nine o'clock, was at the house of an
old Arab historian, Aref el Aref, whom I had been told

was compiling a list of houses destroyed by the Israelis
and an overall history of the occupation. I found him in
a weathered old hermit of a house hiding within a grove
of protective trees. He led me into his "library," a small,
cold room filled with books that all looked about as well-
worn and slightly shabby as he did.

Talking to Aref, it was easy to understand why the
Arabs lost so many wars. He was a charming, roly-poly
little man, with bright, mischievous eyes and white wisps
of hair tufting from the top of his shiny head. He was
slightly antic.

The first thing he did, a little ritual we had to go
through before we could get down to any concrete questions
and answers, was to bring out a little booklet about himself.
It told how he had gone to Turkey as a boy to study, been
inducted into the Turkish Army and sent to fight in Russia;
how he was imprisoned in Siberia, escaped and made his
way back to the mandate of Palestine, where he edited a
revolutionary paper before he became a historian. "It says
here," he said, pointing to the first page of the little booklet,
"that I am one of the most romantic characters in the
Arab world." He looked at me with puckish eyes. I smiled
and nodded. Who had written the book? Who else but
Aref el Aref? "And I am," he added.

Once I managed to start him talking, the man had a
great deal to say. He had compiled a careful list of Arab
houses destroyed by Israel, carefully annotated, by town,
owner and resident. By the end of 1969, it amounted to
approximately seven thousand houses. Moshe Dayan had
said just before this that only 516 houses had been destroyed under "collective punishment." Every foreign diplomat who had made his own check and his own assessment
said that Dayan was frankly misleading in his figures or
simply lying. Aref's figures were just about right. And we

were back to where "worlds of illusion" lie again—only
now on the Israeli side.

Aref had a picture book of all the young Arabs imprisoned. At one point, he brought out of his top drawer
a white head shawl. "This was from a young Arab girl
imprisoned by the Israelis," he said. "She gave this to her
mother one day when the mother was visiting, and on it
she had written about how she was tortured."

Like most of the leaders or elite on the West Bank, Aref
was in constant contact with the Israeli officials, who were
trying, albeit in their own dogmatic ways, to keep the
doors open between the two peoples. And like most of
these leaders, he was proudly, vainly, melodramatically
shutting the doors of *rapprochement* in their faces.

"The military governor of Ramallah came here recently,"
Aref proudly related to me, "and he asked me what I
thought of the Israeli occupation. I told him that I am an
old man. I've seen the Turks come here, and I worked
with them. I've seen the British during the mandate, and
I worked with them. I've seen the Jordanian government
administration, and for them I was military governor of
Ramallah and mayor of Jerusalem. Now, after the fifth of
June, 1967, I've seen the Israeli government, and I did
not work with them. I can honestly testify without prejudice that the Israeli government is the worst—and I
have reason to say so. . . ."

Before I left, Aref, who was then seventy-seven, asked a
favor; asked it shyly, as the "romantic figure" he was.
"May I be permitted to kiss you on the cheek?" he said.
I must admit I felt a little as if I were giving a lollipop
to a child. He tottered across the room toward me,
creaked his cherubic form over, and planted a rather damp,
childlike kiss on my cheek. His breath trembled, not, I
am sure, from any ecstatic thrill but from the strain on

his fat old heart. "Oh," he said, a sad note to his voice, "I can't any more . . . I can't. . . ."

When I left Ramallah and drove north, the landscape became more cavernous, more riven with uninhabited canyons and stark cliffs. Here there were few gardens, little greenery, and few towns. Eventually, I came to Nablus and looked for the house of Heckmat Almosary, a noted Arab educator who was principal of the high school there—a school where the students had been constantly on strike. Some Arabs on the street pointed out his house, and I drove in the front gate to find a beautiful modern mansion with flowers and orange groves surrounding it. A pretty but rather petulant-looking girl with her dark hair in large curlers came out to meet me. She spoke such good English that I asked her where she was educated. "Why, I'm American," she said. "I'm married to a Palestinian now, and we live in Amman." Her husband was Almosary's nephew.

From my viewpoint, I had certainly been exposed to enough of the irrational, infectious hate that permeates this part of the world. But somehow this girl—not even Arab or Jew—made it all snap inside me. She was so rabid in her feelings against the Jews, her voice was so high-pitched and wild, that I left, finally, with feelings of utter despair.

She spat—belched—out every word, making her basically pretty features deformed and twisted as she spoke. "I sat next to a woman in Tel Aviv one day and she said she was Jewish. I said where did she come from and she said Great Britain. God dammit, I told her, you're British. You don't have any right to this country. . . . A friend of ours was in their jail here. They made him sit on hot coals. His entire scrotum is destroyed. He walks around like a cripple." There was so much hate in her voice, and so little reason, that I did what journalists are not supposed to do—I acted on my feelings and I left. I could have waited the two hours until the time Almosary came back, but I couldn't take much more of this.

As I drove through the increasingly barren lands and mottled landscape, I shuddered inwardly at such bitterness. But then, I thought, too, about the other side of the coin: the peculiar yearning that many Palestine Arabs had for the Jews. I had read some of the poems that poets in the occupied territories, like Mahmoud Darwisch, had written and they were extraordinary. They spoke of the days when the two people had loved each other. One was about a Jewish girl, Rita, whom the Arab poet had loved for two years when they were young—now Rita carried a gun against him, he said. Another spoke of how he could never hate people who had been through Auschwitz. Those poems gave me hope, if nothing else did, and I wished that there were more of this spirit on the Israeli side.

Eventually I drove up to Nazareth, and across to Tiberias where I checked into the Galei Kinneret Hotel for the night. It was 3 P.M. and I still wanted to drive up to the Golan Heights, that high tableland overlooking Israel which had been Syria's heavily armed military staging area before 1967. I knew it was late, but nevertheless I decided to take the chance, as I was due early the next morning at a kibbutz to the south.

And so I drove up, up, up. And the higher and the farther I drove up into Golan, the emptier and the more eerie it got. First it was quite beautiful, with the robin's-egg blue of the Sea of Galilee beneath me and the stark, climbing canyons all around me. Then, at dusk, I began to go past bunker after abandoned Syrian bunker and army post after abandoned army post. They were all shot to pieces. The translucent early evening sky shone beautifully at me from between gaping holes and around shattered jagged ends of walls. I wondered what would happen

if I ran out of gas . . . wondered how many fedayeen
were hiding in those abandoned wrecks of buildings . . .
wondered whether I should go back to my good dinner at
Galei Kinneret while there was still some light left in the
sky.

It was here, from the now ruined Syrian Army posts,
that the Syrians had started the six-day war—they had
said that the Israelis were "massing" here that June of
1967, a charge that was palpably untrue. So when the
Israelis took the heights on Saturday, June 10, they took
it to keep it. Golan and Jerusalem, from that point on,
were non-negotiable, non-exchangeable. Soon the Israelis
were establishing nahals—military-agricultural settlements
of farming soldiers—and soon there was a ten-year master
plan for resettlement of sixty thousand Israelis there by
1979.

I pushed on and on, despite the gathering darkness,
which began to seem quite threatening, because I wanted
to see Kuneitra. This had been the largest Syrian town in
Golan and one of the largest of Syrian cities. Now it was
a ghost town. When the war reached Golan, all the Syrians
had fled. Or so I had heard.

When I finally reached Kuneitra, it had just grown dark.
Darkness had fallen, within seconds, with the suddenness
of a blanket being thrown over your head. I drove into the
emptiness—shattered houses and gaping, open windows—
emptiness, emptiness, emptiness. It was in ruins like these
that the Syrian commandos from Saiqa hid before hit-and-
run attacks on the Israelis.

Suddenly, at the end of one street, I met three Israeli
soldiers. They were horrified—that is the only word for
it—to see me there, and the officer was angry. I showed
him my Israeli press card, and he said, urgently, "Go . . .
go back. Get out of here. And go fast. The road is closed
after dark. Please." His voice was frightened. It was a

frightening place. I thought of Joseph in Gaza, who had said, "And they think we are the victors." And I thought of all the Arabs who thought all the Jews were cold and unfeeling supermen.

I drove back to Tiberias as fast as I could get the car to go, down the ravines, curve after sinuous curve, nothing on either side but threatening brush and shadowy darkness and those occasional eerie, hideous ruins. As I swerved and curved my way back, the lights of Israel were turning the valleys and hills around Galilee into a Christmas tree of technology. And I realized that it is this that the surrounding Arabs, in their relative darkness, saw every night. It reminded them every minute, every hour, every day, that they hadn't "done it" and Israel had.

I remembered that when New York Congressman James Scheuer had visited Cairo he had talked to an Egyptian commentator about the advantages that peace would bring to the U.A.R. The Egyptian shook his head. "If we had peace," he said, "we would be invaded economically and culturally. Israel would be all over the place, competing. Look. We love sailing, tennis, going to cocktails. The Israelis don't understand that. They'd be swarming all over Cairo, doing nothing but work, work, work."

It was clear—if Israel were poor, its presence would not irritate so unceasingly. If Israel were not so able and aggressive—what difference would it make? The Arabs had finally got rid of the West, with all its affronts to Moslem sensibilities and all its threats to Arab pride, and they had a little time to make their own peace with themselves and to begin to construct their own balances. Then in the midst of this came Israel, showing them by its very existence that "it" could be done and why hadn't they done it? It altered their own measure, already deeply challenged and troubled, of themselves. It was a new affront, even more unbearable than the first. It was a psychic threat to their

own being. It was not a balance-of-power crisis, this conflict in the Middle East, but a conflict of psyches . . . a
conflict of ways of being.

An hour later, I felt a certain Alice-in-Wonderland quality. I was sitting having dinner in the hotel on the lake
as American and European Jewish couples chattered at
tables around me. Later, when the waiter brought a half
bottle of red wine to my room—when my stomach's be-
having I often sip red wine while I'm reading before going
to sleep—he sat down in that nice informal way Israelis
have and chatted. "I came from Yugoslavia," he said. "It's
a wonderful country." He kept repeating this, "It's a wonderful country."

He was so enthusiastic, so obviously happy with his
"adopted" or "real country," however you want to think
about it, that he made me think of an Israeli cabdriver I
had hired one afternoon in Tel Aviv. He was a young
man, gay and exuberant. I didn't even notice his dark skin
and oriental features until he told he was from Yemen,
he had so absorbed the Israeli "look" of energy and dash.
He stopped at nearly every other corner to wave and chat
with some other driver in the most friendly and open manner. "They're all my friends," he told me in his gay, likable
way. "Everybody in this country is friends. That's why we
all cry when one boy is killed."

From so many Israelis, but from these two men in particular, I realized how much the Israelis love this country—in much the same way as the Palestinians love it.

The next day, after a good night's quiet sleep, I drove
back to Jerusalem along the Jordan River side, stopping
at kibbutzes and various places along the way. One kibbutz
was Gesher, close to the Sea of Galilee and lying right on

the Jordan River border. It was typical of the Maginot
line of kibbutzes manning the border with their guns, their
fields, their barns and their bodies. I wrote about Gesher:

Kibbutz Gesher, Israel—from the hillock where this
handsome kibbutz lies, you look out across the golden
Jordan Valley, across the luxuriant Gesher cotton fields
and the fishponds that glitter like gems in the afternoon
sunlight.

It all looks so peaceful at moments like that.

But the appearance is misleading, for the 21,000
acres of Gesher are now under almost daily fire. On an
average of twice a week, the kibbutz is shelled by Arab
commandos from across the Jordan River.

Commandos also sneak across, mine the fields and
sometimes kidnap workers. Gesher has lost two men
killed and countless of the soldiers who patrol the area
have died.

The 140 children on the kibbutz of 200 adults now
sleep every night in underground shelters—ever since
a shell landed within a few feet of a baby napping
in the sun.

Gesher, in short, is one of a necklace of kibbutzim
which line the border with Jordan and Syria and have
become the working fortresses which are the human
Maginot line between the Israelis and the Arabs.

"All the settlers who live in the border are like soldiers," said Mrs. Edna Solodar, secretary of the kibbutz,
with sadness in her voice. "We sometimes ask ourselves
where else in the world people live like this," added
Mrs. Anne Netzer. "The answer is Vietnam."

The kibbutzniki of Gesher yearn for the old days,
before 1967, when they exchanged pleasantries with
the Arab farmers across the river. "We could talk to
them then," Mrs. Solodar said thoughtfully.

Now the farmers have fled, and the fields are empty

except for commandos. Of them, she murmured: "They behave like people with nothing to lose."

A lot of things have changed in the kibbutz movement in Israel, that idealistic form of communal farming where everyone shares and shares alike. For one thing, today the 200 kibbutzim which exist are enormously prosperous.

In addition to farming, they are becoming industrialized and the level of education of all the kibbutz workers has risen substantially.

"We are not a closed movement," said Mrs. Solodar, a tiny woman who directs her kibbutz. "Things change, the situation changes, but the deeper roots do not change. We say that in the kibbutz, life is built around helping each other. That has not changed. Now we have more beautiful apartments, but the roots of everything are the same. Each person gives what he can and receives what he needs."

"The kibbutz today is more popular than it ever was," said Dr. Yehoshua Arieli, head of the History Department at the Hebrew University in Jerusalem. "Not because everybody wants to become kibbutzniks —only about four per cent of the country actually lives on kibbutzim—but because of the security of the country.

"The kibbutzim line the borders and protect them. And their youth are first-rate fighters. Twenty-nine per cent of the killed and wounded in the war were from the kibbutzim."

One of the major things that worries the people of the kibbutzim today is how to train their children for the war that seems to go on forever.

"If we say that our babies are soldiers, the difference is we teach them to fight and not to hate," said Mrs. Pnina Gazit. "They are soldiers because of the situation. The other side teaches hate. There are cases where our soldiers have found babies in battle. They always care for them. We fight only to protect our lives.

"Even now, if you talk to our children, you never hear them say they hate the Arabs. I hate Fatah and the shelling. But we always hope that when there is peace we will meet the people on the other side again."

Then she looked troubled. "You do find feelings changing toward Arabs. They place mines. What if they do it here? But when I think deeply, I know that not every man is a murderer. We must be careful not to make the same criticism of everybody."

Gesher, now thirty-one years old and settled originally by Jewish children sent away from Nazi Germany by their parents, is typical of the many kibbutzim. The houses are well cared for and attractive, the lanes are filled with blooming flowers.

But the entire complex of housing, dining halls and work buildings is laced with underground tunnels for air raids, and all the children's sleeping rooms have been moved under the earth.

Even the underground rooms where the children sleep are decorated cheerfully with bright pictures of animals and children. Some have movie screens to show movies during shellings. But the bright colors and cheerfulness seem, at times, almost grotesque, for in some kibbutzim the children's bunkers are gasproof. The Israelis know that Egypt's President Gamal Abdel Nasser used poison gas against his own people, Arabs, in Yemen.

When I left Gesher, after a good half a day there, I started off across a particularly bleak section of no man's land along the Jordan. Before, there had been towns, but now there was nothing. Just the empty sand that rose in gentle hills and then soared in the cliffs on both sides of the Jordan. It was eerily beautiful, but for the first time since Golan I felt just a little frightened. I kept gazing off to the left to the other side of the river, and I judged that Karameh and the other ruined towns we had visited with fedayeen on "the other side" must be almost directly across the valley from me. It was weird—I felt as if I were two thousand miles away.

Then two things happened. Suddenly I came to signs which read in several languages: "Danger. You are at the border. Go no farther." The way they were placed, I couldn't tell whether they were referring to the road I was traveling on or to the side roads. Moreover, I wasn't at all sure in the first place whether I was on the right road to Jericho or not. Then I glanced at my gas meter and discovered I was all but out of gas.

In this wilderness I was not about to find a gas station, so I decided to take the chance of driving the eight or ten miles back to the nearest town. As I drove back, I stopped to ask several men who were standing alongside the road how far back the city was. I had assumed they were Israelis, but to my surprise—and then distress—they turned out to be Arabs.

They were voluble, happy sorts, and within minutes they were all ensconced in the back seat of my car, laughing, joking, pointing out things to me in a mixture of Arabic and English. I don't remember exactly how they got in or whether they asked me whether they could; I do remember my extreme sense of unease. Indeed, I was frightened. Even when I criticized the Israelis for certain policies and outlooks, I trusted them. They were like us.

And then I realized something further. Here I was, an opened-minded, liberal person to whom all human beings were basically good and ultimately understandable, and yet it had even got to me. . . . I remembered that when I had first come to Israel, after those months of being stuffed full of Arab hatred and propaganda, that I felt a sense of uneasiness with the Israelis. Now I had been on this side for a while, and I felt the same sense of distrust toward the Arabs, who only a few weeks before I had been with, on good and friendly terms, on the other side of the river.

I was disgusted with myself . . . and disgusted with the whole damned Middle East.

I dropped the three Arabs off at the gas station which they and I were seeking and they were embarrassingly grateful. And when I found myself questioning how wise it was for me to be seen with Arabs in an Israeli town, I was enraged with myself.

They waved me cheerfully away after they had directed me back on my path. They were good, kindly men, certainly nothing to be afraid of.

Nor was the other side.

I mean this side. . . .

I mean . . .

Oh God!

The poison had got even to me.

CHAPTER XII

Arab Summit Conferences Never Die, They Just . . .

▼▼▼

There is a nagging inevitability about the reappearance of certain things—marriage, death, taxes and Arab summit conferences. All are things to be tolerated and things to be survived, if only at great cost.

But it was not in such a resigned, even negative, spirit that I set out for my first Arab summit conference in Rabat, Morocco. I was cheerful and even (God help me!) eager. The paper had even put my picture on the cover of the media's magazine, *Editor and Publisher,* with a Palestinian commando and the title "Our man at the summit."

I was our man, *not* the commando.

For weeks, there had been tremendous propaganda on the part of the Arabs involved as to what would ensue when they all got together. Arab unity would descend upon the assembled states there like a sudden arrival of manna from heaven. They would co-ordinate their military actions against Israel, perhaps even put them under a unified Arab command for the first time in history. There would be a great escalation of their all-out, never-ending, total war against Israel, for all time. Allah be praised!

When I landed in Casablanca, a big, modern city where you wouldn't go to the Casbah with anyone if you were in your right mind, I was even pleased to be going to Rabat. And as I drove down the long, flat, handsome road that stretches along the sea from Casablanca, I had to ask myself—is *this,* too, the Arab world?

This, of course, is the Mahgreb, part of that half circle of states that crooks from Algeria, through little Tunisia, to Morocco and down to Mauritania. Moslems they are, and they speak Arabic! But in terms of "Arab" blood or character, they are totally different people. Being short and stubby and generally with poor, sallow skin, they are not so handsome as the real "Arab" of the Arabian peninsula. But they appeared to be much calmer, much less tormented people, and it seemed to me that to them Israel must be very far away.

Rabat itself, the capital of Morocco and seat of the wily King Hassan II's monarchy, is a modern, startlingly white city with red roofs and broad boulevards. Its natural attractiveness was enhanced by flags flying everywhere, while the shiny black limousines of kings and revolutionaries sped through the streets.

Covering the three-day conference was a slightly curious affair, since the Arabs are about as keen in the ways of public relations with their suspicion of everyone and everything, as the African Bantu. No, that is doing a rhetorical disservice to the Bantu.

The Arab *wants* publicity; he regales you endlessly— hurt, and at the same time, cunning eyes focused pointedly on you about how the world ignores him—but when he has a chance to *get* publicity, when he has something, for instance, to "sell" to the world press, he suddenly conjures up every jinni in him to permit him to thoroughly botch it up.

The way they did it at *this* Arab summit (the last traumatic one had been in Khartoum in 1967 after the six-day war) was to take over the Hilton Hotel for all the Arab representatives and to close it off completely to everyone else. The two hundred or so of the visiting international press (seldom, if ever, had they got so many in one place and with such possibilities for exposure) were housed around town and were permitted to enter the Meccalike fortress of the Hilton only through a special channel and go . . . to the swimming pool.

What was in the swimming pool? Nothing! Not even water, for it was December and cool, though bright. We were, however, permitted to view each other around the swimming pool, always an edifying sight.

Occasionally, too, we were permitted to stand out in front in between the soldiers of Morocco's famous and beautifully costumed regiments who blew horns and did all manner of curious thing to welcome the panoply of Arab leaders. I must admit it was exciting to watch Nasser, oozing charm and assurance, marching in with King Faisal, Arafat and Algeria's Houari Boumedienne. I could not take my eyes off Faisal—his face was the most demanding combination of asceticism, cunning and savagery. His heavy eyelids gave him the appearance of being always slightly sleepy . . . or was it the meetings? Arafat invariably bounced in on his tennis shoes, giving that incongruous "V for Victory" sign, and Boumedienne, slightly crouched, gave the impression of a man about to spring on any enemy.

Our problem was getting news, and it was a problem. Occasionally an Egyptian correspondent would pass through—Arab correspondents *were* permitted in the inner sanctums of the hotel—and brief us. The story was always basically the same: Nasser was still, actually, holding out for some kind of peace; he hadn't closed the doors; he wasn't so "crazy" and unbendable as the West thought; we should "watch and see."

And then occasionally someone would deign to descend from the upper heights of the Hilton to the empty swimming pool, around which we sat like empty chalices waiting to be filled, and talk to us. The omnipresent Palestinian poet and other things, Kemal Nasser, my friend from the afternoon in Damascus, came down once, for instance, wearing his most ironic Rhodes scholar cloak of arrogance and, on behalf of the commandos, showed his utter contempt for the whole charade.

"We have submitted a memorandum in the Defense Council," he said in that clipped English he speaks and always with that bemused, slightly contemptuous smile on his lips, "and we hope to get thirty million pounds sterling—fifteen million for the occupied lands and the rest for escalation."

"And how much will you take?" came a wary journalistic voice.

"Eight to ten million," Nasser rejoined. He smiled. That was the kind of thing he could appreciate, not this absurd summit conference. "The Arab regimes have not been very generous with us," he went on, "but we have our own means to get money. . . ." Indeed they did. Arafat had not wanted the summit, of course; he and the commandos got their money and did their work privately and personally and seductively and with threats and body chops, not in semipublic spectacles like this. But if they had to humor the children, well . . .

And then—the last day, after some of the correspondents had gone home for Christmas—the dam broke and

the Arabs, always so secretive, always so concerned for
face and prestige, always so fanatically desirous *not* to let
the West see their dirty laundry, hung all their petty
squabbling and bickering out on the line where it bobbed
and danced in front of the entire Western world.

Like most things in the Middle East it started over
money, and it ended in . . . bankruptcy. The first the
swimming-pool press got wind of the tragedy was when
someone lurking at the front of the hotel saw who else but
President Nasser, far and away the most important leader
there, stalk—in midmorning, two hours before "closing
time"—out of the meeting. Close behind the tall, imposing-
looking Nasser waddled little roly-poly Yasir Arafat with
his *fetiyah* flying behind him and his tennis shoes strain-
ing from the pace. You didn't need to consult the Koran
to know that something was up.

What had happened—it soon became known even out
in the Sinaic wastelands of the swimming pool—was that
those couple of desert foxes, King Faisal and the Sheikh
of Kuwait, had suddenly, inexplicably, even selfishly, told
the gathered assemblage that they would no longer unquestioningly bankroll the war that Nasser and the commandos seemed to be losing so doggedly . . . and, moreover, expensively. A furious Nasser stood up, his voice
shaking, in the attractive conference room where the meeting was held and said, "We will have to go it alone. Very
well then, if you do not want to support us in the war
against Israel, let us put that in the final communiqué.
Let us announce it to the Arab world."

"Why do you need money," was the Saudis refrain,
"when you're not going to do anything anyway?"

"This is the biggest disaster yet," one Egyptian journalist told me.

As the day wore on, the leaders tried to smooth things

over—which at that point was like trying to smooth over
the Pacific in heat. Nasser, indeed, came back for the afternoon session, ready to make concessions so there could be
a "final communiqué," but by then the two "crazies," as
President Nixon once undiplomatically called them—
Syria and Iraq—had staged *their* walkout; they didn't think
Nasser was radical enough and at one point they were
quoted as saying that they should wage all-out war immediately, even if it resulted in Damascus and Cairo being occupied. Biting your nose off to spite your face is one other
thing the Arabs have perfected to a fine art.

The finale? One of the few things the visiting correspondents had been scheduled to actually *see* was the closing session, beginning at 5:30 P.M. that evening, December
24, 1969. Not only had this been a scheduled *public* event
from the beginning, but additional announcements of the
acceptability of our presence were sent out that very afternoon, even after the Nasser walkout; this occurred because
the secretariat *thought* that Nasser had returned and that
everything was going as scheduled in the final event,
which was to present a grand spectacle of Arab unity to
the world. They didn't know—indeed, no one knew—that
Iraq and Syria were nowhere to be found. And it wasn't
until we were all assembled in the theater and the leaders
had assembled and begun looking around them that they
found the two mavericks were not there. In something akin
to panic, they all filed out, and the place fell apart.

It is at moments like this that being a journalist is most
fun. After days of banishment to the swimming pool, with
properly aloof and amused mien, we coolly observed their
disaster and, from the melancholy and degraded upper
rows to which we had been relegated, watched them
scamper, wild-eyed, impotently, fruitlessly, attempting to
put Humpty Dumpty together again, all under the huge

sign in Arabic that hung over the hall and read: "You
will be the best of nations among humans. You will be the
implementation of good and the rejection of evil."

Until 11 P.M., the meeting was a shambles. All the
closed areas were suddenly open. The sheikhs' turbans all
seemed to be at unruly angles. A carnival atmosphere
reigned. The boys at the front desk were telling me about
who had tapped whose phones.

At 11 P.M., the roster of leaders—Nasser, Arafat, Faisal
with his evil and ascetic face, Khadafi—filed soberly, with
edges of desperation around their eyes, into the conference
room. With Iraq and Syria still unconvinced and not present, King Hassan got up and announced there would be
no final communiqué. It looked like a strain even on the
wily face of the young king, a man so cunning he keeps
summit conferences meeting in his own very conservative
country in order to keep his (i.e., his secret police's) eye on
them. It ended with a King Hassan little press conference
in the same room and he said simply that there had been
"differences over the tactics to be adopted" and that that
was "why Iraq and Syria felt they couldn't attend and
why there was no communiqué" but it was "no reflection
on the achievements which had taken place in secret."

I bet, I thought, as I went out into the cool night to
file my story.

As I left the hall, I ran into one of the Russian Tass
men, who was looking very glum, and asked him what *he*
thought of it all. "They shouldn't do it in public," he said
glumly.

And the next day old crafty Arafat commented, drily, "I
will only say our people have never put their confidence
in summit meetings. Lord preserve me from my friends!
As for my enemies, I can take care of myself."

That same morning I had breakfast with several of my
colleagues and a German correspondent who worked for

the Springer newspapers. We were all in ebullient good
spirits, talking and joking about the spectacle of the pre-
vious day. In the midst of all the humorous banter, the
Springer man, who had been more serious than the others,
looked up suddenly and said without warning:

"The Arabs are suffering from a tremendous case of humiliation. It is not so funny. I can tell you that nations and
people will do anything when they are humiliated. My
country had been strong and secure. I can tell you they
will do anything."

We were all a little more serious then.

But Arab fighting was only beginning. Nasser showed,
just a little later that he would go along, at least within
the limits of his own political possibilities, with a cease-
fire. There seemed to be hope, that summer of 1970, when
the United States extended its plan for stopping hostilities
and finally got both Israel and Egypt to agree with it. And
it seemed for a moment as though perhaps the tangle, so
twisted and deformed through all those endless decades of
history, might gradually straighten itself out, albeit gradually, into some fine, straight healthy line.

Was it possible that the sick inward turning toward one's
own darkest inner swamps could eventually be transformed
into a healthy outgoing regard for others? That some of
the patriotism toward the larger world, that was beginning
to stir in the rest of the world, might replace the atavistic
patriotism toward tribe that still strangles the Middle East?

Even at the outset, of course, there were doubters, persons who in themselves were whole choruses of doom. One
of these, who believed simply that the Arabs could not be
thought of as people, was the columnist Joe Alsop, that
hawk of hawks. I happened to be having a drink that fall
in his stylish Georgetown house one night with Keyes

Beech, the *Daily News'* eminent Asian correspondent, and I was trying to be nice because Alsop was a friend of Keyes.

But Alsop was at his most paranoid. We sat in his beautiful garden. His eyes stared and at times rolled. He felt the whole world was against him on Vietnam—had abandoned him—and he had become even more feverish since the satiric columnist Art Buchwald had written a play in which Alsop was not kindly satirized. Now his passion was the Middle East.

"We're giving in to the Russians," he kept saying. "They have no other desire in the world but to destroy us. You can't trust them on anything."

"But, Joe," I tried to reason once, "there wouldn't be any Russians in the Middle East if it were not for the Palestinian problem . . . unless something is done for them, there will be no peace in the Middle East."

"I don't care about the Palestinians," he shouted. "All that is is emotional claptrap. I can't stand emotional decisions." Now he was shrieking in a high-pitched voice.

"Emotional . . ." I started to say. Then I bit my lip. But I did add, as calmly as I could, "You do have to take into consideration national mentality."

At this, he exploded. "I don't care about national mentality. That's so ridiculous." He was looking at me now with contempt. His lip was quivering. Then he said something about "women" and made a gesture with his jaws to indicate, I supposed, a chicken clucking.

"Tell me, Joe," Keyes interjected, rather tensely, "what are you doing these days?"

"I'm writing a book," Alsop said.

"About what?" Keyes again.

"Art." He said it with a modish pose. "Art Buchwald?" I asked.

This story is interesting, I think, because having written

so much about the irrationality of the Arabs, it is a reminder of how many Americans—in high places, in influential places—are also irrational in *their* reactions.

Worlds of illusion. They work so many ways.

Eventually—too soon, so much too soon—my time in the Middle East was to end. It had been a good time for me, despite the depressions that set in every time I came up against one more of the area's unreasoning, virulent hatreds. It had been, too, a very special time, when every feeling of the Middle East seemed to be heightened, when all the elements were unusually active, and when many things came to a head. It was, in short, an illustrative time, a special time which symbolized all the times that had been and all the times to come.

What was to happen next? Many things *did* happen. The United States pulled back slightly from its total support of Israel, and told both sides they must give in to get peace. Saying that "We think the proposals are fair," Secretary of State William Rogers helped prepare the new proposals that would go into the attempts at a cease-fire, with new negotiations in 1970. Israel was to cede most of the occupied areas in exchange for peace and recognition of its borders. Jerusalem was to be unified. The Palestinian question was to be solved through compensating or repatriating refugees. An international military force would be established as a buffer force and negotiations would be carried through by Gunnar Jarring.

Part of it was that the great powers saw things going too far, too fast, in the Middle East. Men like Secretary of State Rogers saw that by isolating the United States from the Arab world it was encouraging Arab intransigence and Russian domination and thus not helping Israel or anyone else. Or, as George Ball said in a prophetic speech in

Chicago as early as May 1970, "We are encouraging the
Soviet build-up of strength and influence in the Middle
East. That is a development which poses far more danger
for American interests and for the peace of the world than
anything that could possibly occur five thousand miles
away in Asian jungles."

To the astonishment and joy of many, both sides finally
accepted the peace plan in the summer of 1970 and the
fighting stopped at Suez. But as always, the fighting never
stopped. Within hours, the Israelis were accusing the
Egyptians of sneaking missiles up to the canal in the dark
of night, *after* the hour of the cease-fire. It was true, so
the Israelis balked and refused to go to the talks.

But before they could *not* go to the talks, something
even more dramatic occurred. The radical Popular Front
began hijacking planes as though they were kites, bringing
them down in Cairo and in the deserts outside Amman,
holding hostages as though they had the right to do anything in the world to further their cause, and blowing up
planes as if they were matchboxes. Jordan burst into civil
war, as King Hussein's troops battled Palestinian commandos, and Amman was embraced by a dark inner holocaust. The old stone houses were left with gaping holes
from the mortars of both sides, and brutality ran rampant.
Jordanian troops, living out years of repressed fury against
the Palestinians who had taken over their country so recently and so highhandedly, did not take captives among
the commandos—they murdered them, brutally, on the
streets. By the end of two weeks of this, the hundreds of
dead—no one will ever know how many died—were buried near the refugee camps, which had been the wombs
of their refusal to be forgotten and were now their graves.

Several weeks after the civil war in Jordan, I received
a postcard from Amman. It was from my friend Habeeb
Husseiny, the Oxford-educated censor, and it had been

postmarked at the height of the revolution. "Dear Georgie," he wrote. "Where are you now? Why don't you answer my letters? Twice I wrote to your private postal address. No answer from you yet. Anything wrong?"

Right on top of the Jordanian civil war came an even greater trauma: the sudden death of Nasser. The Great Leader was dead, his overwhelming spirit wailed and sung out of this world by five million screaming Egyptians rending their garments before the television screens of a darkly fascinated world. "Why do you leave us alone, Gamal?" came the plaintive cry in Cairo, as millions went out to mourn him and lugubrious voices from the mosques chanted verses from the Koran. "Nasser is not dead," they cried. "Each of us is Nasser." Even in Israeli-occupied Jerusalem, 75,000 Arabs paraded through the old city chanting "Nasser will not die" . . . in Arabic *and* Hebrew, so no one could misunderstand.

Would a new period in the Arab world be ushered in? It seemed as if it might be. Nasser, after all, had been the single guiding spirit in the Arab world—the man who filled the "role wandering aimlessly in search of a hero," as early in his life he characterized in his writings the need for a great leader who would give back to the Arabs their dignity. But he had also been the man who could never be satisfied with just Egypt—Nasser had to have the world.

Now what? Soon it was announced that Anwar Sadat, the vice-president, would succeed Nasser. A soldier, truck driver, journalist, historian, conspirator and terrorist who had wooed the Germans in World War II against the British, Sadat was one of Nasser's original collaborators and one of the most bold and ruthless men. He took part in assassinations and much of the intrigue that surrounded the early years—he was a man to be reckoned with.

It looked for a while as though the endless cycle of retribution might possibly have been broken, or at least arrested. But when I was back in Egypt in June of 1971, it was clear that the same bittersweet air—the same dire contradiction between the stirrings of hope and the dull paralysis that comes from any knowledge of Middle East realities—was still there. Only now it was even sadder than before.

Peace was still being maintained, but the hope for its continuation was as fragile as the lotus blossoms that lined the Nile. To most Egyptians, I soon found, it was just as sure to die once the winter of war came again.

On the one hand, everywhere there was this euphoria that the Egyptians were feeling in the wake of President Sadat's advancement of his peace initiatives and his plans to "democratize" the country. "He will be our most beloved President," Kemal Al Mallakh said, with an emotion strange for him. "He is a man of peace, and men of peace have strengths that men of war do not have. He is expressing what the people want."

"It is a new breath of fresh air on the Nile," an American-educated women's leader told me, nearly breathlessly. "Can't you notice the change? People are not afraid to speak now. We have such hope that we can turn this into a democracy again."

The man who had authored all this naïve but touching hope was a fifty-two-year-old, dusky-skinned, immaculately dressed political unknown when he took over the United Arab Republic after Nasser's death, for in Nasser's all-encompassing shadow, no political flowers blossomed. But Sadat seemed 1.) to sense the deep need of the Egyptian people to return to Egyptian values by ending the war and by ending the increasing totalitarianism of Nasser's regime in its later years and 2.) to see the need to concentrate on the burgeoning internal problems instead of posturing one's way expensively through international problems.

He put forward a daring new peace proposal—Egypt

would recognize Israel and open the canal and sign a peace treaty if Israel would withdraw from all the occupied Arab territories. He called for re-elections to Parliament, a total reorganization of the Arab Socialist Union and the writing of a constitution, as he surrounded himself not with the political hacks of later Nasserism but with idealistic young professors and professional men. He even planned to introduce the jury system (something he had admired on a State Department-sponsored trip to the United States in 1966) to Egypt. Moreover, he began, quite literally, to sweep out the old. When some of the old Nasser hangers-on, men who did not like Sadat, began plotting against him in the spring of 1971, he moved forcefully and cleverly against them. In one fell swoop, he arrested ninety of them, thus clearing the system of all the intelligence chiefs and such men as former Secretary General of the Arab Socialist Union, Aly Sabry. In the summer, they were charged with high treason—an event which further frustrated the Russians, whose friends these men were. Clearly, the country was starting to turn its eyes back toward the West again, where its heart had always been.

Sadat's Egypt was characterized by its rationality. "He has given the people faith in building a modern society based on conscience and technology," said one diplomat. Sadat himself was characterized by being extremely daring and by being deeply, devotedly Egyptian. Unlike Nasser, he had roots in the village. Fridays he prayed at his village mosque. And village life was basically democratic life. "Sadat appeals to the self-respect of the village man," said government spokesman Tahseen Basheer, "and to the desire for law on the part of the intellectuals." It even seemed that Egypt finally would come under the rule of law.

But how long could it last? That was the other side of the coin. Even while the Egyptians were praising their new prince-Pharaoh, they were saying in the next breath that, no, there really was no hope. Over and over, they blamed Secretary of State William Rogers for coming there that spring and giving them so much hope and then going home and giving Israel even more military aid. Again it was, "The United States could stop Israel in a moment by withholding aid, but it won't. How stupid—when there are 120 million Arabs and two million Israelis. The United States is becoming the most hated nation in the world. Soon there will come a time when Americans will be unwelcome everywhere."

Secretary Rogers had made a courageous effort. The Rogers plan was well balanced and fair. At its heart, the idea was to avoid the polarization of the great powers in the Middle East, to re-establish American influence and presence in the Arab countries, and to pave a long road toward peace by slowly removing the poison from both sides. But if it failed, the United States would be hated more, for the failure would seem another slap at Arab dignity.

And if war broke out again? Then the internal reforms in Egypt would die, too. Like Nasser, Sadat would be driven to give all his attention to the war. Then there would be no time for "democratization," for the war machine would grind such foolish idealism to bits. Then there would be even closer relations with the Soviets, and the "opening of the West" would be just one more dead dream left over from this summer of Egyptian content.

Clearly the Middle East had entered a new stage. It was a stage that was even more dangerous than the last, for if this moment was allowed to pass, it would probably never return. Many things changed, but really did not change. The Palestinian commandos were fighting for their lives in Jordan against King Hussein's angry Bedouins, and at times it looked as though their magic was a moment that had passed. Yet if war started again, they would certainly rise even stronger and more determined than before (a "more austere" movement was the way the precise Clovis Maksuud put it). Moreover, the Palestinian problem remained the core problem of the entire conflict: Nothing would ever be settled without *it* being settled.

The Palestinian commandos, so infinitely sure of themselves before, began re-evaluating in order to build themselves up again—stronger and more realistic. "The lesson of 1970," one commando leader told a correspondent from England's *The Guardian,* "is that after all we are not a new departure. We have not risen above our environment. We belong to Arab society and share its characteristic political, cultural and psychological defects. We have proved just another regime, just another Egyptian army. Our achievement was an inflated balloon. It has burst. We shall recover, but it will be a long struggle."

A lot of things happened, that summer of 1971. First the Sudan was taken over by ultra-leftists in a coup inspired by that country's large and always influential Communist Party. General Numeiry, the man I had not recognized even after talking with him for two full hours, was imprisoned in his undershorts (this, some of the correspondents opined waggishly, was probably what enraged him the most) and looked like a goner.

Then suddenly everything reversed itself. Libya's volatile young President Khadafi, a friend of the unclad Numeiry, threatened to shoot down a British airliner flying over Libyan territory if it didn't land. It was carrying two leaders of the coup back to Khartoum. When the plane landed, he arrested the two and presented them on a platter to Numeiry, who by now had his pants on, who was back in power and who soon had the two executed.

Since it was the Moscow-line Communist Party which attempted to overthrow him, Numeiry soon got into a spirited argument with the Russians who had ostensibly been backing his government. He went so far as to throw a couple of Soviet diplomats out and to threaten to break relations.

This immediate event—showing so clearly the tensions always underlying relations between the Arabs and the Soviets—was mirrored in events in Cairo as well. I was in Cairo the end of July while this was going on and from all sides and all sources came whispered accounts of President Sadat's angry dealings with the Soviets over the Sudan affair.

Immediately after the Communist coup there on July 20, I learned, the Soviet ambassador in Cairo asked Sadat to recognize the new Communist government immediately. Sadat not only refused, he sent an Egyptian unit toward Khartoum to help reinstate Numeiry. A week later came a second plea, this one from top-ranking Soviet ideologue Boris Ponomarev, secretary of the Central Committee of the U.S.S.R., who was visiting Cairo. Ponomarev begged Sadat to prevail upon the reinstated Numeiry to stop the outcry in the Sudan against the Communists and to stop the execution of the Communists.

Sadat's answer was brief. "We are not going to have Communism in the Middle East," he answered tersely. Then he went before the Arab Socialist Union meeting and angrily told the assemblage how the Soviets had tried to "order" him to do these things . . . and how he had refused.

I remember the evening, at twilight, when I walked down along the Nile to take my story about this—the first one to get out—to the censor's office. "Oh my," the censor said, as he read the relation of those two events, "I can't let this go through. We have specific instructions that nothing on the two Soviet requests go through." Then—very Egyptian—his eyes lit up and he said, "You know, there's more. Would you like to hear the rest?"

He filled me in on a lot of details I hadn't known, and eventually I talked the Ministry of Information into letting the story go through.

But the spat with the Russians was temporary. For Sadat, to placate the Soviets, whom he needed regardless of likes or dislikes, had already signed a fifteen-year treaty of friendship with them in June.

For its part, Israel was in more torment than ever—unable to live in peace in the Middle East because it was not an island, yet unwilling to give up anything for a peace that would allow it to live with its neighbors; driven by ancient demons and desperations to fear that any step forward might carry it into one of the old abysses; turning in upon itself as it blamed the world for letting it perish and then vowing to fight alone if necessary. Now the world was even more critical of Israel. Nagging questions began to be asked: Was she really *not* prepared to give up the occupied territories?

No question about it, Sadat's offers of recognition of Israel and of a peace treaty in exchange for a return of Arab lands put Israel on the offensive diplomatically. More and more criticisms of the "brave little country" began to be voiced abroad. This was what Israel had said it wanted all these years—this was *all* it wanted, it had said—and now it quibbled pettishly instead of grasping the moment.

Instead of accepting the general offer with a flourish and then working out the details later, Israel fretted about whether Egyptian troops would cross the canal. She talked openly about sabotaging the American plan. Dredging out her own deepest fears, she thought of "security" only in terms of land, not realizing that Israel is and always will be in the Middle East, not in Central Europe; that she will have to learn to live with the Arabs and not to stand in such unbecoming contempt of them; that the best and *only* security is peace and friendship with the Arabs.

Of course, the world expected more of Israel—Israel had

more to give. Israel was the advanced country, the rational country in the equation—yet at this crucial moment, she was not giving positive leadership, she was a bottomless pit of negativisms. She was being less rational than the Egyptians.

Inside the country, the year of peace had brought unexpected internal problems. The "Black Panthers"—dark-skinned Jews from Arab countries—rioted against a government it said gave all the advantages to the immigrants from Eastern Europe and Russia. Strikes paralyzed the country. From abroad came criticisms that many of Israel's most tenaciously held tenets of foreign policy—such as the argument, for American consumption, that Isreal was a "bastion of democracy" against Russian expansion in the Middle East—were simply absurd. Anyone could see it was Israel and her effect on the Arab countries which had brought Soviet expansion into the Middle East.

American diplomats admitted too, belatedly, that, in the summer of 1970 on the eve of the cease-fire, the Israelis had violated the cease-fire—by building permanent roads, by strengthening bunkers and by moving military equipment—just as much as the Arabs had. Only the Arab movements had been heralded throughout the world and the Israelis had refused to begin negotiations because of them, while no one said a word about the Israeli violations.

Why? I asked a top American negotiator when he was in Cairo. "Because we always like to think there's a Russian conspiracy out there and that they're taking advantage of us" was his wry reply.

Myths? Illusions? They were everywhere.

Some Israelis saw the ironic tragedy of the moment. My friend Amnon Rubinstein, dean of the Law School at Tel Aviv University, wrote at the time: "The Arab refusal to make any sort of peace with Israel—or even to mention her by name—became the rock upon which Israel built her foreign policy." When Sadat made his proposals, "the rock began to crumble and the carefully built house seemed to be on the verge of collapse. The immediate reaction in Israel was expressed by Ephraim Kishon, Israel's leading humorist." Rubinstein then quoted Kishon:

"During the last few years, when the whole civilized world was monolithic in its categoric demand for an Israeli withdrawal to unsafe and unrecognized borders, in exchange for the Arabs' willingness to call the old armistice agreement a peace treaty, in those fateful days our harassed glances turned toward the valley of the Nile and our parched lips mumbled a mute supplication: Gamal, where are you?

"And he came. Gamal was always in the right place at the right time. . . . 'No peace, no negotiations, no recognition!'

"Now the great man has gone and left us orphaned. . . . Anwar, that nincompoop, needed only a few months to discover the basic gimmick: the world expects deeds from Israel but only words from Egypt, and in exchange for the old borders, he is willing to supply an unlimited quantity of new words. We have lost our last and most faithful ally. One can no longer rely on the Arabs."

By September, there were sporadic outbursts of fire along Suez. Planes on both sides were shot down. It was obvious that if there was no progress on a political settlement, the fighting would, accidentally at first, deliberately at last, start again.

Above everything hung the relentless tyranny of the steadily passing moment. "If this time is lost, it won't easily come again," warned a Western diplomat. "This part of the world will go on changing in ways unfathomable to us now."

But no one had the courage to grasp and hold fast the moment. We all felt it slipping through our hands.

CHAPTER XIII

They All Love Jerusalem

▼▼▼

It was Christmas again in Jerusalem, the Holy City. A dim winter sun struggled up through the bitter cold every morning at 6 A.M., throwing a gently beautiful glow over the city where Christ, Mohammed and the Jewish prophets taught their followers to love their fellow man. By eight o'clock everything was suffused with a soft pink radiance that by noon had turned into a cool sand color and by dusk was a tired rose.

Certainly, the city was exquisitely beautiful. In the mornings, the sun sparkled on the silver dome of Al Aksa Mosque, which the Moslems built over such Jewish religious sites as the palaces of the Kings of Judah and the holy of holies spot where Abraham prepared to sacrifice Isaac. The seventh-century Christian Dome of the Rock cohabited on the same site and caught the sun lingeringly in its robin's-egg-blue dome. During the day, the city, encircled by crenelated medieval walls and battlements that were cut by such gates as Herod's and the Gate of Dung,

turned a golden shade that, had one not known the spirit
of the city better, would remind you of the golden hair of
some beautiful fairy princess.

Everyone was preparing to celebrate Christmas in his
own way. Arabs, Jews and Christians, even if not going
to the "church, mosque or synagogue of their choice,"
were headed for the "event of their choice." Everybody was
busy. The air rang with speculation about what awful
thing would happen *this* Christmas.

But as I stood in my neat, modern room on the Mount
of Olives, it was not only ancient Christian lore and love
that gripped me. Recent history was there, too. Was I not,
after all, standing on the very spot where the Jordanians
and foreign capitalists who had built the hotel had demolished part of an ancient Jewish cemetery in order to
construct their access road? And could I not look directly
across the relic-filled ravine to the spot where the Israelis
had wiped out a couple of hundred Arab homes—the
Israelis called them "slums"—in order to build a Jewish
plaza in front of the holy Wailing Wall?

Long, long ago, Bethlehem's Church of the Nativity had
been carefully carved up by the major faiths. Now, on
Christmas Eve, the time in the church was meticulously
scheduled so one Christian sect would be walking *out* one
gateway at the precise moment the other group was walking
in another. This way they were not faced with the necessity
of greeting each other on the birthday of Christ, their
Saviour.

No question about it, Christmas is somehow the time
when Jerusalem is most itself. Each year, for instance, lest
the Arab commandos again cut the telephone lines on
Christmas Eve or throw a bomb through a pilgrims' bus,
security grows tighter and tighter.

Now the religious processions were trailed by jeeps with
machine guns mounted on them while army helicopters

circled overhead. In the Church of the Nativity, which is built over the grotto where Christ presumably was born, armed Israelis stood on the rooftops all around as protection against terrorists.

As the octogenarian patriarch Archbishop Alberto Gori arrived, he was flanked by five Israeli mounted police bearing lances and pennants, helmeted Israeli troops with automatic weapons and civilian police who seemed to outnumber the pilgrims in Manger Square. At times, it was hard to hear the music because of the low-flying military helicopter.

This year, the courtyard of the church and the streets were filled with hippies, many of them bored with the rest of the world and seeking a quick thrill in the Holy Land. While the church service was being projected on closed circuit TV on the side of a building and as pilgrims knelt reverently on the stones, one hippie girl rounded the corner and cried, "Oh look, they're showing a movie. I hope it's something I haven't seen."

But it was not only at Christmas that the "Holy Land" outdid itself. The Orthodox Easter in Jerusalem that year was just as eventful. While Israeli riot police attempted to maintain order, Coptic and Ethiopian Christians battled each other at the Church of the Holy Sepulcher, traditionally known as the tomb of Jesus.

None of this was new, of course. The British pilgrim, Henry Maunfrell, who visited Jerusalem in 1697, wrote scathingly afterward of the "un-Christian fury and animosity between the Greeks and the Latins." In disputing which group should go into the Holy Sepulcher to celebrate Mass, he said, "They have sometimes proceeded to blows and sounds even at the very door of the sepulcher, mingling their own blood with their sacrifices, in evidence of which fury the father guardian showed us a great scar upon his arm, which he told us was the mark of a wound given him by a sturdy Greek priest in one of these unholy wars."

But when I was in Jerusalem at the Christmas season, I realized that it was a mistake to think that only the Christians there were filled with hopes and plans and thoughts of their brothers during the holy season. Moslems and Jews were equally stirred by the spirit of the city, and both were talking in private conversations about the love of human procreation.

One Arab merchant spoke to me ringingly of how the Arabs loved and wanted more and more children. "We need boys to grow up and become commandos and destroy the Jews," he said. "So we have to keep our birth rate up."

A woman at Kibbutz Gesher by the Sea of Galilee was expecting her fifth child and hoped for more. "We want bigger families now," she told me, standing in the kibbutz and looking over the gorgeously golden Jordan Valley, filled with barbed wire fences, mine fields, mortar holes and the constant threat of Arab guerrillas sneaking across to kill the kibbutzniks. "We are so afraid of being alone now," she went on. "All the boys are going off to the army. And they don't say, 'When we come back.' They say, 'If we come back . . .'"

Still, some of the "newer" Christians found today's tolerance in the "Holy City" a sign of remarkable progress. One evening shortly before Christmas, I was at a cocktail party at the residence of Steve Campbell, the American consul general, talking to a British Anglican supercanon, named Canon Avery. He was a Dickensian little cleric with the distinct shape of an overblown black triangle, and he was a specialist on the sects, groups, brotherhoods, sisterhoods, guilds, caliphates, and rites which have gone into the "international" city of Jerusalem. He was terribly British and talked in that droll way of caricature country

English priests; in effect, he spat when he spoke, and he was usually speaking.

While dodging Canon Avery's undisciplined spittle, which flew out in all directions as he spoke, I asked him about *his* plans for Christmas Eve. "We Anglicans came late," he said with a sweet smile. "We're permitted to sing carols in the courtyard on Christmas Eve," he added, briskly and juicily. "And if it rains very hard we are permitted to enter the Nativity church. But only if it rains very hard. There's more room out there anyway."

"Say," I went on, dodging discreetly, "you must have known Elia Khoury?" I was curious what *he* would have to say about his Arab Anglican brother, whom I had interviewed in Amman after his deportation by the Israelis from Ramallah, only a half hour's drive from Jerusalem.

Canon Avery smiled a wonderfully . . . beatifically . . . mischievous smile. Then he looked very sober indeed. "They said he was harboring fedayeen," he said. "They said he had money in his safe for them." "Did he?" I asked. Canon Avery looked absolutely devilish. "Of course, he did," he answered.

But why, I asked myself, should all these different peoples and religions, all these human fanatics and saints under one banner or religion or holy war of the moment, have found their one beloved lair, holy place and center in Jerusalem? Why was the rest of the world spared this singular, obsessive devotion? What, in effect, did Jerusalem do to deserve it?

The answer, of course, was easy:

If one goes back, even very briefly, to the history book, it is curious to find that Jerusalem, in its recorded history of more than four thousand years, should have been known in the early Akkadian tongue (in which it was Urusalim) as the "City of Peace." It was not only the magically luminous light of this dry land—a light which seemed to illuminate the city from within with a golden glow. It was not only the fact that here, surrounded by the weird land formations and endless sand seas and hopeless lifelessness of the Dead Sea, one seemed to see more clearly—it was also that one saw ghosts . . . and saviors . . . and wisemen with more alacrity than in those other green, northern damp and cold places where one turned in upon oneself for warmth and succor and shunned sidewalk revelation.

Jerusalem's history is filled with illustrative tales of human events, but who could forget the epic year 198 B.C., when Greek troops practiced heathen rites and sacrificed swine upon the altar of the Jews, destroying the Scrolls of the Law? Or the Roman procurator, Pontius Pilate, who became known for only one act—the execution warrant he signed during his term of office, A.D. 26–36, for one unknown Zealot Jesus Christ? Who can forget the temple of Venus, built upon the place where Christ was crucified, then torn down to build the original Church of the Holy Sepulcher, which was later destroyed by the Persians in 614, restored by the abbot Modestus, destroyed by the caliph Hakim of Egypt, rebuilt by the emperor Constantine Monomachus and reconstructed by the Crusaders in 1144?

This is the way it went for four thousand years and one feels, coming back to the Middle East today and seeing the city of Jerusalem, that perhaps this is—in this part of the world—the way it is always going to be. Only now the symbols are a little—a very little—more modern. The Jordanian Arabs destroyed an old Jewish cemetery on the Mount of Olives to build the Intercontinental Hotel. The Jews took it all back, with the hotel, in the 1967 war. The Arabs wouldn't let the Israelis through old Jerusalem before 1967 to wail at the Wailing Wall. Now the Jews have taken down the Arab houses around the Wailing Wall to build themselves a whole plaza to wail in. When one thinks of Christ and Mohammed ascending into heaven from here

and the Jewish prophets wailing in grief throughout pre-
history, one has a feeling that there was probably some
good reason for getting out fast and for wailing inter-
minably.

Is there, then, really no hope in the Middle East? Does
the "Holy City" really represent the total impossibility of
people ever living together in peace, tolerance and dignity?

Despite this disheartening progression, there *is* a basis
for hope. Underlying all this hateful squabbling, both
Arab and Hebrew nationalism have the identical attributes
of a common linguistic base and of rich cultural and historical heritages that have been constantly interwoven.

All of this is complemented by a strange yearning these
two peoples have for each other—a yearning complicated
by an odd, historic dependency. The Arabs feel the existence of Israel means they can't realize any of their national
objectives; at the same time, they depend upon Israel to
provide the presence against which they can fight to pull
themselves up, to transform themselves. To an almost equal
extent, the Israelis depend upon the exterior Arab threat to
keep their people in a state of urgency and to preserve
Zionist passions.

They are so close and their interactions are so uncannily
intertwined, that each side continuously turns the other into
what it thought it was itself; in effect, one makes the other
into what it hoped—or feared—it was. Most of this is
negative, but it *could just as easily become positive*.

In the 1930s, Arab writers were challenged to define a
revival of Arabism by pitting themselves against the challenge of Zionism. Polk says that "tragically and ironically,
the underlying psychological thrust of all these movements
has been the same for the Arabs as for the Zionists: a

means of creating for themselves a parallel status to other
men." And Max Dimont is even more hopeful: "For seven
hundred years," he wrote, "Arab and Jew lived side by
side in peace and with mutual respect. If Jews today in the
Arabic world live under the most squalid conditions, it is
not because Arabs pushed them there. These conditions
were created for Jew and Arab alike by subsequent conquerors. History has shown that Jew and Arab can live
together without strife and with mutual profit."

Both peoples have gone through an uncannily similar experience. Both today share a nationalism that arose as a
consequence of rejection of their attempts at assimilation—
the Jews by the West, and the Arabs by the Ottoman
Empire and the West. As a consequence of their rejection
elsewhere, they have turned their nationalisms against each
other—against, ironically, the very people they are closest
to. For it is not Palestine or Israel itself, that tiny fingertip
of land, that is important, it is the dignity and the resurrection which that small, tormented piece of land represents
for two peoples, both long humiliated, both long insulted,
both long oppressed.

It is ironic—and infinitely tragic—that today they should
need to seek that manhood that one has achieved and one
has not, in pitting themselves against each other—against
each other's tragedy and against each other's humiliations.
And the people who really crippled them are scot-free and
far away, celebrating Fasching in München, refining heroin
in Marseilles, invading Anguilla and raising poppies in
Turkey.

Even the myths that separate them turn out to be, under
examination, things that should bring them together. This,
of course, is a part of the world where everyone lives by
myths. The Jews, in their return, are pretending that they
are the same people that left in the Diaspora, yet any
historian will tell you they are not even by blood the same

people. During those nearly two thousand years the Jewish people was created anew by Italians, Russians, Spaniards and Middle Easterners of every stripe who converted to the Jewish faith. Nor is the myth of the Bible that Palestine was promised to the "seed of Abraham" relevant as a *sole* claim to Palestine: for Abraham's son Ishmael, being born of the Egyptian woman Hagar, is actually also father of the Arabs who came to Palestine in A.D. 634. Besides few of the people who advance this argument still believe in the Bible—they might as well be quoting *Wind in the Willows*.

On the Arab side there is not even that much attachment to reality. To them, it is perhaps the most cerebral war ever fought. It is obscure, remote from need or threat. The Israelis *need* to fight; their whole being as a nation and their whole existence as a people demand it. But the Arabs do not *need* to fight. Everything they have they would continue to have without the war. And far, far more. Everything they risk and every dead body they bring home is done in the name of something they do not need in order to exist, something that is paralyzing their national development, poisoning their children's minds and stunting their growth as human beings. And yet they persist in this obsessive fight as if it were a fight to the death, instead of some metaphysical need. The Arabs constantly use the word "scientific" to describe the fight; actually, it is atavistic, mired in primeval fears.

Nor does the "myth" that this is at base a religious conflict hold up. Today these primeval war emotions exist without any really deep religious belief behind them. None of the young people on either side is religious—the young Jews and the young Arabs are more like each other in this way than either is like its older generation. Yet whereas their parents' generation knew each other because they once lived together in Palestine, the children are strangers to one another.

So we have a religious war without religion . . . and a time when, increasingly, the young hate each other more bitterly than their parents because they no longer know each other.

Yet even the differences between Arab and Jew have their strangely hopeful side. Certainly they show the predominance of culture in the formation of people over the predominance of race. In a strange, warped way, therefore, the Middle East should give us hope—its saga shows that every racial group can develop and can come to be almost anything it culturally drifts into—or chooses.

And so, yes, there are these hopes and there is unquestionably this yearning that the two peoples have for each other. But every year that the war goes on, it kills it just a little more. It is not that there have not been dreamers on both sides—men of good will who would take the first step toward peace—but that the dreamers were always, and are today, overruled by the hard men of reality, who do such a good job of arranging everything everywhere.

Yes, the dependence and the yearning and even the closely allied hatred could be turned into love—but the spirit would have to cease being demonic and start being creative.

War is easy to risk, but who will risk peace?

Today in Jerusalem? Today, of course, most of the interaction is between Arabs and Jews. The Christians are relatively quiet. They know that they did their part earlier, and they're sitting this one out, calm in the knowledge that their turn will surely come again.

Even today, everybody prizes this golden city. The one sticky point in every talk of negotiation is that the Israelis say they might give up the other Arab territories they took after the 1967 war, but that they'll never give up Jerusalem. The Arabs say they can accept anything but the loss of Jerusalem and they now sign their letters with the centuries-old Jewish ending, "Next year in Jerusalem."

And so, in Jerusalem, during Christmas, or Ramadan, or Chanukah, as dawn breaks over the Mount of Contempt, or the Dung Gate, everybody is momentarily at rest, the better to get his energy back for the eventful year that is sure to follow. In the churches there is a lot of talk about "love," but in actuality there is only one thought on every tongue, regardless of race, religion, creed or national origin: "The only thing the other side understands is force."

God rest ye, merry gentlemen!

INDEX

Mount Hermon, 96, 100, 108
Moyne, Lord, 17
Musa, Omar el Hadj, 46, 146–48
Muscat (enclave), 183–84
Mussolini, Benito, 132
"Musug-musug," 183
Myths, 305–6

Nablus (town) 265, 268
Naji, Abu, 86
Nasser, Gamal Abdel, ix, xii, xv,
xvi, 6, 8, 10–11, 51, 83, 111, 244;
accomplishments, 15, 199; ambi-
tion, 29–30; characteristics, 2, 15,
16, 45, 289; death, xvi, 30, 289;
Egyptians feeling for, 128; followers, 180, 181; "Free Officers,"
203; friends, 33; illusion, 125;
Israel, 16, 50, 125; Libya, 144;
power base, 10; Rabat Confer-
ence, 280–84; "revolution," 15, 16,
17, 18, 29, pattern, 137; rise, 52;
wife, 202; Yemen, 275
Nasser, Kemal, 93–96, 116, 281
Nationalism, 304; Arab, 83–84;
Jewish, 304, 305; Fatah-Zionist
concepts, 10; Middle East, xii;
"new," 135, 136; Palestinian, xv;
Syria, 88
National liberation movements, 228–
29
NATO, 157
Nazareth, 265, 269
Nazis, 222, 223
Near East Council of Churches,
116
Negroid race, xii, 23
Nehruisms, 81
Netzer, Anne, 273
New Guinea, 11
New Left, 213
New Yorker, The, 264
New York *Times,* 33
Nidal, Abu, 62–64, 66, 67. *See* Sar-
tawi, Dr.
Nidal, Omar, 63–64
Nile River, 1, 18, 21–22; cruises,
15, 21ff., 27
Nile Valley, 14
1967 war. *See* Six-day war
Nixon, Richard M., ix, xiii, 283
Nordic race, xii
North Africa, xiii
North Vietnam, ix, 112
North Yemen, 182–83
Nubians, 14, 15, 23–26

Numeiry, Gaafarel, 147, 154, 156–
57, 293–94
Nusseibeh, Anwar, 263–64

Oases, 131, 136, 139
Occupied territories, 224–25, 231,
241ff., 277; Arabs, 264; "collective
punishment," 258–59, 266; extent
of, 253; Israel, 253–54, 291, 295;
mood, 263; after six-day war, 252,
259
Ogonyok (magazine), 37
Oil, xiii, 9, 47–48, 134, 142; Libya,
140–41, 142; Saudi Arabia, 180
Omdurban (Sudan), 152
"100-year war," ix
Orne (Lebanon), 96
Osiris, 15, 20
Ottoman Empire, 305
Oxford University, 7, 76, 288

Palestine, 17, 78–79; Arabs-Israelis,
78–79, 222–23; British Mandate, 77,
81, 102, 248–49; claims to, x–xi, xv,
77–78; Jewish immigration to, 222;
partition (1948); 71, 77; war (1948),
xvi, 102, 215
Palestine Liberation Army (PLA),
80
Palestine Liberation Front, 183
Palestine Liberation Organization
(PLO), 68, 80, 85, 93, 101, 114.
See Arafat, Yasir
Palestine National Assembly, 80
Palestinian Arabs, x–xi, 10, 35, 40,
55, 74ff., 79, 81, 84–86, 182; Arab
states relationship, 78; claims to
Israel, 77ff.; "Diaspora," 78, 79;
force, 84; Jews, 114, 269; leaders,
119, new-style, 103–5; Libya, 142;
number, xvi, who fled after partition, 77; refugees, 70–75, 225–26,
241; "return," idea of, 85; supporters, 157; U.S., 46; women,
114ff., 120, 201. *See* Gaza
Palestinian commandos, xi, xii, xv,
xvi, 3, 58–59, 77ff., 81, 100, 161,
241, 252, 264, 273–74, 281, 282,
292–93; aims, 93, 94; Arab governments, 35; Arab League, 252;
beginning, 80; education, 75; flag,
89; income, 82; Israelis, 226–30;
Jordan, 58ff., 67–69, 80, 288–89;
leaders 9, 75, 80, 93; Lion Cubs,
68; most important (*see* Al
Fatah); Saiqa (Syrian-sponsored),
89–90, 91–92, 97, 109; supporters,

Sea of Galilee, 269, 272, 301
"Secular state," idea, 80–81
Selassie, Haile, 156, 161, 167, 172, 175
Semitic language, 167
Semitic race, xii
Sex(uality), 193; Arabs, 189–90, 192–93
Shab'a, 97
Shagar, Ibrahim Mohammed, 152
Shaheen, Yusif, 30–31
Shalitt case, 236–37
Sharm el Sheikh, 225
Shashar, Michael, 260
Sheba, Queen of, 167, 168
Sheikhs, 2, 198
Shelhi, Omar, 139
Sheuer, James, 271
Shing, Mrs. Chava, 234–35
Shukur, Abdel, 19–20
Shuman, Nicholas, 8, 124
Sinai, 214, 225; occupation, 253
Sinai peninsula, 9
Sirhan, Sirhan, 88
Sisson, David, 56–57
Sisson, Mrs. David, 56
Six-day war (1967), xv, xvi–xvii, 5, 9, 46, 51, 60, 72, 81, 103–4, 114, 142, 213, 216, 223; aftermath, 252ff.; Arab reaction, 51, 82, 224, 280; "Basic Factors in Arab Collapse," 123; jokes about, 6; start, 270. See Occupied territories; Refugees, and under country
Slave trade, 145, 148
Smith, Miss, 57, 72
Social change, 14–15, 17–18, 24–25, 255, 256ff.
Socialist Bloc, 160
Society, unitary spirit, 4
Solodar, Edna, 273, 274
Solomon, King, 167, 168, 237
Somalia, 183
Somaliland, 23
South Africa, 213
South Vietnam, ix, 169
South Yemen, 182, 183
Soviet Union. See Russia
Soviet Writers Union, 38
Spain, 9
Sphinx, 6
Stern Gang, 227, 230
Straits of Tiran, 215
Sudan, xi, 12, 23, 46, 131; British, 145–46, 149–50, 151, 154, 191; communism, 155, 293–94; Dinka

tribe, 145; Eritrean refugees, 163, 170; government, 149–51, 153, 157; history, 148ff.; independence, 145, 149, 150; Information Ministry, 146, 190; Islam, 152; Israel, 153, 168; revolution, 150, 155; Russia, 146; U.S., 155; women, 190–91
Suez Canal, xviii, 205, 288; closing, xvi; invasion, 51; Israel-French-British attack (1956), xvi; nationalization, 51; 1956 war, 223
Sukairy, Ahmed, 80
Sulzberger, Cy, 34
Summit conferences (Arab): Khartoum (1967), 280; Rabat, Morocco (1969), 278–85
Sweden, 230
Switzerland, 26
Sykes-Picot agreement, 78
Symington, Stuart, 174
Syria, xi, 32, 87–88, 119, 129, 264–65; Army, 90; commandos (see Saiqa); education, 127; ELF, 162; Golan Heights, 253, 269, 270; illusion, 126; Israel, 91, 262, 270, 273; Jews, 95; Lebanon border, 100; nationalism, 88; Neo-Ba'athist government, 91; Palestinian refugees, number, 59; Rabat Conference, 283, 284; Russia, 45, 80

Tamini, Kassem Akr, 260–61
Tass, 133, 135, 284
Tel Aviv, 11, 17, 63, 217; Hilton, 99, 210; University, 121, 232, Law School, 126, 218
Terrazzi, Zuhdi, 68, 86, 114
Terrorism (ists), 226–30, 244–45, 247, 250, 252. See Al Fatah; Irgun; Palestinian commandos and Stern Gang
Theodore, Emperor, 165–66
Third World, xi, 38, 76, 79, 80, 83; Nasser, 52; socialism, 84; women, 199
Tiberias, 269, 270; Galei Kinneret Hotel, 269, 270, 272
Tigré language, 170
Time magazine, 77
Tiran, Schmuel, 244–46, 247, 248, 250
Toscanini, Arturo, 17
Trade routes, 23
Tribalism, 158
Tripoli, 105, 133–36
Tripolitania, 131

DATE DUE

7/10			
MAY 2 0 1978			
GAYLORD			PRINTED IN U.S.A.